REALM OF RACKET

REALM OF RACKET

**Learn to Program,
One Game at a Time!**

```
(list

  Forrest Bice
  Rose DeMaio
  Spencer Florence
  Feng-Yun Mimi Lin
  Scott Lindeman
  Nicole Nussbaum
  Eric Peterson
  Ryan Plessner

  David Van Horn
  Matthias Felleisen

  Conrad Barski, MD)
```

**no starch
press**

San Francisco

Printed in USA

First printing

17 16 15 14 13   1 2 3 4 5 6 7 8 9

ISBN-10: 1-59327-491-2
ISBN-13: 978-1-59327-491-7

Publisher: William Pollock
Production Editor: Alison Law
Cover Illustration: Eric Peterson
Illustrations: Feng-Yun Mimi Lin and Eric Peterson
Interior Design and Composition: Rose DeMaio and Nicole Nussbaum
Developmental Editors: Keith Fancher and William Pollock
Copyeditor: Marilyn Smith
Proofreader: Paula L. Fleming

For information on distribution, translations, or bulk sales, please contact No Starch Press, Inc. directly:

No Starch Press, Inc.
38 Ringold Street, San Francisco, CA 94103
phone: 415.863.9900; fax: 415.863.9950; info@nostarch.com; www.nostarch.com

Library of Congress Cataloging-in-Publication Data:

Felleisen, Matthias.
   Realm of Racket : learn to program, one game at a time! / by Matthias Felleisen, Conrad
Barski, Forrest Bice, Rose DeMaio, Spencer Florence, Feng-yun Mimi Lin, Scott Lindeman,
Nicole Nussbaum, Eric Peterson, Ryan Plessner, and David Van Horn.
        pages cm
   Includes index.
   ISBN-13: 978-1-59327-491-7
   ISBN-10: 1-59327-491-2
 1. Racket (Computer program language) 2. LISP (Computer program language) 3. Computer
programming. I. Title.
   QA76.73.R33F45 2013
   005.1--dc23
                                              2013002308

SUSTAINABLE FORESTRY INITIATIVE Certified Sourcing www.sfiprogram.org Label applies to the text stock SFI-00341

To the Memory of John McCarthy
September 4, 1927–October 24, 2011

BRIEF CONTENTS

Preface: Hello World xv

Introduction: Open Paren 1

Chapter 1: Getting Started 19

Chapter 2: A First Racket Program 27

Chapter 3: Basics of Racket 35

Chapter 4: Conditions and Decisions 51

Chapter 4½: define define 'define 71

Chapter 5: big-bang 79

Chapter 6: Recursion Is Easy 95

Chapter 7: Land of Lambda 111

Chapter 8: Mutant Structs 127

Chapter 9: The Values of Loops 153

Chapter 10: Dice of Doom 165

Chapter 11: Power to the Lazy 193

Chapter 12: Artificial Intelligence 203

Chapter 13: The World Is Not Enough 213

Chapter 14: Hungry Henry 231

Good-Bye: Close Paren 265

CONTENTS IN DETAIL

PREFACE
HELLO WORLD   **xv**

Why Would I Want to Learn About Racket?...xv
Who Should Read This Book?...xvi
What Teaching Approach Is Used?...xvi
Can I Skip Chapters?..xvi
Anything Else I Should Know?...xvi

INTRODUCTION
OPEN PAREN   **1**

(.1   What Makes Lisp So Cool and Unusual?..2
(.2   Where Did Lisp Come From?...2
(.3   What Does Lisp Look Like?..5
(.4   Where Does Racket Come From?..7
(.5   What Is This Book About?..9
`Halt`—Chapter Checkpoint..10

1
GETTING STARTED   **19**

1.1   Readying Racket..19
1.2   Interacting with Racket..21
`Raise`—Chapter Checkpoint...23

2
A FIRST RACKET PROGRAM   **27**

2.1   The Guess My Number Game..27
2.2   Defining Variables...29
2.3   Basic Racket Etiquette...30
2.4   Defining Functions in Racket...30
        A Function for Guessing..31
        Functions for Closing In...32
        The Main Function..33
`Resume`—Chapter Checkpoint...34

3
BASICS OF RACKET   **35**

3.1   Syntax and Semantics...35
3.2   The Building Blocks of Racket Syntax...36
3.3   The Building Blocks of Racket Semantics..38
        Booleans...38
        Symbols..39

        Numbers 39
        Strings 40
3.4   Lists in Racket 41
        CONS Cells 42
        Functions for CONS Cells 42
        Lists and List Functions 43
        The CONS Function 43
        The LIST Function 45
        The FIRST and REST Functions 45
        Nested Lists 46
3.5   Structures in Racket 47
        Structure Basics 47
        Nesting Structures 49
        Structure Transparency 50
`Interrupt`—Chapter Checkpoint 50

4
CONDITIONS AND DECISIONS   51

4.1   How to Ask 51
4.2   The Conditionals: IF and Beyond 56
        One Thing at a Time with IF 56
        The Special Form that Does It All: COND 58
        A First Taste of Recursion 59
4.3   Cool Tricks with Conditionals 61
        Using the Stealth Conditionals AND and OR 61
        Using Functions that Return More than Just the Truth 63
4.4   Equality Predicates, Once More 64
4.5   Comparing and Testing 68
        Writing a Test 68
        What Is Not a Test 69
        Testing in the Real World 69
        More Testing Facilities 70
`Call-with-current-continuation`—Chapter Checkpoint 70

4½
DEFINE DEFINE 'DEFINE   71

4½.1 Module-Level Definitions 71
        Variable Definitions 71
        Function Definitions 73
4½.2 Local Definitions 73
`Abort`—Chapter Checkpoint 75

5
BIG-BANG   79

5.1   Graphical User Interface 79
5.2   Landing a UFO 80
5.3   Using big-bang: Syntax and Semantics 83

5.4 Guessing Gooey 85
        The Data 85
        The Main Function 86
        Key-Events 87
        Rendering 88
        Time to Stop 88
Exit—Chapter Checkpoint 89
Chapter Challenges 89

6
RECURSION IS EASY   95

6.1 Robot Snake 95
6.2 A Data Representation for the Snake Game 96
6.3 The Main Function 97
6.4 Clock Ticks 98
        Eating and Growing 99
        Slithering 100
        Rotting Goo 102
6.5 Key-Events 103
6.6 Rendering 105
6.7 End Game 107
6.8 Auxiliary Functions 108
Return—Chapter Checkpoint 109
Chapter Challenges 109

7
LAND OF LAMBDA   111

7.1 Functions as Values 111
7.2 Lambda 113
7.3 Higher-Order Fun 114
7.4 Two More Higher-Order Functions 118
7.5 Derive This! 121
7.6 apply 122
Break—Chapter Checkpoint 123

8
MUTANT STRUCTS   127

8.1 Chad's First Battle 127
8.2 Orc Battle 128
8.3 Setting Up the World, a First Step 128
8.4 Action: How Structs Really Work 131
8.5 More Actions, Setting Up the World for Good 135
8.6 Ready, Set, big-bang 136
8.7 Initializing the Orc World 140
8.8 Rendering the Orc World 142
8.9 The End of the World 146
8.10 Actions, A Final Look 147

`Throw`—Chapter Checkpoint 151
Chapter Challenges 151

9
THE VALUES OF LOOPS   153

9.1   FOR Loops. 153
9.2   Multiple Values 155
9.3   Back to FOR/FOLD 156
9.4   More on Loops 157
`Waitpid`—Chapter Checkpoint 160

10
DICE OF DOOM   165

10.1   The Game Tree. 165
10.2   Dice of Doom, The Game. 166
10.3   Designing Dice of Doom: Take One 166
            Filling in the Blanks 167
            Simplifying the Rules 167
            End of Game 167
            Controlling the Game 168
10.4   How Game Trees Work. 168
10.5   Game States and Game Trees for Dice of Doom 171
10.6   Roll the Dice 174
10.7   Rendering the Dice World 176
10.8   Input Handling. 179
10.9   Creating a Game Tree 181
            The Game Tree. 182
            Neighbors 184
            Attacks 187
10.10   The End Game 189
`Kill`—Chapter Checkpoint 190
Chapter Challenges 190

11
POWER TO THE LAZY   193

11.1   Doomsday 193
11.2   Lazy Evaluation 194
11.3   Memoized Computations. 196
11.4   Racket Can Be Lazy 198
`Delay`—Chapter Checkpoint 198

12
ARTIFICIAL INTELLIGENCE   203

12.1 An Intelligent Life-form. 203
12.2 Lazy Games 204
12.3 Adding Artificial Intelligence 206

`Stop-when`—Chapter Checkpoint 208
Chapter Challenges 209

13
THE WORLD IS NOT ENOUGH   213

13.1 What Is a Distributed Game? 213
13.2 The Data 215
     Messages. 215
     Previously Fabricated Structures 215
     Packages. 216
     Bundles. 216
     Mail. 216
     iworld Structures 216
13.3 The Network Postal Service 217
13.4 Organizing Your Universe. 218
13.5 Distributed Guess. 219
     The State of the Client and the State of the Server 221
     The Server 222
     The Client 224
     Running the Game 225
`Error`—Chapter Checkpoint 225
Chapter Challenges 226

14
HUNGRY HENRY   231

14.1 King Henry the Hungry 231
14.2 Hungry Henry, the Game 232
14.3 Two United States. 232
14.4 Henry's Universe 233
     Message Data and Structures. 233
     Complex Numbers Are Good Positions 236
     A Day in the Life of a Server 236
     A Day in the Life of a Client. 236
14.5 State of the Union 236
     State of Henry 237
     State of the House 237
14.6 Main, Take Client 238
     The Appetizer State 239
     The Entree State 242
14.7 Main, Take Server. 245
     The Join State and Network Events 247
     The Join State and Tick Events 249
     The Play State and Network Events 251
     The Play State and Tick Events 253
14.8 See Henry Run 257
`On-disconnect`—Chapter Checkpoint. 258
Chapter Challenges 258

GOOD-BYE
CLOSE PAREN   265

).1   Run Racket Run 265
).2   Racket Is a Programming Language 266
).3   Racket Is a Metaprogramming Language 270
).4   Racket Is a Programming-Language Programming Language 274
So Long 281

;; Preface
(Hello World)

```
#|
Step into Realm of Racket, a book that takes you on a unique
journey into the land of computer programming. In the style
of Conrad Barski's Land of Lisp, this book teaches you how to
program in Racket by creating a series of games. Racket is a
friendly mutation of Lisp that's perfect for all, from those who
want to launch their education in computer science to those look-
ing to expand their knowledge and experience in programming.
|#
```

Why Would I Want to Learn About Racket?

You've certainly heard of JavaScript, Perl, Python, and Ruby. But what about Racket? Just because it's not the most mainstream programming language doesn't mean you should discount its capabilities. Racket allows functional programming and other different paradigms that even hard-core programmers have never seen before. Get ready for the excursion. Even after you get through *Realm of Racket*, there is a lot to explore.

Who Should Read This Book?

Our mantra is "by freshmen, for freshmen," but that doesn't mean you should drop this book if you are a sophomore or an industry professional. True, we were freshmen when we started writing this book, but our mantra means only that this book was written for you by peers who have a special interest in programming and want to explore it in a new, fun way. So you see why our mantra is what it is—it would have been a bit of a mouthful to say, "By people who have a special interest in programming and want to explore it in a new, fun way, for people who have a special interest in programming and want to explore it in a new, fun way." And our recent expedition into the realm of Racket has enabled us to write this book with genuine empathy for a novice learner.

Regardless of your programming background, many of the topics in this book will be new to you, and much of what you've learned before will appear in a new light. This book is written for those who are truly inquisitive and interested in exploring a unique world of programming, so really we are all "freshmen" in this context.

What Teaching Approach Is Used?

It won't take you long to realize that this is not your typical programming textbook. We decided to present the material in a way that is engaging and really sticks—with games and comics.

In this book, we will teach you various topics through coding games, including a text-based game, some old-school games like Snake, and others that we invented ourselves. Along the way, you will need to use your programming skills to help a character named Chad navigate the dungeons of DrRacket.

Can I Skip Chapters?

You might think you can skip ahead and save Chad right away, but we highly recommend that you read this book from front to back. Each chapter depends on the knowledge you learned from the previous one, and we don't want you to miss out on any of Chad's adventures.

Anything Else I Should Know?

The source code of our games is available with the code base of Racket. Once you download Racket, navigate to the Racket installation and look for the **collects/realm/** folder. All the game code is there for you to explore, modify, and experiment with.

Finally, the book comes with its own website. Visit `realmofracket.com` and keep visiting—you never know what you'll find there. Onward!

;; Introduction
(Open Paren)

```
#|
```

So you think you know how to program because you took an introductory course or two. Or perhaps you read a book that taught you
programming in 13 days. And then you picked up this book, which
is full of parentheses and comics. Doesn't it look different from
what you have seen in the past?

The programs you see here look like those that we encountered
in our first programming courses. You might be wondering why anyone would teach such a weird-looking programming language and why
we find it so exciting that we would write a whole book about it.

Or maybe you've heard others rave about the Lisp language and
thought, "Boy, Lisp sure looks different from other languages that
people talk about. Maybe I should pick up a Lisp book." Either way,
you're now holding a book about a programming language in the Lisp
family. And that whole family is very cool and unusual and fun.
You won't regret it.

```
|#
```

(.1 What Makes Lisp So Cool and Unusual?

Lisp is a highly expressive language. With Lisp, you take the most complicated problems and express their solutions in a clear and appropriate way. If Lisp doesn't have the means to do so, you change Lisp.

Lisp will change your mind, too. Eric Raymond, a well-known "hacker"—in the original, positive sense of the word—once wrote that "Lisp is worth learning for a different reason—the profound enlightenment experience you will have when you finally get it. That experience will make you a better programmer for the rest of your days, even if you never actually use Lisp itself a lot."

Here is what we did with Lisp in the very first class of our very first course: we launched a rocket. Well, we didn't launch a real rocket, but the animation looked cool, and it was just a few lines of code. After a couple of weeks into the course, we wrote our first interactive graphical game. Yes, our program used mouse clicks, clock ticks, and keyboard events to control a nifty little Snake game. Then we wrote an interpreter for the language that we used in the course. Did you get to write an interpreter for your language in your course? And before we knew it, we wrote distributed games. In case you don't know what "distributed" means, our games ran on many computers, and at each computer, some person interacted with the game or some program played the game, and all these computers exchanged messages to make everything work together. And can you believe that some of us had never programmed before?

So Lisp is different. And the Lisp we use is Racket, with which even children can quickly feel at home. Once you have experienced this kind of programming, it will become a part of you, and you will dream about it. You will always strive to mimic this style in the languages you must use to earn a living. You'll say to yourself, "That's kind of how I'd do it in Lisp." That's the power only Lisp can give you.

(.2 Where Did Lisp Come From?

At this point, you may start wondering why your instructor didn't tell you about Lisp. You may think that it may be something new that he hadn't heard of yet. Sadly though, it's the opposite. The idea of Lisp is truly ancient, and yet, in some ways, most existing flavors of Lisp are more advanced than any other kind of language. But Lisp's history is very different from that of other languages, and that could be why people overlook it.

Here is what we know from the anecdotes our professors told us. Way back in the 1930s, the first True Wonk of Programming walked the Earth. His name was Al—though his birth certificate said Alonzo Church—and he invented a new kind of calculus: **lambda calculus**. In this calculus, everything was a function, and every function that counted was something. All in all, it was functional and it functioned, although all this programming happened with paper and pencil because people had just figured out electricity.

Soon enough, the Earth was aflame in a great war with serious consequences on the world of programming. Governments sponsored science projects, and several of these projects created real computers. All computers, and especially the very first ones, are plain, dumb pieces of electrical hardware. As a matter of fact, the early computers—with names such as ENIAC and Zuse's Z3—were so primitive that "programming" them involved flipping switches or patching cables to physically encode each operation. Those dark days saw a lot of experimentation with different computer architectures and an explosion of different ways of "programming" them.

Naturally, people invented the idea of a programming language because it is the only way to make dumb computers truly useful. However, "language" meant nothing but a fairly thin veil over the underlying hardware. With these languages, programmers gave machines instructions. It made programming easier than flipping switches and patching cables, but it didn't make it easy. Programmers had to think about the machine when they programmed, and their programs remained tied to specific computers.

Programming languages needed to evolve to survive beyond the confines of a specific machine. Thus, the 1950s saw the arrival of new types of software, including the most important: compilers and interpreters. A compiler can take something that looks like plain arithmetic and convert it automatically into a format that the computer can execute. An interpreter is similar, although it performs the actions described in a human-written program directly; there is no intermediate step that converts it all the way down to a computer format. Best of all, compilers and interpreters are software. This means that a competent programmer can change an existing compiler or interpreter a bit to make it work on a different computer, without changing the language that programmers use to interact with the compiler or interpreter. As a result, computer programmers could suddenly write programs in a notation that was mostly independent of a specific computer.

Nevertheless, programming remained a task of giving machines instructions. Take FORTRAN, the earliest language with a compiler. Its designers created it to help scientists program, and scientists still use FORTRAN today. Just typing a FORTRAN program makes you shuffle bits and bytes in the machine, and once you're finished, you can barely see the mathematical problem you wanted to solve.

Another early language in the same mold as FORTRAN is ALGOL 60. While FORTRAN was made in America, ALGOL emerged in Europe, designed by a committee of computer scientists from all over the world. Together, FORTRAN and ALGOL spawned a long series of programming languages, called the ALGOL family. All members of this family are made from more or less the same material and for the same kind of programmers—those who love the machine more than the problem. You may have heard of some of these languages, such as C, Pascal, C++, and Java. To this day, most college courses use the ALGOL family to teach the first course on programming. Your instructors may even have told you that all languages are so similar that once you have seen one of them, you have seen all of them. Although this statement might be true for the ALGOL family of languages, it isn't true for Lisp, a language nearly as old as FORTRAN and ALGOL.

Lisp's beginnings are quite humble. Also in the late 1950s, John McCarthy—a computer scientist who worked at MIT, the best college in East Cambridge—came across Al's old papers on lambda calculus. The papers were difficult to read because they had been written in the days before people had real computers. They sent John daydreaming. When he woke up, he knew that he was sick of programming computers in the dumb ways of machine language or FORTRAN. He wanted an intelligent way to go about it. So one day he gathered together his researchers and challenged them to build a programming language that wasn't about the bits and bytes in a computer. Instead, he wanted to create a language that would help programmers solve problems without forcing them to think about the elements of a machine.

John's first example was about lists: lists of ideas, lists of tasks, lists of insights, and even lists of programs. To deal with lists, a program should provide lists and functions for processing lists—never mind how the computer really deals with all of this inside. Better still, a language should be able to "talk" about itself and about programming. In short, he wanted Lisp, a language so elegant and powerful that even writing an interpreter for Lisp in Lisp itself would take only about 50 lines of computer code.

Before John knew it, his people made Lisp real. The language was indeed small, and it was really possible to write a Lisp interpreter in Lisp in a few dozen lines of code. Because it was so easy to write a Lisp interpreter, many people wrote one. As it turned out, everyone tinkered with the original small Lisp interpreter. Soon enough, there wasn't just one Lisp but a lot of Lisps. Fortunately, all these Lisps shared the essential traits of John's original ideas so that Lisp programmers could easily exchange ideas. That's why Lisp is a family of programming languages, not just a single programming language.

(.3 What Does Lisp Look Like?

Now you know that Lisp is cool, old, and an entire family of languages. You also know that we are totally excited about one member of this family: Racket. Before you become impatient with us, let us show you some Lisp code so that this introduction doesn't become all talk and no action.

At some level, Lisp code isn't as different as it may seem at first. Here are some valid Lisp expressions, and we're sure you can guess what they compute:

```
(* 1 1)
(- 8 (* 2 3))
(sqrt 9)
```

If you answered 1, 2, and 3, then you've already figured out how to read Lisp code. It looks like arithmetic, except that the functions—addition, subtraction, multiplication, and square root—come before their operands, and expressions are surrounded by parentheses.

You may wonder why in the world Lisp breaks with the centuries-old tradition of infix notation, but take a look at this:

```
(+ 1 2 3 4 5 6 7 8 9 0)
```

For many functions, it makes a lot of sense to supply a lot of arguments at once, and with prefix notation, doing so is easy. But programming is also about defining your own operators and writing expressions that use these and the ones that come with the language. So in C++ programs, you may see things like this:

```
(foo<bar>)*g++.baz(!&qux::zip->ding());
```

Can you explain the order in which the subexpressions of this complex beast are evaluated? No one can. Everyone must dissect the expression first to understand it. Dissecting means putting in more parentheses, either in your head or on paper, after looking up which operators have the highest precedence. Do you recall your struggles with precedence in grade school? When you read Lisp code, this confusion never happens:

```
(sqrt (+ (sqr 3) (sqr 4)))
```

Here, you see a deeply nested expression, and yet the parentheses immediately tell you in which order things are evaluated. The parentheses also tell you that the operators—sqrt, +, and sqr—are involved, because you know that every left parenthesis—called "open" when Lispers speak—is followed by an operator. And guess what the right parentheses are called in Lisp-speak? You got it: "close." That's how easy it is to read Lisp. Once you're used to it, which may take a day or two, you will see its advantages.

However, Lisp isn't just about numbers or arithmetic; it's also about list processing. So you should be curious about what lists look like in Lisp. Here are some examples:

```
(list 1 2 3 4 5 6 7 8 9 0)
(list (list 1 3 5 7 9) (list 2 4 6 8 0))
(list (list 'hello 'world)
      (list (list 'it 'is) 2063)
      (list 'and 'we 'love 'Racket))
```

The first list consists of 10 digits; the second one groups these digits into two lists, which then become the elements of another list; and the third example shows that while lists can be deeply nested, Lisp comes with symbolic values, too.

Of course, a language that is about lists has even better ways to write lists:

```
'(1 2 3 4 5 6 7 8 9 0)
'((1 3 5 7 9) (2 4 6 8 0))
'((hello world)
  ((it is) 2063)
  (and we love Racket))
```

These first three examples should look familiar; they are abbreviations for the preceding list examples. See how little you need to write for a list of lists with symbolic information inside? One last example should inspire some awe:

```
'(sqrt (+ (sqr 3) (sqr 4)))
```

By adding a quote to the left of a piece of Lisp code, we turn it into a piece of data. Because the two expressions are equivalent, we could have written this:

```
(list 'sqrt
      (list '+
            (list 'sqr 3)
            (list 'sqr 4)))
```

Both create lists that contain a list, which contains a symbolic representation of addition and two more lists. The quoted expression creates a piece of data that captures all the structure that is in the program expression itself: its nesting structure, its numbers, and its symbols. If you had used string quotes to turn the expression into a piece of data, all you would have is a string. Before you could recover the expression's structure and organization, you would need to complete your entire computer science undergraduate major.

In Lisp, all it takes is one keystroke on your keyboard—one character on the screen. You cannot do anything like this without a Lisp. Now that's cool. And it's powerful.

(.4 Where Does Racket Come From?

Now back to 1972. Object-oriented programming had made an appearance. What we call the Smalltalk and Simula programming languages were up and running, and they suggested the object-oriented way of programming. People at John's old place began to study these ideas. Guy Steele and Gerry Sussman were two of these programmers. Here is how it all went down when they took this topic into their own hands:

What's an object?

An object computes something if you send it different kinds of messages.

Do we really need to understand how objects work with many different messages?

No way. A scientist just needs to know how objects deal with one message, and that shows how all messages work.

So what are objects that understand one kind of message?

Functions! Objects that understand only one message—"run your code on the following arguments"—are functions.

How about all these loops?

Al already knew in the 1930s that loops are just abbreviations for recursive functions.

You mean loops are like frosting on the cake when an object can send a message to itself?

Absolutely, loops are like adding sugar to soda.

Are conditionals fundamental?

Nope, not even they are. Al showed that such things are just functions and compositions of functions.

Guy and Gerry went back and forth for a while in this fashion. When they were done, they had extended Al's programming language of functions with just two ideas: assignment statements and jumps in control flow. Everything else was **syntactic sugar**, that is, shorthand for a combination of concepts from this tiny core language. The language drew its power from Guy and Gerry's efforts to make everything simple and regular.

The two also understood that this collection of ideas was close to John's idea of Lisp and that Lisp was really good for prototyping new languages. And so they prototyped their language in Lisp and called it Scheme. Because of that, people started thinking of Scheme as just another form of Lisp.

From Guy and Gerry's MIT AI Lab, Scheme quickly spread to several other places. Dan Friedman and Mitch Wand picked it up at Indiana University, and their research group built a version called Scheme84. They used Scheme to conduct programming language research. Because Scheme is so small and regular, it is easy to study the effects of adding one more idea or whether a new idea is just syntactic sugar for Scheme. A team of Yale researchers, under Paul Hudak's leadership, created another flavor, dubbed T. They looked at T as a compiler project, figuring out how to compile an expressive language into fast machine code. On top of that, individuals all over the world constructed their own variants of Scheme. Soon enough, dozens of Scheme implementations existed, all with their own small mixins and little extensions and tiny add-ons.

One of these Scheme implementations emerged at Rice University in Houston, Texas. Matthias Felleisen, Robby Findler, Matthew Flatt, and Shriram Krishnamurthi wanted to use Scheme to teach children math in a creative way. Children in middle school and high school could write computer games in plain arithmetic and algebra, which is easily expressed in a Scheme-like language. The four researchers also wanted to build all the necessary software in Scheme, and then they quickly realized that Scheme was too small to build real systems. They added structures, a class system, exceptions, fancy loops like you've never seen before, modules, custodians, eventspaces, libraries for building graphical-user interfaces, and many other things. Yes, some of these additions can be understood as syntactic sugar, but others introduced fundamentally new ideas into the world of programming languages.

Eventually, Matthias and Robby and Matthew and Shriram and everyone else who used this flavor of Scheme decided that their language was quite different from the original Scheme. After a lot of loud and wild arguing, they decided to give it a new name. This is where Racket comes from.

But don't worry—just because Racket is a large, useful language doesn't mean it is difficult to learn. Remember that Matthias, Robby, Matthew, and Shriram had middle school students in mind when they launched the Racket project. Because of this, learning Racket is like walking up a gentle slope; you should never feel like you have to climb a straight wall—unlike in your class, perhaps.

(.5 What Is This Book About?

So this book is *for* freshmen and it is written *by* freshmen, with a little help from some sophomores and professors. We assume that you have programmed somewhere, somehow—most likely in a freshman course at college. Our goal is to show you our own world of programming, one game at a time. We hope that this will open your mind about programming and that it will get you in touch with your inner Racketeer. If you like it, this book is a platform from which you can easily work your way into the rest of Racket and a whole new world of understanding programs.

Halt—Chapter Checkpoint

This introduction acquainted you with some historic background about programming and the Lisp family of programming languages:

- Computers are dumb pieces of hardware.
- Programmers use programming languages to turn computers into useful and entertaining gadgets.
- One of the oldest high-level languages is Lisp, which is more than 50 years old.
- There are many related flavors of Lisp, and we call Lisp a family of languages.
- To this day, Lisp offers programmers a way to experience programming as poetry.
- Racket is our chosen flavor of Lisp. Racket is relatively new, and it is especially well suited for novice programmers who want to ramp up gradually.

THIS IS CHAD.
Chad looks sad.

Maybe that's because he feels lost.

After his first year in college, he still feels unsure about his future.

He has not declared a major yet and didn't find any of his first-year courses exciting.

His good friends, Matt and Dave, suggested that he should check out programming, but Chad can't understand why.

Chad is going to do some research.
How exciting can programming really be?

Who are you?

Me?
OPEN PARENTHESIS!

define me
    "I am DrRacket! Now that you have entered my dungeons, you shall be my minion!
    The only way you can escape is by using your mind to defeat my traps and puzzles. Your life now depends on your thinking and creativity.
    Abandon all hope, ye who...who...just...uh...um...argh, nevermind.
    It's going to be really difficult from now on! MUAHAHAHAHA!"

CLOSE PARENTHESIS!

;; Chapter 1
(Getting Started)

```
#|
You need a Racket before you can launch a rocket, so the first
thing you need to learn is how to download and install DrRacket.
Once you have it on your computer, you will learn how to experi-
ment. Racket is all about experimenting with expressions and
creating your programs from these experiments. After some quick
demonstrations, you'll be ready to write a game!
|#
```

1.1 Readying Racket

Racket is a programming language. In principle, the Racket compiler is all you need to write Racket programs. You could—and die-hard Lispers would—launch the Racket compiler in an interactive mode, type in the program, and voilà, you'd have a running program. Or you'd get an error message saying that something isn't quite right, and you'd have to retype a part of your program. After a while, this gets bothersome. Just as you need a comfortable seat to work, you need a convenient "software seat" to develop your programs, to experiment with pieces, to run your test suites, and to explore the partially finished game. We call this place a **program development environment** (**PDE**); others refer to it as an **interactive development environment** (**IDE**).

DrRacket—pronounced "Doctor Racket"—is the PDE for Racket, and it is bundled with the Racket programming language. The original Racketeers—the people who created and use DrRacket—wanted to have a PDE where everyone—young children, old Lispers, and regular programmers—could quickly feel comfortable. Therefore, DrRacket is designed in such a way that you can immediately experiment with expressions and program fragments. You can edit programs and run them. You can write tests for your program and check them. And using DrRacket is quite easy.

So let's get DrRacket. Point your browser to racket-lang.org, and near the top-right area of the page, you will see a download icon. Click the icon, choose your platform, and download Racket from any of the sites that show up.

Racket can run on Windows, Mac, and *nix systems. For Windows and Macs, a software installer takes care of everything that needs to happen. If you're on a *nix box, you are already a hero and don't need instructions. In the end, you will have a folder with several applications. Launch DrRacket as appropriate for your platform: by clicking, from a shell, or whatever.

#|
NOTE: In this folder, you can see another folder called **collects** and within that folder, you can find **realm**. There, you can access all the source code for all the games in this book. We encourage you to open these files in DrRacket and to experiment with the code.
|#

Among other things, Racket is a programming language for making programming languages. Because of that, Racket comes in many flavors. Some flavors are for beginners; they are called **teaching languages**. Others are for writing small shell scripts or large applications. A third kind is for old people who wish to program in long-gone languages. And there are many more flavors beyond this short list. As far as this book is concerned, however, we will show you just one flavor: plain Racket.

You choose which Racket flavor you want to use with these four steps:

- Select the "Language" menu of DrRacket.
- Select the "Choose Language..." menu.
- Enable the option "The Racket Language."
- Click "OK" and then click "Run," the little green go icon.

Now take a closer look at DrRacket. You should see these primary pieces:

- Some buttons, including "Run" and "Stop"
- A **definitions panel** where you see the text `#lang racket`, which means you are using the Racket programming language
- An **interactions panel** labeled "Welcome to DrRacket" with another line of text that says your chosen language is "racket" and a third line with just one symbol: ">"

1.2 Interacting with Racket

DrRacket displays the ">" prompt in the interactions panel. The prompt signals that DrRacket expects you to enter an expression, say `(+ 1 1)`. DrRacket reads this expression, evaluates it, prints the result, and then displays its prompt again. Old Lispers call this mechanism a **read-eval-print loop**, but we are sticking with the Racketeer term **interactions panel**.

Go ahead. Enter an expression. Use `(+ 1 1)` if you can't think of anything better. Here is what happens:

```
> (+ 1 1)
2
```

As soon as you hit the "Enter" key, DrRacket becomes active and prints the result. Let's try another expression:

```
> (+ 3 (* 2 4))
11
```

The interactions panel works! Hooray! You type expressions and Racket evaluates them. Experiment some more—that's what the interactions panel is for. You could, for example, play with expressions like these:

```
> (sqrt 9)
3
> (sqrt -9)
0+3i
```

Yes, Racket knows about complex numbers. How about this:

```
> (+ 1 2 3 4 5 6 7 8 9 0)
45
```

Calling + on many numbers actually works. And so do nested expressions:

```
> (sqrt (+ (sqr 3) (sqr 4)))
5
```

Lists are a pleasure, too:

```
> '((1 3 5 7 9) (2 4 6 8 0))
'((1 3 5 7 9) (2 4 6 8 0))
```

They come back out just as you put them in, because there is nothing to evaluate with lists.

How about expressions as nested lists?

```
> '(sqrt (+ (sqr 3) (sqr 4)))
'(sqrt (+ (sqr 3) (sqr 4)))
```

Okay, enough of that. We need to move on to the definitions panel.

Take a look at the sketch below. We entered (+ 3 (* 2 4)) into the definitions panel, hit "Enter," and nothing happened. While the interactions panel is for experimenting with expressions, the definitions panel is where you record your code.

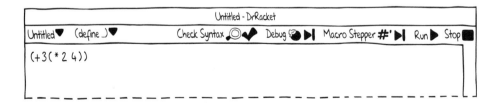

To make something happen, click the "Run" button. DrRacket will evaluate the expression and then print the result 11 in the interactions panel. You could also enter this in the definitions panel:

```
'(hello world)
```

Click "Run," and you'll see '(hello world) in the interactions panel. DrRacket does all the printing for you; there's no need for you to specify such mundane things. Also, note that your cursor is back in the interactions panel. You can now enter expressions there again and experiment some more.

Before we forget, click the "Save" button—the one with the disk icon. DrRacket will ask you to select a file name and folder on your computer where it will save the current contents of the definitions panel. Racketeers use file names that end in **.rkt** and you should do so, too:

my-first-program.rkt

You could run the program in this file in stand-alone mode now, or you could open the file in DrRacket and run things there.

Say you closed DrRacket and, before you know it, panic strikes. You just discovered that your first program wasn't supposed to add 3 to the product of 2 and 4. It was supposed to say '(hello world) and nothing else. Launch DrRacket again. Use the "File" menu and choose "Open Recent" from the available options. When you mouse-over this option, you can see **my-first-program.rkt**, and you should click it. The program is back in the definitions panel, and you are now free to change it to '(hello world). And that's why we place everything we wish to keep in the definitions panel.

Any questions? Oh yes, it's called the definitions panel because you actually write down definitions for variables and functions. But the best way to show you how to do this is by writing our first simple game together. Ready?

Raise—Chapter Checkpoint

In this chapter, you learned a few basics about Racket and DrRacket:

- DrRacket is the PDE for Racket. It runs on most computing platforms. Both Racket and DrRacket are available for free online at racket-lang.org as one package.

- You can enter expressions and evaluate them in the interactions panel.

- You can edit programs in the definitions panel and run them, and the interactions panel shows what they compute.

;; Chapter 2
(A First Racket Program)

```
#|
You've installed DrRacket, learned that programs go into the
definitions panel, and experimented with Racket in the interac-
tions panel. You are now ready to write your first real program,
a simple game for guessing numbers.
|#
```

2.1 The Guess My Number Game

The first game we will write is one of the simplest and oldest games around. It's the classic Guess My Number game. In this game, the player thinks of a number between 1 and
100. Our program will then figure out that number by repeatedly making guesses and
asking the player if her number is bigger or smaller than the current guess.

The following piece shows what a game might look like in the interactions panel if the player chose 18:

```
> (guess)
50
> (smaller)
25
> (smaller)
12
> (bigger)
18
```

The above interactions involve three different kinds of expressions: (guess), (smaller), and (bigger). You can probably imagine what they mean. The first one tells the program to start guessing; the second one says that the guess is too high, so a smaller number needs to be guessed; and the third one commands the program to look for a bigger number.

Everything to the immediate right of "(" is a function, which means that we are dealing with three functions here: guess, smaller, and bigger. All you need to do is define these functions, and you have programmed yourself a first game. The player calls these functions in the interactions panel, starting with the `guess` function.

Now, let's think about the strategy behind this simple game. The basic steps are as follows:

- Determine or set the upper and lower limits of the player's number.
- Guess a number halfway between those two numbers.
- If the player says the number is smaller, lower the upper limit.
- If the player says the number is bigger, raise the lower limit.

By cutting the range of possible numbers in half with every guess, the program can quickly home in on the player's number. Cutting the number of possibilities in half at each step is called a **binary search**. As you may know, binary search is frequently used in programming because it is remarkably effective at finding answers quickly. Even if we played the game with numbers between 1 and 1,000,000, a binary strategy could guess the right number in about 10 guesses.

At this point, you know almost everything there is to know about the game. We just need to introduce a few more Racket mechanics, and you will have Guess My Number going.

2.2 Defining Variables

As the player calls the functions that make up our game, the program will need to update the lower and upper limits at each call. One way to do so is to store the limits in variables and to change the values of the variables during the game. For Guess My Number, we'll need to create two new variables called `lower` and `upper`.

The way to create a new variable is with `define`:

```
> (define lower 1)
> lower
1
> (define upper 100)
> upper
100
```

We weren't completely honest with you. In addition to functions, it is also possible that "(" is followed by a **keyword**, such as `define`. Expressions that start with a keyword work in their own special way, depending on the particular keyword. You'll just need to remember the rules for each keyword. Fortunately, there is only a very small number of them.

The `define` keyword is quite important for understanding Racket programs, as it is used to define variables and functions. Here we are using it to define variables. The first part of the `define` expression is the name of the variable, and the second is an expression that produces the value we want the variable to have.

What may surprise you is that a definition does not evaluate to anything. Don't worry. We will explain. Oh, and do place those two definitions where they belong—in the definitions panel.

2.3 Basic Racket Etiquette

Racket ignores spaces and line breaks when it reads code. This means you could format your code in any crazy way but still get the same result:

```
> (                          define
                   lower 1)
> lower
1
```

Because Racket code can be formatted in such flexible ways, Racketeers have conventions for formatting programs, including when to use multiple lines and indentation. We'll follow common conventions when writing examples in this book, and you're better off mimicking them. However, we're more interested in writing games than discussing source code indentation rules, so we won't spend too much time on coding style in this book.

```
#|
NOTE: Pressing the "Tab" key in DrRacket automatically indents your
code to follow common convention. You can auto-indent a chunk of code
by highlighting it and then pressing the "Tab" key. You can auto-
indent an entire Racket program just by pressing Command+i on a Mac
or Ctrl+i on Windows and *nix.
|#
```

2.4 Defining Functions in Racket

Our Guess My Number program defines `guess` to start the game and responds to requests for either `smaller` or `bigger` guesses. In addition to these three functions, we also define a function called `start` that starts the game for a different range of numbers.

Like variables, functions are defined with `define`:

```
(define (function-name argument-name ...)
  function-body-expression
  function-body-expression
  ...)
```

First, we specify the name of the function and the names of its arguments and put all of them in a pair of parentheses. Second, we follow it up with the expressions that comprise the function's logic.

The dots mean that the preceding entity occurs an arbitrary number of times: zero times, one time, two times, and so on. It is thus possible that a function may have zero arguments, but it must have at least one expression in its body.

A Function for Guessing

The first function we'll define is `guess`. This function uses the values of the `lower` and `upper` variables to generate a guess of the player's number. In our definitions panel, its definition looks like this:

```
(define (guess)
  (quotient (+ lower upper) 2))
```

To indicate that the function does not take any arguments, we place a closing parenthesis directly after the function name `guess`.

```
#|
NOTE: Although you don't need to worry about indentation or line
breaks when entering code snippets, you must be sure to place paren-
theses correctly. If you forget a parenthesis or put one in the wrong
place, you'll most likely get an error; if you don't, you're in trou-
ble. But there's no need to worry: as you have probably noticed by
now, DrRacket helps you with this task.
|#
```

Guess what this function does. As discussed earlier, the computer's best guess in this game is a number halfway between the two limits. To accomplish this, we choose the average of the two limits. If the average number ends up being a fraction, we choose the nearest whole number.

We implement this in the `guess` function by first adding the numbers that represent the upper and lower limits. The expression `(+ lower upper)` adds together the value of those two variables. We then use the `quotient` function to divide the sum in half to get an integer.

Let's see what happens when we call our new function after clicking "Run":

```
> (guess)
50
```

Since this is the program's first guess, the output we see when calling this function tells us that everything is working as planned. The program picked the number 50, right in between 1 and 100.

When programming in Racket, you'll almost always write functions that won't explicitly print values on the screen. Instead, they'll simply return the value calculated in the body of the function, and DrRacket prints it for you. For instance, let's say we wanted a function that just returns the number 5. Here's how we could write the return-five function:

```
(define (return-five)
  5)
```

Because the value calculated in the body of the function evaluates to 5, calling (return-five) in the interactions panel returns 5, and DrRacket prints that:

```
> (return-five)
5
```

This is how guess is designed; we see this calculated result on the screen not because the function displayed the number, but because this is a feature of DrRacket's interactions panel.

```
#|
NOTE: If you've used other programming languages before, you may
remember needing to write something like "return" to cause a value
to be returned. This is not necessary in Racket. The final value
calculated in the body of the function is returned automatically.
|#
```

Functions for Closing In

Now we'll write our smaller and bigger functions, which update the upper and lower variables when necessary. Like guess, these functions are defined with the define form. Let's start with smaller:

```
(define (smaller)
  (set! upper (max lower (sub1 (guess))))
  (guess))
```

First, we use define to start the definition of any new function. Because smaller takes no parameters, the parentheses are wrapped tightly around smaller. Second, the function body consists of two expressions, one per line.

Third, the function uses a set! expression to change the value of a variable. In general, a set! expression has the following shape:

```
(set! variable expression)
```

The purpose of set!, pronounced "set bang," is to evaluate the *expression* and set the *variable* to the resulting value. With this in mind, we can see that the set! expression in the definition of smaller first computes the new maximum number, and then it assigns that number to upper, giving us the new upper bound.

Since we know the maximum number must be smaller than the last guess, the biggest it can be is one less than that guess. The code (sub1 (guess)) calculates this value. It calls our guess function to get the most recent guess, and then it uses the function sub1 to subtract 1 from the result. By taking the max of lower and (sub1 (guess)), we ensure that bigger is never smaller than lower.

Finally, we want our smaller function to show the player a new guess. We do so by putting a call to guess as the final expression in the function body. This time, guess calculates the new guess using the updated value of upper.

The bigger function works in the same manner as smaller, except that it raises the lower value instead:

```
(define (bigger)
  (set! lower (min upper (add1 (guess))))
  (guess))
```

After all, if the player calls the bigger function, she is saying that her number is bigger than the previous guess, so the smallest it can now be is one more than the previous guess. The function add1 simply adds 1 to the value returned by guess.

Here we see our functions in action, with the number 56 as the player's number:

```
> (guess)
50
> (bigger)
75
> (smaller)
62
> (smaller)
56
```

The Main Function

It is practical to have one **main function** that starts—or restarts—the whole application. Placing the definition of the main function at the top of the definitions panel also helps readers understand the purpose of the program.

For Guess My Number, this is a simple feat:

```
(define (start n m)
  (set! lower (min n m))
  (set! upper (max n m))
  (guess))
```

As you understand by now, start takes two arguments, which are the numbers we want to set as the lower and upper bounds. By using the max and min functions, we cut down on the instructions that we need to give any player. It suffices for a player to put in any two numbers in any order, and the function can determine the lower and upper bounds. For example, you could start the game using a small range of numbers, like this:

```
> (start 1 30)
15
```

```
#|
```
NOTE: As we continue to more challenging games, you will see how a main function makes our games much more user friendly.
```
|#
```

The other functions continue to work as advertised:

```
> (bigger)
23
> (smaller)
19
```

Now go ahead and do some guessing yourself.

Resume—Chapter Checkpoint

In this chapter, we discussed some basic Racket forms. Along the way, you learned how to do the following:

- Use define to define a variable or function.
- Use set! to change the value of a variable.
- Use the interactions panel for experimentation.
- Copy and paste successful experiments to the definitions panel.

;; Chapter 3
(Basics of Racket)

```
#|
You've written your first program. It consisted of a few functions
that dealt with numbers. You've seen the basics of expressions
and definitions. You know there are a lot of parentheses.
   Now it's time to bring some order to chaos. In this chapter,
we'll show you other kinds of data, as well as the general struc-
ture and meaning of Racket programs.
|#
```

3.1 Syntax and Semantics

To understand any language—be it a human language or a language for programming—requires two concepts from the field of linguistics. Computer scientists refer to them as "syntax" and "semantics." You should know that these are just fancy words for "grammar" and "meaning."

Here is a typical sentence in the English language:

```
My dog ate my homework.
```

This sentence uses correct English syntax. Syntax is the collection of rules that a phrase must follow to qualify as a valid sentence. Here are some of the rules of sentences in the English language that this text obeys: the sentence ends in a punctuation mark, contains a subject and a verb, and is made up of letters in the English alphabet.

However, there is more to a sentence than just its syntax. We also care about what the sentence actually means. For instance, here are three sentences that, roughly, have the same semantics:

My dog ate my homework.

The canine, which I possess, has consumed my school assignment.

我的狗吃了我的家庭作業。

The first two are just different ways of saying the same thing in English. The third sentence is in Chinese, but it still has the same meaning as the first two.

The same distinction between syntax and semantics exists in programming languages. For instance, here is a valid line of code written in C++:

```
((foo<bar>)*(g++)).baz(!&qux::zip->ding());
```

This line of code obeys the rules of C++ syntax. To make the point, we put in a lot of syntax that is unique to C++. If you were to place this line of code in a Python program, it would cause a **syntax error**.

Of course, if we were to put this line of code in a C++ program in the proper context, it would cause the computer to do something. The actions that a computer performs in response to a program make up its semantics. It is usually possible to express the same semantics with distinct programs written in different programming languages; that is, the programs will perform the same actions independent of the chosen language.

Most programming languages have similar semantic powers. In fact, this is something that Al and his student Alan Turing first discovered in the 1930s. On the other hand, syntax differs among languages. Racket has a very simple syntax compared to other programming languages. Having a simple syntax is a defining feature of the Lisp family of languages, including Racket.

3.2 The Building Blocks of Racket Syntax

From the crazy line of C++ code in the previous section, you can get the hint that C++ has a lot of weird syntax—for indicating namespaces, dereferencing pointers, performing casts, referencing member functions, performing Boolean operations, and so on.

If you were to write a C++ compiler, you would need to do a lot of hard work so that the compiler could read this code and check the many C++ syntax rules.

Writing a Racket compiler or interpreter is much easier as far as syntax is concerned. The part of a Racket compiler that reads in the code, which Racketeers call the **reader**, is simpler than the equivalent part for a C++ compiler or the compiler for any other major programming language. Take a random piece of Racket code:

```
(define (square n)
  (* n n))
```

This function definition, which creates a function that squares a number, consists of nothing more than parentheses and "words." In fact, you can view it as just a bunch of nested lists.

So keep in mind that Racket has only one way of organizing bits of code: parentheses. The organization of a program is made completely clear only from the parentheses it uses. And that's all.

A FORM IN RACKET

In addition to parentheses, Racket programmers also use square brackets [] and curly brackets {}. To keep things simple, we refer to all of these as "parentheses." As long as you match each kind of closing parenthesis to its kind of opening parenthesis, Racket will read the code. And as you may have noticed already, DrRacket is extremely helpful with matching parentheses.

The interchangeability of parentheses comes in handy for making portions of your code stand out for readers. For example, brackets are often used to group conditionals, while function applications always use parentheses. In fact, Racketeers have a number of conventions for where and when to use the various kinds of parentheses. Just read our code carefully, and you'll infer these conventions on your own. And if you prefer different conventions, go ahead, adopt them, be happy. But do stay consistent.

```
#|
```
NOTE: Code alone doesn't make readers happy, and therefore Racketeers write comments. Racket has three kinds of comments. The first one is called a **line comment**. Wherever Racket sees a semicolon (;), it considers the rest of the line a comment, which is useful for people and utterly meaningless for the machine. For emphasis, Racketeers use two semicolons when they start a line comment at the beginning of a line. The second kind of comment is a **block comment**. These comments are useful for large blocks of commentary, say at the beginning of the file. They start with #| and end with |#. While you may recognize the first two kinds of comments from other languages, the third kind is special to Racket and other parenthetical languages. An **S-expression comment** starts with #; and it tells Racket to ignore the next parenthesized expression. In other words, with two keystrokes you can temporarily delete or enable a large, possibly nested piece of code. Did we mention that parentheses are great?
```
|#
```

3.3 The Building Blocks of Racket Semantics

Meaning matters most. In English, nouns and verbs are the basic building blocks of meaning. A noun such as "dog" evokes a certain image in our mind, and a verb such as "ate" connects our image to another in a moving sequence.

In Racket, pieces of data are the basic building blocks of meaning. We know what 5 means and we know that 'hello is a symbol that represents a certain English word. What other sorts of data are there in Racket? There are many, including symbols, numbers, strings, and lists. Here, we'll show you the basic building blocks, or **data types**, that you'll use in Racket.

Booleans

Booleans are one of Racket's simple data forms. They represent answers to yes/no questions. So when we ask if a number is zero using the zero? function, we will see Boolean results:

```
> (zero? 1)
#f
> (zero? (sub1 1))
#t
```

When we ask if 1 is zero, the answer is #f, meaning false or no. If we subtract 1 from 1 and ask if that value is zero, we get #t, meaning true or yes.

Symbols

Symbols are another common type of data in Racket. A symbol in Racket is a stand-alone word preceded by a single quote or "tick" mark ('). Racket symbols are typically made up of letters, numbers, and characters such as + - / * = < > ? ! _ ^. Some examples of valid Racket symbols are `'foo`, `'ice9`, `'my-killer-app27`, and even `'--<<==>>--`.

Symbols in Racket are case sensitive, but most Racketeers use uppercase sparingly. To illustrate this case sensitivity, we can use a function called `symbol=?` to determine if two symbols are identical:

```
> (symbol=? 'foo 'FoO)
#f
```

As you can see, the result is `#f`, which tells us that Racket considers these two symbols to be different.

Numbers

Racket supports both **floating-point numbers** and **integers**. As a matter of fact, it also has **rationals**, **complex numbers**, and a lot more. When you write a number, the presence of a decimal point determines whether your number is seen as a floating-point number or an integer. Thus, the exact number 1 and the floating-point number 1.0 are two different entities in Racket.

Racket can perform some amazing feats with numbers, especially when compared to most other languages. For instance, here we're using the function `expt` to calculate the 53rd power of 53:

```
> (expt 53 53)
24356848165022712132477606520104725518533453128685640844505130879576720609150223301256150373
```

Isn't that cool? Most languages would choke on such a large integer.

You have also seen complex numbers. Consider this example:

```
> (sqrt -1)
0+1i
> (* (sqrt -1) (sqrt -1))
-1
```

Racket returns the imaginary number `0+1i` for `(sqrt -1)`, and when it multiplies this imaginary number by itself, it produces an exact `-1`.

Finally, something rational happens when you divide two integers:

```
> (/ 4 6)
2/3
```

The / function is dividing four by six. Mathematically speaking, this is just two over three. But chances are that if you've programmed in another language, you would expect this to produce a number like 0.66666...7. Of course, that's just an approximation of the real answer, which is the rational number two over three. Numbers in Racket behave more like numbers that you are used to from math class and less like the junk other languages try to pass off as numbers. So Racket returns a rational number, which is written as two integers with a division symbol between them. It is the mathematically ideal way to encode a fraction, and that is often what you want, too.

You will get a different answer if your calculation involves an inexact number:

```
> (/ 4.0 6)
0.6666666666666666
```

Compared with the previous example, this one uses 4.0 in place of 4. You might think 4.0 and 4 are the same number, but in Racket, the decimal notation indicates an inexact number; 4.0 really means some number that is close to four. Consequently, when you divide a number that is close to four by six, you'll get back a number that is close to ⅔, namely 0.6666666666666666.

Inexact numbers, like 4.0, are called floating-point numbers, and basically they don't behave like any kind of number you've seen in a math class. But the important thing to remember is that if you never use decimal notation, you won't need to worry about how these kinds of numbers behave. Exact numbers in Racket are honest numbers like the ones you learned about in grade school.

```
#|
NOTE: People invented floating-point numbers because computer pro-
grams that use ordinary (also called "precise") numbers can sometimes
be too slow for scientists and engineers. For us, precise numbers are
usually fine, and when they are not, we'll dive into floating-point
numbers.
|#
```

Strings

Another basic building block is the **string**. Although strings aren't really that fundamental to Racket, any program that communicates with a human may need strings, because humans like to communicate with text. This book uses strings because you are probably used to them.

A string is written as a sequence of characters surrounded with double quotes. For example, `"tutti frutti"` is a string. When you ask DrRacket to evaluate a string, the result is just that string itself, as with any plain value:

```
> "tutti frutti"
"tutti frutti"
```

Like numbers, strings also come with operations. For example, you can add two strings together using the `string-append` function:

```
> (string-append "tutti" "frutti")
"tuttifrutti"
```

The `string-append` function, like the + function, is generalized to take an arbitrary number of arguments:

```
> (string-append "tutti" " " "frutti")
"tutti frutti"
```

There are other string operations like `substring`, `string-ref`, `string=?`, and more, all of which you can read about in Help Desk.

```
#|
NOTE: An easy way to look up something in Help Desk is to move your
cursor over a name and press "F1."
|#
```

3.4 Lists in Racket

Lists are a crucial form of data in Racket. Racket data is like a big toolbox, and you can make amazing things if you know how to utilize your tools. You can't do anything without a trusty hammer, an ever-helpful screwdriver, and some needle-nose pliers. These basics are symbols, numbers, and strings in Racket. Then you have all the power tools—chain saws, drills, planers, and routers—that take everything to the next level, just like Racket lists and structures. Well, you really can't make anything in Racket without the basic cons cell, which is actually one of the most powerful tools Racket offers.

CONS Cells

Lists in Racket are held together with **cons cells**. Understanding the relationship between cons cells and lists will give you a better idea of how complex data in Racket works.

A cons cell is made of two little connected boxes, each of which can point to any other piece of data, such as a string or a number. Indeed, a cons cell can even point to another cons cell. By being able to point to different things, it's possible to link cons cells together into all kinds of data, including lists. In fact, lists in Racket are just an illusion—all of them are actually composed of cons cells.

For instance, suppose we create (list 1 3). It's created using three cons cells. Each cell points to a number, as well as the next cons cell for the list. The final cons cell then points to empty to terminate the list, such as (cons 1 (cons 2 (cons 3 empty))). If you've ever used a linked list in another programming language, this is the same basic idea. You can think of this arrangement as similar to a calling chain for your friends. "When I know about a party this weekend, I'll call Bob, and then Bob will call Lisa, who will call . . ." Each person in a calling chain is responsible for only one phone call, which activates the next call in the list. In the Realm of Racket, we also like to think of them as nesting dolls that shed layers until the last doll, which is rock solid.

Functions for CONS Cells

In this day and age, it is rare for a Racket programmer to manipulate cons cells as dotted pairs. Most of the time, these cells are used to build lists and nested lists, and there are great functions for dealing with all kinds of lists.

On some rare occasions, you may want to play with plain cons cells. So here is how you create a **raw cons cell**:

```
> (cons 1 2)
'(1 . 2)
```

As you can see, the result is a list with a dot. You can give a cons cell a name with define:

```
> (define cell (cons 'a 'b))
```

And you can extract the pieces of data that you stuck into a cons cell:

```
> (car cell)
'a
> (cdr cell)
'b
```

That is, if x is the name for a cons cell, car extracts the left piece of data from x and cdr extracts the right one.

Now you may wonder how anyone can be so crazy as to come up with names like car and cdr. We do, too. Therefore we focus on cons cells as the building blocks of lists and move on.

Lists and List Functions

Manipulating lists, not nested cons cells, is important in Racket programming. There are three basic functions for manipulating lists in Racket: cons, first, and rest. But to get started, you want to know that empty, '(), and (list) are all ways to say "empty list."

The CONS Function

If you want to link any two pieces of data in your Racket program, regardless of type, one common way to do that is with the cons function. When you call cons, Racket allocates a small chunk of memory, the cons cell, to hold references to the objects being linked. Here is a simple example where we cons the symbol chicken to the empty list:

```
> (cons 'chicken empty)
'(chicken)
```

Notice that the empty list is not printed in the output of our cons call. There's a simple reason for this: empty is a special value that is used to terminate a list in Racket. That said, the interactions panel is taking a shortcut and using the quote notation to describe a list with one element: 'chicken.

The lesson here is that Racket will always go out of its way to hide the cons cells from you. The previous example can also be written like this:

```
> (cons 'chicken '())
'(chicken)
```

The empty list, '(), can be used interchangeably with empty in Racket. Thinking of empty as the terminator of a list makes sense. What do you get when you add a chicken to an empty list? Just a list with a chicken in it. Of course, cons can add items to the front of the list. For example, to add 'pork to the front of '(beef chicken), use cons like this:

```
> (cons 'pork '(beef chicken))
'(pork beef chicken)
```

When Racketeers talk about using cons, they say they are **consing** something. In this example, we consed 'pork on to a list containing 'beef and 'chicken. Since all lists are made of cons cells, our '(beef chicken) list must have been created from its own two cons cells:

```
> (cons 'beef (cons 'chicken '()))
'(beef chicken)
```

Combining the previous two examples, we can see what all the lists look like when viewed as conses. This is what is really happening:

```
> (cons 'pork (cons 'beef (cons 'chicken '())))
'(pork beef chicken)
```

Basically, this is telling us that when we cons together three items, we get a list of three items.

The interactions panel echoed back to us our entered items as a list, '(pork beef chicken), but it could just as easily, though a little less conveniently, have reported back the items exactly as we entered them. Either response would have been perfectly correct. In Racket, a chain of cons cells and a list are exactly the same thing.

The LIST Function

For convenience, Racket has many functions built on top of the basic three—cons, first, and rest. A useful one is the list function, which does the dirty work of building our list all at once:

```
> (list 'pork 'beef 'chicken)
'(pork beef chicken)
```

Remember that there is no difference between a list created with the list function, one created by specifying individual cons cells, and one created with '. They're all the same animal. But consider the following before you rush out and buy all available quotes.

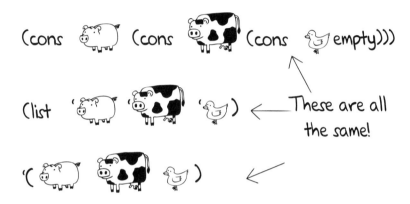

The FIRST and REST Functions

While cons constructs new cons cells and assembles them into lists, there are also operations for disassembling lists. The first function is used for getting the first element out of a list:

```
> (first (cons 'pork (cons 'beef (cons 'chicken empty))))
'pork
```

The rest function is used to grab the list out of the second part of the cell:

```
> (rest (list 'pork 'beef 'chicken))
'(beef chicken)
```

You can also nest `first` and `rest` to specify further which piece of data you are accessing:

```
> (first (rest '(pork beef chicken)))
'beef
```

You know that `rest` will take away the first item in a list. If you then take that shortened list and use `first`, you'll get the first item in the new list. Hence, using these two functions together retrieves the second item in the original list.

Nested Lists

Lists can contain any kind of data, including other lists:

```
> (list 'cat (list 'duck 'bat) 'ant)
'(cat (duck bat) ant)
```

This interaction shows a list containing three elements. The second element is `'(duck bat)`, which is also a list.

However, under the hood, these nested lists are still just made out of cons cells. Let's look at an example where we pull items out of nested lists.

```
> (first '((peas carrots tomatoes) (pork beef chicken)))
'(peas carrots tomatoes)
> (rest '(peas carrots tomatoes))
'(carrots tomatoes)
> (rest (first '((peas carrots tomatoes) (pork beef chicken))))
'(carrots tomatoes)
```

The `first` function gives us the first item in the list, which is a list in this case. Next, we use the `rest` function to chop off the first item from this inner list, leaving us with `'(carrots tomatoes)`. Using these functions together gives the same result.

As demonstrated in this example, cons cells allow us to create complex structures, and we use them here to build a nested list. To prove that our nested list consists solely of cons cells, here is how we could create the same nested list using only the `cons` function:

```
> (cons (cons 'peas (cons 'carrots (cons 'tomatoes '()))) 
        (cons (cons 'pork (cons 'beef (cons 'chicken '()))) '()))
'((peas carrots tomatoes) (pork beef chicken))
```

Since various combinations of `first` and `rest` are so common and useful, many are given their own name:

```
> (second '((peas carrots tomatoes) (pork beef chicken) duck))
'(pork beef chicken)
> (third '((peas carrots tomatoes) (pork beef chicken) duck))
'duck
> (first (second '((peas carrots tomatoes)
                   (pork beef chicken)
                   duck)))
'pork
```

In fact, functions for accessing the `first` through `tenth` elements are built in. These functions make it easy to manipulate lists in Racket, no matter how complicated they might be. If you are ever curious about built-in list functions, look in Help Desk.

3.5 Structures in Racket

Structures, like lists, are yet another means of packaging multiple pieces of data together in Racket. While lists are good for grouping an arbitrary number of items, structures are good for combining a fixed number of items. Say, for example, we need to track the name, student ID number, and dorm room number of every student on campus. In this case, we should use a structure to represent a student's information because each student has a fixed number of attributes: name, ID, and dorm. However, we would want to use a list to represent all of the students, since the campus has an arbitrary number of students, which may grow and shrink.

Structure Basics

Defining structures in Racket is simple and straightforward. If we wish to make the student structure for our example, we write the following **structure definition**:

```
> (struct student (name id# dorm))
```

This definition doesn't actually create any particular student, but instead it creates a new kind of data, which is distinct from all other kinds of data. When we say "creates a new kind of data," we really mean the structure definition provides functions for constructing and taking apart student structure values. Within `struct`, the first word—in this case, `student`—denotes the name of the structure and is also used as the name of the constructor for student values. The parentheses following the name of the structure enclose a series of names for the components of the structure, and the constructor takes that many values.

Let's create an **instance** of student:

```
> (define freshman1 (student 'Joe 1234 'NewHall))
```

Since the structure definition mentions three pieces, we apply the student constructor to three values, thus creating a single value that contains them all. This value is an instance, and it has three **fields**. Just as with any other kind of value, we can give names to structures for easy reference. If we ever need to retrieve information about our freshman1 student, we just use the **accessors** for student structures:

```
> (student-name freshman1)
'Joe
> (student-id# freshman1)
1234
```

To access the information in a structure field, we call the appropriate accessor function. In this case, we want to pull the name from the student structure that we already created, so we'll use student-name. As you can see, the interactions panel shows 'Joe, which is the value in freshman1's name field. When you want to access a different field, you use the function for that field instead, say student-id#. As you may have guessed by now, the structure definition creates three such functions: student-name, student-id#, and student-dorm. We sometimes call them **field selectors** or just **selectors**.

In Racket, it is common practice to store data as lists of structures. Say we wanted to keep a list of all the freshman students in a computer science class. Since we could have anywhere from a handful to hundreds or thousands of students in the class, we want to use a list to represent it:

```
> (define mimi (student 'Mimi 1234 'NewHall))
> (define nicole (student 'Nicole 5678 'NewHall))
> (define rose (student 'Rose 8765 'NewHall))
> (define eric (student 'Eric 4321 'NewHall))
> (define in-class (list mimi nicole rose eric))
> (student-id# (third in-class))
8765
```

Here, four students are listed and combined in a list called in-class. All of the list functions we discussed in the previous section still apply, and we see that we can still access the fields of the student structures.

Nesting Structures

It can come in handy to have structures within structures and even within lists. For instance, in our previous example, we could keep all the students in one centralized `student-body` structure for freshmen, sophomores, juniors, and seniors, where each year stands for a list of student structures:

```
> (struct student-body (freshmen sophomores juniors seniors))
> (define all-students
    (student-body (list freshman1 (student 'Mary 0101 'OldHall))
                  (list (student 'Jeff 5678 'OldHall))
                  (list (student 'Bob 4321 'Apartment))
                  empty))
```

Here, we create the `student-body` structure with fields for the four different years. Next, we give the name `all-students` to one specific instance of `student-body`. As you can see, we expect lists of students in each of the four fields of a `student-body` instance.

To retrieve the name of the first freshman in the list, we need to properly layer our accessors:

```
> (student-name (first (student-body-freshmen all-students)))
'Joe
> (student-name (second (student-body-freshmen all-students)))
'Mary
> (student-name (first (student-body-juniors all-students)))
'Bob
```

We want the `student-name` of the `first` of the `student-body-freshmen` list. As we can see, `'Joe` is the name of the first freshman we created before. This also works to get `'Mary` and `'Bob`.

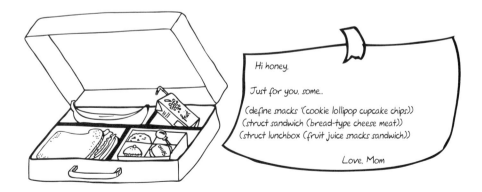

Hi honey,

Just for you, some...

(define snacks '(cookie lollipop cupcake chips))
(struct sandwich (bread-type cheese meat))
(struct lunchbox (fruit juice snacks sandwich))

Love, Mom

Structures and lists are useful for many different cases, such as organizing data into meaningful compartments that can be easily accessed. In this book, we will be using structures and lists for almost all programs.

Structure Transparency

By default, Racket creates opaque structures. Among other things, this means that when you create a specific structure and use it in the interactions panel, it does not print just as you created it. Rather, you will see something strange:

```
> (struct example (x y z))
> (define ex1 (example 1 2 3))
> ex1
#<example>
```

If you want to look inside structures, you must use the #:transparent option with your structure definition. By some sort of magical process, you will then be able to see your structures in the interactions panel:

```
> (struct example2 (p q r) #:transparent)
> (define ex2 (example2 9 8 7))
> ex2
(example2 9 8 7)
```

All of the structures in this book are supposed to be transparent, and therefore we don't bother to show the option when we define structures.

Interrupt—Chapter Checkpoint

In this chapter, you saw most of the building blocks of Racket's syntax and semantics:

- There are many kinds of basic data, like Booleans, symbols, numbers, and strings.
- You can make lists of data.
- You can make your own, new kinds of data with structures.
- You can mix it all up.

;; Chapter 4
(Conditions and Decisions)

```
#|
```
You've now seen Racket's simple syntax and a bunch of different
kinds of data. But can you write a program that answers a question about some piece of data? And can you write a program that
chooses different values depending on the answers to these questions? In this chapter, we'll look at predicates and different
forms of conditional evaluation. Among them is an extremely elegant multi-branch conditional that Racketeers use as their major
workhorse for many of their programming tasks.
```
|#
```

4.1 How to Ask

Racketeers think of a conditional as a form that asks questions about values and, depending on the answers, evaluates the appropriate expression. It is therefore natural that this
chapter shows you how to ask questions before it introduces conditionals.

A Racket program can ask many kinds of questions, but it always asks questions with
predicates. You may have heard of predicates in English class, but a Racket predicate is
just a function that returns either true or false, which are conventionally written as #t

and #f, but `true`, `#true`, `false`, and `#false` also work. The preceding chapter introduced several such functions, including

- `zero?`, which checks whether its argument is 0
- `symbol=?`, which compares symbols
- `student?`, but nobody told you that it was there

Let's check out the first two functions in the interactions panel:

```
> (zero? 42)
#f
> (zero? 0)
#t
> (symbol=? 'a 'b)
#f
```

The first three questions are obvious and so are the answers. Experiment with other questions, say, `(zero? "hello what's up?")` or `(symbol=? "a" 'b)`. Don't be afraid if it looks like things go wrong; sometimes they are supposed to.

Now let's take a look at this mysterious `student?` function. Recall our first `struct` definition:

```
> (struct student (name id# dorm) #:transparent)
```

It defines several functions, and we told you about four of them: `student`, `student-name`, `student-id#`, and `student-dorm`:

```
> (define sophomore3 (student 'David 100234 'PG))
> (student-name sophomore3)
'David
```

What we didn't tell you is that a structure definition also defines a predicate function. Its name is like that of the constructor but with a "?" added at the end. We pronounce it "huh?," so we read `student?` as "student, huh?" (or "student, eh?" in Canada). Here is what it does:

```
> (student? 'a)
#f
> (student? sophomore3)
#t
> (student? (student 1 2 3))
#t
> (student? "i am student")
#f
```

The `student?` function takes one argument. If the value is an instance of the `student` struct, it returns #t, aka true. Otherwise, it returns #f. Got predicate, huh?

Predicates such as `student?` are often called **type predicates**. These type predicates distinguish one kind of data from all other types of data. Every built-in form of data comes with a type predicate:

```
> (number? 'a)
#f
> (string? "hello world")
#t
> (symbol? 'a)
#t
> (image? 10)
#f
> (boolean? "false")
#f
```

Of course, Racket also has predicates for lists:

```
> (list? 'eh)
#f
> (cons? '(what is that aboot?))
#t
> (empty? 'a)
#f
```

As you can see, it actually has a predicate for lists in general, for non-empty lists, and for empty lists. For numbers, you get even more predicates:

```
> (real? 10)
#t
> (real? (sqrt -1))
#f
> (rational? 2/3)
#t
> (integer? 1.0)
#t
> (integer? 1)
#t
> (exact-integer? 1.0)
#f
```

If you ever need a predicate, guess a name and experiment in the interactions panel. Or look in Help Desk.

So when the preceding chapter says that the struct definition for student introduces an entirely new kind of data, it means that no existing type predicate will ever return #t when given an instance of student and that the new predicate, student?, will return #t for student structs and nothing else.

There is a little bit more to predicates:

```
> (= 1 2)
#f
> (= (sqrt -1) 0+1i)
#t
> (boolean=? #f #f)
#t
> (string=? "hello world" "good bye")
#f
> (equal? (student 'David 100234 'PG) sophomore3)
#t
```

Given that `student?` is called a type predicate, you may have guessed that `symbol=?`, `=`, `boolean=?`, `string=?`, and `equal?` are called **equality predicates**. Most basic forms of data come with functions that compare elements for equality, and for those that don't, there is `equal?`. Indeed, `equal?` is a function that compares absolutely everything:

```
> (equal? '(1 2 3) '(1 2 3))
#t
> (equal? 'a 'b)
#f
> (equal? "hello world" 'a)
#f
> (equal? 10 10)
#t
> (equal? #t 10)
#f
```

It compares lists, symbols, strings, numbers, Booleans, structs, and more. Not only does it compare numbers with numbers, lists with lists, and so on, but it actually compares numbers with lists, Booleans, strings, and everything else. Furthermore, it also compares data within **composite** data, such as elements within a list or pieces of a structure. It is a universal equality predicate.

Now you may wonder why Racket bothers with all these equality predicates. You may have noticed that when it comes to functions, we never really mention types. For example, we could define this kind of function:

```
(define (add-to-front-of-123 x)
  (cons x '(1 2 3)))
```

And then we could do this:

```
> (add-to-front-of-123 'a)
'(a 1 2 3)
> (add-to-front-of-123 0)
'(0 1 2 3)
> (add-to-front-of-123 '(a b c))
'((a b c) 1 2 3)
```

Racket would happily create these lists, while add-to-front would never wonder what type of data it receives. Types don't play a restrictive role in Racket. For this reason, Racketeers tend to use equality predicates that tell the reader of their programs about the kind of data they are dealing with. When you see (equal? x y), you get no hints. In contrast, the program snippet (= x y) immediately conveys that x and y should be numbers, and if they aren't, Racket will let you know. As you will see, these little hints thrown into a program are quite valuable when you try to decipher its meaning.

4.2 The Conditionals: IF and Beyond

Now that you understand predicates, let's look at if, a conditional that you have probably encountered in your previous programming experience.

The basic idea behind a conditional expression is that some code is evaluated *only under some condition*. It's an old idea that goes back to John McCarthy, who first used conditionals in the 1960s as a convenient way to implement mathematical functions. These days, you would be hard-pressed to find a program that doesn't contain a conditional.

One Thing at a Time with IF

An **if expression** can be used to choose between two different computations based on a computation that produces true or false:

```
> (if (= (+ 1 2) 3)
      'yup
      'nope)
'yup
```

```
> (if (= (+ 1 2) 4)
      'yup
      'nope)
'nope
```

In the eyes of Racket's if, as well as all in its other conditional forms, #f is false and anything that is not false is true. It's an old, slightly weird Lisp tradition that Racket kept and that is really convenient once you're used to it. Some examples should clear up any confusion:

```
> (if '(1)
      'everything-except-#f-counts-as-#t
      'aw-heck-no)
'everything-except-#f-counts-as-#t
> (if empty
      'everything-except-#f-counts-as-#t
      'aw-heck-no)
'everything-except-#f-counts-as-#t
> (if false
      'everything-except-#f-counts-as-#t
      'aw-heck-no)
'aw-heck-no
```

Notice how '(1) counts as true according to if. The same is true of empty. Remember, everything that is not #f is true.

Here is an if expression that actually asks a question with a predicate:

```
> (if (odd? 5) 'odd-number 'even-number)
'odd-number
```

All we're doing here is asking whether 5 is odd and then, depending on the answer, evaluating one of the two following expressions in the if form. Since 5 is odd, if evaluates the first such expression, and as a whole it returns 'odd-number.

There's a lot happening in this harmless-looking if expression, and it's all important for understanding Racket. Consider the template of an if expression:

```
(if some-expression
    an-expression
    another-expression)
```

Here, the first of the expressions, some-expression, is called the **test**; the second one is known as the **then** expression; and the third one is dubbed the **else** expression. The last two expressions are also known as **branches**. Knowing these labels for the pieces of an if expression helps us talk about it.

The key observation is that only one of the two expressions that follow the test expression in an `if` form is actually evaluated. Usually, when a function call is executed in Racket, all the arguments are evaluated before the function is called. However, `if` does not follow these rules. Consider this example:

```
> (if (odd? 5)
      'odd-number
      (/ 1 0))
'odd-number
```

Any self-respecting, law-abiding *function* would kick your butt to the curb if you tried to run this code, because the else branch is dividing by zero.

But `if` isn't really a function. Like `define`, it's a special **form**, and all forms have special privileges, such as the right to not evaluate all their arguments in the normal way. This makes sense, since the whole point of a conditional is to evaluate only a certain expression and not the others. In this case, `if` merrily ignores the division by zero because it's in the branch that applies only to even numbers. Conditional expressions in Racket are typically special forms.

The Special Form that Does It All: COND

If you ever want to make more than one decision, you can nest `if` expressions, just as you may have done with other languages.

```
> (define x 7)
> (if (even? x)
      'even-number
      (if (= x 7)
          5
          'odd-number))
5
```

This example consists of an `if` expression nested in the else branch of another `if` expression. The question of the outer `if` finds out whether the value of x is an even number; if not, x is odd, and thus the inner `if` can check whether x is equal to 7.

But what do you do if you're the kind of coder who wants it clear-cut and simple? Well, Racket has you covered.

The **cond expression** is the classic way to do branching in Racket. It can handle many branches instead of just two. Since `cond` has been around since the Racket Stone Age, many Racket programmers consider it to be the one true Racket conditional form.

Here's an example of cond:

```
> (define x 7)
> (cond [(= x 7) 5]
        [(odd? x) 'odd-number]
        [else 'even-number])
```

As you can see, the body of a cond uses layers of brackets to separate the different branches. The first expression of each such branch contains the condition for making that branch active. In our example, we are checking for different qualities about variable x.

The conditions in a cond form are always checked consecutively from top to bottom, meaning the first successful match drives the behavior. So it makes sense that we check first to see if the number is equal to 7 and then if it is odd. Otherwise, cond would never find the case of x equals 7. In this example, the last bracketed part has else as its condition, which catches the rest of the numbers. If the number is not 7 and not odd, then it must be even.

It is a common cond idiom to use else as the last branch because it ensures that the conditional will evaluate some branch. You should experiment and change the value of x in its definition to see what happens with the cond expression. Also, formulate a cond expression that checks conditions in the exact same order as the above nested if expression. Experiment with your revised expression, too. Convince yourself that all three expressions have the same meaning.

A First Taste of Recursion

Because we know about if and cond and how to detect an empty list, we can now process lists using **recursion**. You may have been told to be scared of recursion, but we dealt with it in our third week of programming—if we figured it out, you can figure it out, too. It all just boils down to one point: we can take items from the front of a list and send the rest of the list back to the same function until the list is empty. That process is called a **list-eater**, and it sure is a good thing that detecting empty lists is easy, because so many functions in Racket end up being list-eaters.

Let's look at a common list-eating function:

```
(define (my-length a-list)
  (if (empty? a-list)
      0
      (add1 (my-length (rest a-list)))))
```

You can probably guess what it does, but just to make sure, here are some examples:

```
> (my-length '(list with four symbols))
4
> (my-length '(42))
1
```

As these examples show, this first recursive function calculates the length of a list.

The function is written in classic Racket style. Since a list is either empty or non-empty, the function checks whether its argument, a-list, is empty. If it is empty, we know how many items are on the given list, 0, and that's what the function returns. If a-list is not empty, we know that it contains at least one item. We also know that (my-length (rest a-list)) calculates the length of the rest of the list. To get the length of the entire a-list, the function just needs to add 1.

If these interactions do not make sense to you, try looking at one step-by-step:

```
  (my-length (list 'a 'b))
== (my-length (cons 'a (cons 'b empty)))
== (add1 (my-length (rest (cons 'a (cons 'b empty)))))
== (add1 (my-length (cons 'b empty)))
== (add1 (add1 (rest (cons 'b empty))))
== (add1 (add1 (my-length empty)))
== (add1 (add1 0))
== (add1 1)
== 2
```

For now, this is enough recursion. We will show you more list-eaters in chapter 6 when we discuss how to create a Snake game.

4.3 Cool Tricks with Conditionals

There are two counterintuitive tricks involving conditionals that can help you write concise code. The first involves and and or, which are actually shorthand for conditionals. The second takes advantage of Racket's conception of truth and falsehood.

Using the Stealth Conditionals AND and OR

The conditionals and and or look like simple mathematical operators that allow you to compose complex questions from simple ones. They help you manipulate Boolean values in the same way that you might manipulate numbers with addition and subtraction. For example, here's how we could use and to see if three numbers are odd:

```
> (define x 5)
> (define y 7)
> (define z 9)
> (and (odd? x) (odd? y) (odd? z))
#t
```

Because 5, 7, and 9 are odd, the entire expression evaluates to true. Similarly, we can use or to see whether at least one of a bunch of numbers is odd:

```
> (define w 4)
> (or (odd? w) (odd? y) (odd? z))
#t
```

Because 7 is odd, the or expression still evaluates to true, despite the fact that 4 is even.

But there's something interesting about and and or that you might not notice just by looking at these two examples. So far, these two forms look like ordinary mathematical functions; they do not look like conditional forms, such as if and cond. However, they can be used to code conditional behavior. For instance, here's a variable definition:

```
> (define is-it-even #f)
> is-it-even
#f
```

You can use conditionals to change the value of the variables, like this:

```
> (or (odd? x) (set! is-it-even #t))
#t
> (and (even? x) (set! is-it-even #t))
#f
> is-it-even
#f
```

I guess we're both conditionals on the inside, aren't we?!

When we check on `is-it-even`, the variable remains unchanged. In fact, our `or` expression produces true because of shortcut Boolean evaluation. This means that once Racket determines that an expression in a sequence of `or` values is true, it simply returns true and doesn't bother evaluating the remaining conditions. However, the value of `is-it-even` does change when we use an even number in our first `or` clause:

```
> (or (odd? w) (set! is-it-even #t))
> is-it-even
#t
```

In this case, the first expression produces false, causing the evaluation of the second expression, which changes `is-it-even` to `#t`.

The shortcut evaluation for `and` works in the opposite way. If `and` determines that an early expression of `and` is false, it stops with `#f` without bothering to evaluate the rest of the expressions:

```
> (and (odd? 5) (even? 5) (/ 1 0))
#f
```

While this may seem like an unimportant distinction, it can actually be very useful in many situations. For instance, imagine that you want to save a file to disk, but only if the file is modified and only if the user wants it to be saved. The basic code could be written as follows:

```
> (if file-modified
      (if (ask-user-about-saving)
          (save-file)
          false)
      false)
```

Here, the function `ask-user-about-saving` would ask the user about saving the file, and it would return true or false based on the user's wishes. However, since shortcut Boolean evaluation is guaranteed for Boolean operations, we could write this five-line conditional in one line:

```
> (and file-modified (ask-user-about-saving) (save-file))
```

Using this concise style for conditionally evaluating code is possible only if you think beyond the typical use of the Boolean operators as mathematical operators.

A third way to write this code, which is a compromise between the previous approaches, is as follows:

```
> (when (and file-modified (ask-user-about-saving))
    (save-file))
```

Many experienced Racketeers will consider this version the best because it separates the condition from the action. Specifically, a **when conditional** is like an `if` without an else branch. The keyword signals that the program will test a condition and then perform some action, but only if the condition evaluates to `#t`. Naturally, Racket also comes with an **unless form**, which is the opposite of `when`:

```
> (define filename "my-first-program.rkt")
> (unless (ask-user-whether-to-keep-file filename)
    (delete-file filename))
```

An `unless` form performs some action if its condition returns `#f`.

Using Functions that Return More than Just the Truth

Now let's look at another benefit of Racket's way of thinking about true and false. As we've already discussed, any value other than `#f` counts as true in Racket. This means that functions that are commonly used in conditions have the option of returning more than just the truth. For instance, the Racket function `member` can be used to check for the membership of an item in a list:

```
> (if (member 4 (list 3 4 1 5)) '4-is-in 'not-in)
'4-is-in
```

This seems pretty straightforward. However, once again there is something happening behind the scenes that you may not expect. Let's run the `member` expression in isolation:

```
> (member 1 '(3 4 1 5))
'(1 5)
```

What the heck happened here? Why is `member` returning `'(1 5)`? Actually, there's a perfectly rational explanation for this. Whenever a Racketeer writes a function that returns true or false, she will think to herself, "Is there anything else I could return other than just true?" Since all non-false values in Racket count as true, returning some other value is essentially a freebie. The implementors of the `member` function decided that some crazy Racketeer somewhere may see the value in having the tail of the list for some calculation that uses this function.

Just in case you think they are crazy, here is an example that exploits this trick:

```
> (define tasks '(1 clean 3 homework 4 party))
> (member 3 tasks)
'(3 homework 4 party)
```

The `tasks` list enumerates a sequence of jobs that someone needs to complete. When you now use `member` to look up the task labeled 3, the function doesn't just produce #t, but it produces what the list contains for the task labeled 3 and subsequent tasks in the list. Of course, this list counts as true, too, but it is a more informative kind of truth. From there, you can see that task number 3 is `'homework`, followed by 4 and `'party`. Go party for a while.

4.4 Equality Predicates, Once More

Section 4.1 presents a plethora of equality predicates. There are some that are specialized to particular kinds of data, like `string=?`, and there is also `equal?`, which is not specialized at all. The `equal?` function compares any kind of data, even composite structures. But `equal?` isn't the only universal equality predicate, and it's important to understand the alternatives.

Let's look at another struct definition:

```
> (struct point (x y) #:transparent)
```

```
#|
```
NOTE: Did you notice that we used #:transparent even though we prom-
ised not to bother you with that anymore? In this case, we really
want you to remember it, because it is necessary here. If this seems
opaque, omit the keyword and see what happens.
```
|#
```

It introduces a class of `point` structs, each with two fields: `x` and `y`. You should recall that
this kind of `struct` definition simply defines a bunch of functions for creating, manipulating, and discovering concrete instances:

- `point`
- `point-x`
- `point-y`
- `point?`

With these you could, for example, define a function that determines the distance of a
`point` from the origin; that is, `(point 0 0)`. Here, let's try it:

```
(define (distance-to-origin p)
  (sqrt (+ (sqr (point-x p)) (sqr (point-y p)))))
```

You may recall from high school mathematics how to explore this function after
clicking the "Run" button:

```
> (distance-to-origin (point 3 4))
5
```

Also try it with 12 and 5. What do you expect as the result? Why?
It is possible to give names to points with `define`:

```
> (define pt1 (point -1 2))
> (define pt2 (point -1 2))
```

And yes, `pt1` and `pt2` look equal, and `equal?` says they are:

```
> (equal? pt1 pt2)
#t
```

The reason is that `equal?` checks that both arguments belong to the same class of data,
namely points, and that all their pieces—x and y here—are `equal?`, too.

You may have noticed that the description of `equal?` seems recursive, kind of like `my-length` from before. We tend to think of `equal?` like this:

```
(define (my-equal? a b)
  (cond
    [(and (point? a) (point? b))
     (and (my-equal? (point-x a) (point-x b))
          (my-equal? (point-x a) (point-x b)))]
    ...
    ;; Every struct definition adds a cond clause.
    [(and (cons? a) (cons? b))
     (and (my-equal? (car a) (car b))
          (my-equal? (cdr a) (cdr b)))]
    [(and (empty? a) (empty? b))
     #t]
    [(and (symbol? a) (symbol? b))
     (symbol=? a b)]
    [(and (number? a) (number? b))
     (number=? a b)]
    [(and (boolean? a) (boolean? b))
     (boolean=? a b)]
    ...
    ;; Every primitive form of data has a cond clause here.
    [else #f]))
```

Whenever a program defines a `struct`, the function is updated to contain a line like the one for `point` so that `equal?` can deal with this new kind of data. Subsequent lines compare basic forms of data. In addition to symbols, numbers, and strings, Racket supports other forms of basic data, but we don't need them in this book.

But `equal?` isn't always what you need. Sometimes you don't want to compare the pieces of a structure; instead, you want to know whether the two given concrete structures were created via the exact same call to the constructor. To this end, Racket provides the `eq?` function:

```
> (eq? pt1 pt2)
#f
> (eq? pt1 pt1)
#t
> (eq? pt2 pt2)
#t
```

As these interactions with Racket show, `eq?` recognizes that `pt1` is equal to itself and so is `pt2`, but `pt1` and `pt2` were created at different times.

In Racket, it is also possible to give new names to existing values:

```
> (define pt3 pt1)
```

The `eq?` function knows about such things:

```
> (eq? pt1 pt3)
#t
```

Indeed, it even works through composite data:

```
> (define (eq-first-items list1 list2)
    (eq? (first list1) (first list2)))
> (eq-first-items (cons pt1 empty) (cons pt3 empty))
#t
> (eq-first-items (cons pt1 empty) (cons pt2 empty))
#f
```

Chapter 8 will introduce a way to change the values of the fields of structures. Once this additional expressive power is available, the difference between `eq?` and `equal?` becomes critical. While `equal?` compares whether two values consist of identical pieces, `eq?` compares whether changing one structure changes the other structure, and that happens only when the structures were created with the exact same call to the constructor function.

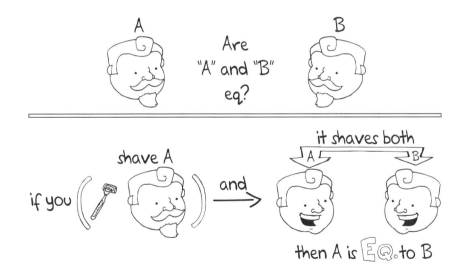

In summary, equality is a subtle property. Almost all programming languages offer functions such as eq? and equal?, and it is important to appreciate the differences. Most of the time, the equality predicates discussed in section 4.1 will serve your programming needs just fine. But for some occasions, you need eq?, and here we have prepared you for just those occasions.

4.5 Comparing and Testing

Equality matters a lot when it comes to testing. When you write programs, you should create tests for almost all the functions in your code. As a matter of fact, you should write tests before you even write the functions.

In principle, a **test** consists of two pieces: a function call and an expected result value. Racket evaluates the function call and then compares the result with the expected value. If they are equal, you learn that the function works correctly on that input. If not, something is wrong: your function, your test, or both.

Racket provides several libraries for testing. One such library is rackunit. Whenever you need to use one of Racket's provided libraries, you **require** that library:

```
> (require rackunit)
```

This makes all the functionality of rackunit available in the interactions panel. If you want this functionality in your programs, you add the line to the definitions panel. You can find documentation for rackunit in Help Desk by pressing the "F1" key on most computers. Browse the docs at your leisure. Here we cover just the basics.

Writing a Test

When testing in rackunit, the most commonly used function is check-equal?, which takes two expressions, evaluates them, and compares them for equality using the equal? function. So suppose you want to test the add1 function. You know that whenever you apply add1 to 5, you expect 6 back, and here is how you write down this expectation:

```
> (check-equal? (add1 5) 6)
>
```

Notice how the expression seems to do nothing. But it really does check whether (add1 5) and 6 are equal, and you can see so for yourself by entering a test that fails:

```
> (check-equal? (add1 5) 7)

FAILURE
name:       check-equal?
location:   ...
```

```
expression: (check-equal? (add1 5) 7)
actual:     6
expected:   7
```

Since (add1 5) evaluates to 6 and not 7, check-equal? signals that this test has failed. The call to a function has produced an actual result that differs from the expected result. And that is what a test is all about.

What Is Not a Test

Sometimes you may wish to test the composition of functions. Nevertheless, even in these cases, a test consists of an expression and its expected outcome. For example, the following test says that sub1 is the inverse of add1, at least for the number 5:

```
> (check-equal? (sub1 (add1 5)) 5)
```

When you run a function or a program, you are not testing it—you are exploring its behavior. You may have certain ideas in mind of how it should behave, but as long as you don't write down this expectation beforehand, and as long as there is no automatic comparison, it is *not a test*.

Testing in the Real World

Any testing function can take an optional third argument: a string. This is a helpful way to clarify what the test means:

```
> (check-equal? 5 6 "NUMBERS MATTER!")

FAILURE
name: check-equal?
location: ...
expression: (check-equal? 5 6)
params: (5 6)
message: "NUMBERS MATTER!"
actual: 5
expected: 6
```

When a test fails, this string is displayed in a prominent position. You will find that when a program comes with a few hundred tests, these messages can be very handy.

All of the programs that come with the book have extensive test suites. Indeed, in our freshman year, we always wrote tests before starting on our functions. We are now real believers—there simply is no other way to write good programs. But we don't have the space in this book to explain the tests for the programs. We suggest that you open some of our games in DrRacket and look at the test suites so that you get a sense of what test suites look like.

More Testing Facilities

Here are a few more testing functions from `rackunit` that you may find in our code.

Name	Purpose	Example (all pass)
`check-not-equal?`	Checks for inequality	`(check-not-equal? 5 4)`
`check-pred`	Checks the second argument against the predicate	`(check-pred number? 5)`
`check-=`	Checks if two numbers are within a certain range of each other	`(check-= 1 3 2)`
`check-true`	Checks if the argument is #t	`(check-true (odd? 71))`
`check-false`	Checks if the argument is #f	`(check-false (odd? 42))`
`check-not-false`	Checks if the argument is not #f	`(check-not-false (member 5 '(1 2 5)))`

`Call-with-current-continuation`—**Chapter Checkpoint**

In this chapter, you learned about predicates, conditionals, and testing:

- Racket has predicates, including type and equality predicates.
- There are many conditionals, but `if` and `cond` are the most important ones.
- Conditionals tend to use predicates to ask questions about values, and the rest of the computation depends on the questions' outcomes.
- The `rackunit` library is for writing tests.
- To test means to compare the outcome of expressions with expected answers.
- All of our programs come with tests, but we don't show the tests in the book.

;; Chapter 4½
(define define 'define)

```
#|
So far, we have covered the basics of defining variables and
functions. Did you wonder if there was more to it? In this
chapter, we will show you everything you need to know about
definitions.
|#
```

4½.1 Module-Level Definitions

The most common kind of definitions are **module-level definitions**. These introduce names that can be accessed anywhere in the module. For now, think of a module as the definitions panel. There are two kinds of module-level definitions: variable definitions and function definitions.

Variable Definitions

Let's begin with variable definitions. Suppose we were to develop a graphical version of the Guess My Number game from chapter 2 that displays its results on a window of some fixed size. The right approach in this scenario is to define variables for the width and height of the window.

```
(define WIDTH 100)
(define HEIGHT 200)
```

By convention, we use uppercase for the names of module-level definitions that introduce **constants**. Doing so makes constants stand out. These constant definitions can also name computed values instead of hard-coded ones:

```
(define X-CENTER (quotient WIDTH 2))
(define Y-CENTER (quotient HEIGHT 2))
```

Defining a constant and referencing it throughout the program is highly preferable to using literal constants everywhere. Once you have done so, you can change the value where it is defined, and then everything else that references the constant will use the new value as well. This provides a single point of control. For example, if we defined the constant WIDTH to be 100 and later we realize that the resulting image is too small, we could simply change the definition of WIDTH to 200, and this value will be used as the width throughout the whole program. In particular, X-CENTER would change from 50 to 100.

A more feeble-minded programmer might have instead first littered the program with 100s. After deciding the window was too small, he would need to change all of those 100s to 200s. Being lazy, he might just search and replace 100 with 200, which has the intended effect of making the window bigger, but also has the unintended effect of making the game start by guessing 100 instead of 50. Can you figure out why?

To avoid these kinds of issues, we define constants for elements of our game that do not change throughout the code. For example, these elements could be image size, instructions, colors, and so on. Another benefit of coding this way is that if someone wants to play our game in Arabic or Zulu instead of English, all he needs to do is look for the section in the code where the strings are defined and change these constant strings to his preferred language.

We define constants separately from code for every single program in this book. However, we will not show you all the constant definitions because we're more interested in talking about games than constants. The constants are available in the source code, which is only a few keystrokes away.

At times, we must impose some limits on these constants. We wouldn't want someone to replace the height of our screen with a negative number. To check that the constant is always appropriate, we can provide a section of code below the constant definition that will raise an error if the value we have provided is inappropriate:

```
(unless (> HEIGHT 0)
  (error 'guess-my-number "HEIGHT may not be negative"))
```

This check works because any code that is placed in the definitions panel is executed when we hit "Run." It will be as if that portion of the code had been typed in the interactions panel. In this case, we tell DrRacket to signal an error and inform the programmer that a constraint has been broken.

Function Definitions

The other kind of module-level definition is a function definition, and we've already seen several of these. These defined functions can be called anywhere in the module:

```
(define SQR-COLOR "red")
(define SQR-SIZE 10)
(define (draw-square img x y)
  (place-image (square SQR-SIZE "solid" SQR-COLOR)
               x y
               img))
```

As we saw before, a function definition is composed of the keyword define, followed by the name of the function and any arguments, all enclosed in parentheses. This function header is followed by the expressions that will be executed when the function is called.

4½.2 Local Definitions

In Racket, you can place the same kind of definition that you placed at the module level inside function definitions. More precisely, a definition may show up within any sequence of expressions inside function definitions and conds, as long as it's not the last expression.

Such **local definitions** are useful if you don't want to compute a value multiple times or if you don't want to nest expressions too deeply. These definitions exist only within the pair of parentheses in which they are defined and cannot be accessed anywhere else. We call this the **scope** of the definition. For instance, consider this program fragment:

```
(struct posn (x y))
(struct rectangle (width height))
(define (inside-of-rectangle? r p)
  (define x (posn-x p))
  (define y (posn-y p))
  (define width (rectangle-width r))
  (define height (rectangle-height r))
  (and (<= 0 x) (< x width) (<= 0 y) (< y height)))
```

The scope of x, y, width, and height is the entire body of the inside-of-rectangle? function. We introduce these variable definitions to eliminate some nesting from the and expression. We assume you figured out that this function computes whether a given point is within a rectangle.

Local definitions even work within a cond:

```
(define (random-stars n)
  (cond
    [(zero? n) '()]
```

```
[else (define location (random-location 200 300))
      (if (inside-moon? location)
          (random-stars n)
          (cons location (random-stars (sub1 n))))]))
```

This function is a natural number–eater. When it is given a natural number—zero, one, two, and so on—random-stars checks whether the number is zero. In the else case, it will recur with one less than the given number, so sooner or later, the function will pick the first case. It is more important, however, to understand the local definition in the else case. It names a random place in a 200×300 grid location, and this name stands for the random position between the brackets [ ] of the second arm in the cond. Conversely, location is not available elsewhere in the scope of the function definition or the module itself.

Why do we name the random place location? The whole point of random-location is to pick some place out of 60,000 possible places, choosing a random one every time the function is called. Hence, if we wrote this . . .

```
(if (inside-moon? (random-location 200 300))
    (random-stars n)
    (cons (random-location 200 300) (random-stars (sub1 n))))
```

. . . it's very likely that the two calls would pick two distinct locations. Worse, the second time it picks a place, it may appear within the shape of the moon, which we wish to avoid.

Here is another example of a local definition:

```
(define (winners lst pred)
  (cond
    [(empty? lst) (list pred)]
    [else
     (define fst (first lst))
     (if (score> (record-score pred) (record-score fst))
         (list pred)
         (cons pred (winners (rest lst) fst)))]))
```

The purpose of the function is to pick the first-place finishers from a list of game records. As you can see, the function definition relies on several assumptions. First, its code suggests that we have a struct definition of the following shape:

```
(struct record (name score))
```

The name field records the name of the player, and the score field records the player's performance. Second, lst is a list of such records, and pred is one such record. Indeed, the original list is (cons pred lst), and it is sorted according to score. Somehow, winners is applied to the first and the rest of the list. Now in this context, you understand that winners is a list-eating function and goes through one record at a time. When there is at least one other record, it picks the first one, names it `fst`, and compares the scores of `fst` and its predecessors. Depending on the outcome, all winning records have been picked off or `winners` has to continue the search for equal-scoring players.

In this case, we use the local definition of `fst` only to make the code more readable. While we could avoid the definition and copy the expression wherever `fst` appears, it would make the code look large and bulky. Because Racket delimits the scope to the brackets of the second arm of the `cond`, there is also no harm in introducing yet another name into the world. If we need to use it again, we can do so outside this small scope.

Finally, you may be wondering who guarantees that `winners` is always applied to the `rest` and the `first` of some sorted list. To avoid any mistakes, we need to show you *locally defined* functions:

```
(define (winning-players lst)
  (define sorted-lst (sort lst ...))
  (define (winners lst pred)
    (cond
      [(empty? lst) (list pred)]
      [else
  (define fst (first lst))
  (if (score> (record-score pred) (record-score fst))
      (list pred)
      (cons pred (winners (rest lst) fst)))]))
  ;; START HERE:
  (winners (rest sorted-lst) (first sorted-lst)))
```

This form of local function definition is a common idiom. Since `winners` shouldn't be applied to arbitrary lists and records, we hide it by defining it within the scope of some other function that consumes a list of records. Then this function sorts the list and applies `winners` to the appropriate pieces. As you know by now, the function named `winners` can be accessed only between `(define` and its closing parenthesis, and therefore no one can apply this function in the wrong way.

Abort—Chapter Checkpoint

In this chapter, you learned:

- How to write module-level variable and function definitions
- The advantages of introducing constant definitions
- How to write local, variable, and function definitions
- Where to place local, variable, and function definitions
- The benefits of defining variables and functions locally

;; Chapter 5
(big-bang)

```
#|
While Guess My Number may not be the world's most exciting game,
it was easy to write. Obviously, it doesn't look anything like
the software apps you use on your laptop or phone. Now think
about how amazing it would be if Guess My Number came with a
full-fledged graphical user interface. In this chapter, we'll
give it exactly that. As it turns out, this is super easy.
|#
```

5.1 Graphical User Interface

Text-based games can be fun and rouse our inner geek, but they are so '70s. Let's move on to at least the '80s where, at a minimum, software needs a **graphical user interface** (**GUI**), which we endearingly pronounce as "gooey." Intuitively, you know what a GUI is because you have used a lot of graphical software applications. These are programs that react to mouse events, keystrokes, and many other things, including clock ticks. Every computer comes with a clock—a little device that ticks every so often. If your program reacts to these clock ticks, it can create the illusion of continuously moving objects.

Racket provides several libraries for creating GUIs, and here we will combine two of these libraries to create animations and games: 2htdp/universe and 2htdp/image.

The first library defines a special form called `big-bang` that creates interactive programs, which we call **worlds**. The second one provides a bunch of functions for manipulating images. From now on, most of your programs will start with these two lines:

```
#lang racket
(require 2htdp/universe 2htdp/image)
```

The first line says that we're using the Racket programming language, and the second tells Racket that our program needs all the functionality from the two libraries.

```
#|
NOTE: The 2htdp in the name of the library refers to the second edi-
tion of the textbook for our course, "How to Design Programs," avail-
able online at htdp.org.
|#
```

We mentioned that `big-bang` creates worlds. But what exactly is a world? There are two ways to describe it: the state and the view. The states of a world refers to a class of data, each element of which we can meaningfully interpret in the context of the animation or game. A specific state is an element of this class, and it is `big-bang`'s task to know the current state. For example, if you have an animation of a descending UFO, then you might say that any positive integer is a state, and its meaning is the distance that the UFO has traveled toward Earth. Of course, players want to see the world, not some piece of data, and that is what we call the **view** of the world. In our example, this could be a picture of a little cartoon UFO flying across the screen.

5.2 Landing a UFO

To get from the state of the world to its view, you need a function that renders the state as an image. For the UFO animation example, a state of 42 can mean that your program should place the image of a UFO 42 pixels from the top of some background image.

However, rendering a world isn't enough. Your program must change the state of the world on occasion. For example, you may wish to lower the UFO by three pixels every time the clock ticks. If the initial state of the world is 0, it will be 3 after one clock tick, 6 after two, 9 after three, and so on. Can you imagine the images that come with these states of the world? In the first image, the UFO is 0 pixels from the top. In the second image, it is 3 pixels down. And by the third tick, it is already 6 pixels down. Now imagine that the clock ticks every 1/28 second, and your program makes the computer render an image every time the clock ticks. When you display a sequence of still frames at this rate, you get a movie—that is, you get the impression of movement on the screen. An animation is simply the rapid-fire display of plain old still images.

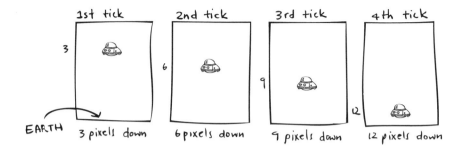

With `big-bang`, we can create an animation of a UFO landing in a snap:

```
(big-bang 0
          (on-tick add-3-to-state)
          (to-draw draw-a-ufo-onto-an-empty-scene))
```

Here we are using two functions we haven't defined yet: `add-3-to-state` and `draw-a-ufo-onto-an-empty-scene`. Each function will take in the current state of the world as an argument. The first function, `add-3-to-state`, adds 3 to the state it gets, and it returns the result, which `big-bang` turns into the next state:

```
(define (add-3-to-state current-state)
  (+ current-state 3))
```

The second function, `draw-a-ufo-onto-an-empty-scene`, places the image of a UFO onto an empty scene at `current-state` pixels from the top. Our world's state doesn't tell us how far from the left or right the UFO is placed, so let's just put it in the middle. You may have a different number in mind, and that's totally fine with us:

```
(define (draw-a-ufo-onto-an-empty-scene current-state)
  (place-image IMAGE-of-UFO (/ WIDTH 2) current-state
               (empty-scene WIDTH HEIGHT)))
```

Like a painter, we can create our images on empty canvases. Luckily, we don't need to do the stretching and stapling. All we have to say is `(empty-scene WIDTH HEIGHT)`, and DrRacket will give us a white rectangular image that is WIDTH by HEIGHT pixels with a thin black border around it. Neat, huh? Then we call `place-image` to place our `IMAGE-of-UFO` at `(/ WIDTH 2)` pixels from the left margin and `current-state` pixels from the top margin of the scene.

You might be wondering why the coordinates of `place-image` go top down and not bottom up, as with ordinary mathematics. Well, hardware people decided long ago that this is how they wanted coordinates to work on computer monitors. Here's a diagram that shows how the coordinate system works:

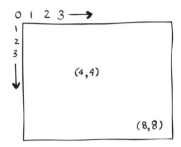

Now there is only one thing left to do:

```
(define IMAGE-of-UFO ...)
```

We want you to insert your favorite image of a UFO in lieu of the dots. Go find one on the Web. Save it on your computer. Then use DrRacket's "Insert" menu to put it in the right place. Yup, it works! Or use your epic artistic skills to draw one with the functions in 2htdp/image. That's right, you can use the interactions panel to make a UFO of your own. Images really are just values in Racket, and with DrRacket, you can easily experiment with image compositions. Every expression that you evaluate in the interactions panel is printed, where "printing" means rendering for images. Go ahead, try out some other image functions from 2htdp/image.

Let's experiment with the two functions in the interactions panel:

```
> IMAGE-of-UFO
```

```
> (draw-a-ufo-onto-an-empty-canvas 33)
```

We could, and you should, call the function on 36, 39, 42, and so on. These would show us more of the still images that make up the animation.

So here's the complete program:

```
(define (add-3-to-state current-state)
  (+ current-state 3))

(define (draw-a-ufo-onto-an-empty-scene current-state)
  (place-image
   IMAGE-of-UFO (/ WIDTH 2) current-state
   (empty-scene WIDTH HEIGHT)))

(define IMAGE-of-UFO ...)

(big-bang 0
          (on-tick add-3-to-state)
          (to-draw draw-a-ufo-onto-an-empty-scene))
```

Click "Run" and watch the descent of the UFO to Earth. But see how it goes right through the bottom of the scene? Stop the program with the "Stop" button.

Our animation isn't any good because we want the UFO to land on Earth. Let's make it stop with a little help from big-bang:

```
(define (state-is-300 current-state)
  (>= current-state 300))

(big-bang 0
          (on-tick add-3-to-state)
          (to-draw draw-a-ufo-onto-an-empty-scene)
          (stop-when state-is-300))
```

With stop-when, your program will tell big-bang when it's time to stop the animation. In our animation, we picked the height of the scene as the final state of the program. You should try out other numbers and see what happens.

5.3 Using big-bang: Syntax and Semantics

You have seen one example of how to write a nifty animation with just two or three function definitions and one big-bang expression. It is time to look at the details of big-bang.

The general syntax is this:

```
(big-bang state-expression
            (to-draw draw-function)
            (on-tick tick-function)
            (on-key key-function)
            (stop-when stop-function optional-last-scene))
```

The value of `state-expression` is the initial state of the world. As mentioned before, the state of the world can be any piece of data. For our UFO animation, we started with 0 and used non-negative integers to represent the distance that the UFO has traveled. But note that since a typical game has many more "moving" pieces than a UFO, lists and structures are great ways to represent our world state.

Each of the parenthetical elements that follow the initial `state-expression` are called **specs**, which is short for specifications. We also call them **clauses** on occasion. Each spec designates a **handler function** that consumes the current state of the world as its first argument. Here are brief explanations of the most important specs:

- `to-draw` tells DrRacket to use its handler to render the state of the world as an image.

- `on-tick` orders DrRacket to call its handler function every time the clock ticks.

- `on-key` specifies a handler that DrRacket employs when a key has been pressed. The function will take two arguments: the current state of the world and a string, which represents the key that was pressed. It produces the next state of the world.

- `stop-when` provides a function that checks whether the program evaluation should stop. This function is called every time the clock ticks or when a key is pressed. It consumes the current state of the world and produces a Boolean. The evaluation of the `big-bang` expression will stop if the `stop` function returns `#t`; otherwise, it carries on.

As its name implies, the `optional-last-scene` argument is an optional function that you may or may not supply. It will render the very last world in your program when the `stop-function` has returned true. It's helpful to supply this function so that the player knows when the program has ended.

If you look up `big-bang` in Help Desk, you will find that it can deal with many more specs, and we will discuss those when we need them.

By now, you may wonder what keeps track of the state of the world. The answer is `big-bang`. It knows the initial state of the world and hands the current state of the world to its specified handlers. When a handler function, such as the function that comes with `on-tick`, returns a new state as needed, `big-bang` will make it the current state of the world. And from there the cycle resumes.

5.4 Guessing Gooey

Let's write a GUI version of our Guess My Number game. It should display the program's guesses and respond to the player's key presses. We want the player to be able to press the up and down arrow keys to instruct the program. He will use the "↑" key if the program's guess should be higher and the "↓" key if the number should be lower. If his number has been guessed, he can press "=" to terminate the game. The player can also press "q" to quit the game at any point. Throughout the game, we would also like to display the playing instructions on the scene. Overall, the game console will look something like this:

The Data

As with all the games in this book, it is important to clearly identify and interpret the data we use to represent the states of the world before we start coding. A well-chosen data representation makes all the difference, because it almost always dictates how the code will be organized.

Since we need to keep track of the lower and upper bounds in this game, we'll create a structure with two fields, called `small` and `big`:

```
(struct interval (small big))
```

We use the word "interval" for this structure because the number we are guessing must be in the interval. We also define a number of constants, as discussed in chapter 4½:

```
(define HELP-TEXT
  (text "↑ for larger numbers, ↓ for smaller ones"
        TEXT-SIZE
        "blue"))
(define HELP-TEXT2
  (text "Press = when your number is guessed; q to quit."
        TEXT-SIZE
        "blue"))
(define COLOR "red")
```

The constants `HELP-TEXT` and `HELP-TEXT2` are the instructions for the game, and the sizes of these texts are determined by `TEXT-SIZE`. Note that `text` translates the instruction strings into images. The size of the game window is defined by `WIDTH` and `HEIGHT`. For the definitions of `WIDTH` and `HEIGHT`, see the code that comes with this chapter. The constant `COLOR` determines the display color.

Finally, we'll define a background scene as a constant:

```
(define MT-SC
  (place-image/align
    HELP-TEXT TEXT-X TEXT-UPPER-Y "left" "top"
    (place-image/align
      HELP-TEXT2 TEXT-X TEXT-LOWER-Y "left" "bottom"
      (empty-scene WIDTH HEIGHT))))
```

We use `place-image/align` to place and align the images created with `HELP-TEXT` and `HELP-TEXT2` on top of an empty scene. The image `HELP-TEXT2` will be aligned along the bottom left of the screen, and `HELP-TEXT` will be aligned along the top left of the screen.

The Main Function

To explain the code, we start with the main function:

```
(define (start lower upper)
  (big-bang (interval lower upper)
```

```
(on-key deal-with-guess)
(to-draw render)
(stop-when single? render-last-scene)))
```

As with our text-based version of Guess My Number, we let the player supply the lower and upper limits of the guesses. The initial world is created with these arguments. When the player presses a key, big-bang calls deal-with-guess to create a new state of the world if necessary. Furthermore, we use the handler function render to draw the state of the game. If the program guesses the player's number, single? returns #t and render-last-scene produces the last scene of the game. That's all—except for an explanation of how these functions work.

Key-Events

The key-handler for on-key takes in a world and a key-event. It then returns a new world or the world that it has been given, depending on which key has been pressed:

```
(define (deal-with-guess w key)
  (cond [(key=? key "up") (bigger w)]
        [(key=? key "down") (smaller w)]
        [(key=? key "q") (stop-with w)]
        [(key=? key "=") (stop-with w)]
        [else w]))
```

All key-events are strings, but not all strings are key-events, so we use key=? instead of string=? for comparisons. This function is provided by 2htdp/universe and checks for equality between keys. We need the program to increase its guess when the player presses the "↑" key, represented by "up", so we send the input world to our bigger function. Conversely, when the player presses the "↓" key, represented by "down", we send the world to the function smaller so that a smaller number can be guessed. When the guess is correct, the player may press "=" or "q" to end the game.

You might be wondering what the stop-with function is all about. This function consumes a world state and creates a special kind of world state. When big-bang receives this special state, big-bang stops running. If an optional rendering function is present in a stop-when spec, big-bang will use this function to render the world given to stop-with. Otherwise, it uses the normal rendering function that we gave on-draw to render the last scene.

Our smaller and bigger functions are almost exactly the same as those of the text-based version, but instead of using set! to change the lower or upper bounds of the guesses, we have them create new interval structures:

```
(define (smaller w)
  (interval (interval-small w)
            (max (interval-small w) (sub1 (guess w)))))
```

```
(define (bigger w)
  (interval (min (interval-big w) (add1 (guess w)))
            (interval-big w)))
```

The guess function is also similar to that of the previous version of the game, except it now consumes the state of the world and uses its fields to calculate the next guess:

```
(define (guess w)
  (quotient (+ (interval-small w) (interval-big w)) 2))
```

So our guess function picks out the values in the small and big fields of the world state it has been given. It then adds them up and divides the sum by 2 to get the average of the lower and upper bounds.

Rendering

Now let's define the handler function for the to-draw clause, which draws a scene every time big-bang's world is updated:

```
(define (render w)
  (overlay (text (number->string (guess w)) SIZE COLOR) MT-SC))
```

The render function places the program's guess onto the background scene. In this case, we have overlayed an image of the program's guess in its predefined size and color onto MT-SC, which is the background scene that includes instructions on how to play.

We also want to render a scene when the game has ended:

```
(define (render-last-scene w)
  (overlay (text "End" SIZE COLOR) MT-SC))
```

This rendering function will simply display the text "End" onto the background scene using overlay.

Time to Stop

Finally, the program needs to know when to stop the game. Logically, the player's number has been guessed when the lower and upper bounds are equal:

```
(define (single? w)
  (= (interval-small w) (interval-big w)))
```

The single? function compares the two bounds of the world. If they are equal, the game is over.

```
```

And that's all there is to it. Now you have your first interactive graphical program. As you can see, upgrading the Guess My Number game from a text-based version to a graphical one is really not that complicated. The `big-bang` library is a powerful tool, and it comes with many other exciting features that we have yet to discuss.

```
#|
NOTE: If you don't like how the game ends when the software has
guessed your number, feel free to change the program. You may wish
to change the render function. Or you may wish to change what we
call states of the world. Or you may change both. Go ahead and
experiment!
|#
```

Exit—Chapter Checkpoint

In this chapter, we described how to create animations and games:

- The `2htdp/image` library is for creating graphics.
- In Racket, graphical shapes are values just like numbers in other languages.
- You can use `big-bang` from the `2htdp/universe` to create animations and games.
- Tick handlers are functions that step a world from one moment to the next.
- Key-event handlers compute new worlds in response to keyboard events.

Chapter Challenges

- **Easy**   Find an image of a locomotive. Create an animation that runs the locomotive from just past the left margin to just past the right margin of the screen. Next, modify your program so the locomotive wraps around to the left side of the screen after passing the right margin.

- **Medium**   Change the Guess My Number game so that it displays the number of guesses the program takes to find the player's number. Hint: you might need to change the data used to represent the world's state.

- **Difficult**   Add a feature to the UFO animation so that you can control the UFO using direction keys. Once you've done this, make the UFO leave a trail of gray circles when it moves so that it looks like smoke is coming out of it.

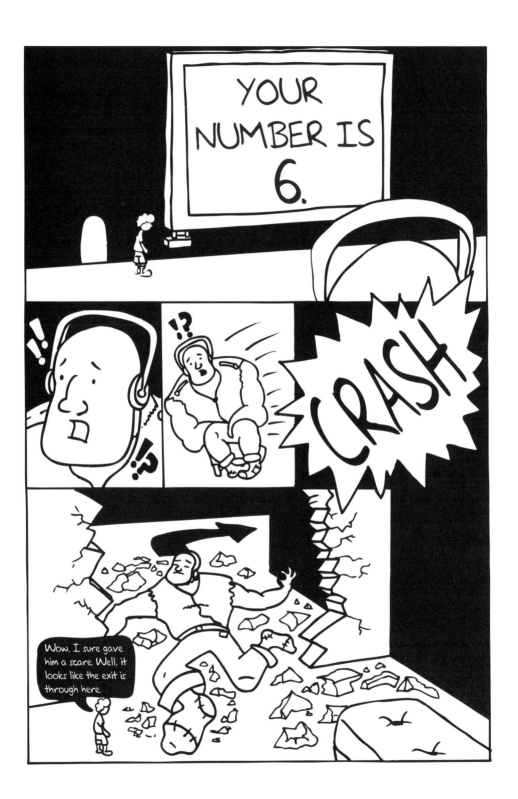

ROBOT SNAKE

Whoa, what is this place?

And what are these creatures?

Well, looks like the only way out is across this room, but it's covered by all these little monsters and their gooey slime!

;; Chapter 6
(Recursion Is Easy)

```
#|
You've seen lists, you've seen very basic recursion, and you know
how to use big-bang to create a simple game. You are probably
wondering when we get to make an interesting game. The answer is
right now. In this chapter, we will use lists and leverage the
full power of recursion to make the classic Snake game.
|#
```

6.1 Robot Snake

Walking along a dark corridor, Chad suddenly finds himself in a deep pit among DrRacket's mischievous minions. The crazy critters are out of control and have scattered radioactive goo all over the place. He sees a tunnel on the other side of the pit and considers jumping over the dangerous, glowing puddles—but there are too many! Chad then stumbles across a jittering, broken robotic snake. Upon closer inspection, he finds a panel on the snake that houses its instruction manual. As it turns out, the snake is designed to dispose of radioactive goo by gobbling it up. As the snake eats more goo, it becomes larger. Chad looks at the snake again. Its segments are falling apart and its wiring is haphazard. He guesses that as long as the snake does not bump into the walls or itself, it will work just fine. Can you help Chad operate the snake?

In this chapter, we turn Chad's encounter into an interactive game. The player uses the arrow keys to control a snake, which is placed in a rectangular pit. Appearing and disappearing goo items are scattered all around the pit, and it's up to the snake to devour them. When the snake eats a piece of goo, though, a new one appears at a random position in the pit. In order for the snake to eat, its head must be over a piece of goo.

6.2 A Data Representation for the Snake Game

Before we develop a data representation, let's look at an example. In the situation on the right, the snake is moving upward and has nearly hit the edge. The player can move the snake either right or left by hitting the arrow keys. If she doesn't, the game will end on the next clock tick. The best option is for her to move to the right, so that she doesn't become trapped in the corner. Also, turning right means her snake can easily eat that nearby piece of radioactive goo by moving down.

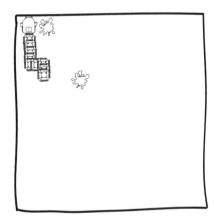

Let's begin by considering how we will represent elements of the game as data. In the previous chapter, we used structures to represent our world, and we will do the same here:

```
(struct pit (snake goos))
```

This structure definition helps us represent the state of the world as a pit structure with two fields. The first field, snake, keeps track of the current state of the snake. The second field, goos, tells us about the pieces of goo in the snake pit.

Our representation choice for the snake pit implies that we need a snake representation. Again, we use a struct:

```
(struct snake (dir segs))
```

The snake structure has two fields: dir, which is the direction in which the snake is slithering, and segs, which is a list of segments. A direction is one of the following strings: "up", "down", "left", or "right". These correspond to the four arrow keys on your keyboard. We think of segments as a non-empty list of posns. The list can never be empty because, at the very least, the snake must have a head. As the game progresses and the snake eats more, this list will grow.

A posn is simply a point in two-dimensional space:

```
(struct posn (x y))
```

As in physics, we think about any object—snake segments or goos—as a point in the plane. With this representation, a check for collisions becomes especially easy. Objects collide when they both occupy the same point. We do pay a price for this simplicity, however. In particular, the segments of a snake cannot be arbitrary posns. Two neighboring segments may differ in at most one direction, not both, and the difference must be 1. Fortunately, the game creates snakes so that this is always true.

We also need the data representation for goo:

```
(struct goo (loc expire))
```

The loc field contains a posn representing the goo's location. The expire field represents the number of clock ticks left before this goo expires.

Now we have introduced all of the structs needed to represent a world, and we can experiment with some simple worlds. Here is one:

```
> (define snake-example
    (snake "up" (list (posn 1 1) (posn 1 2) (posn 1 3))))
> (define goo-example
    (list  (goo (posn 1 0) 3) (goo (posn 5 8) 15)))
> (define pit-example
    (pit snake-example goo-example))
> pit-example
(pit
 (snake
  "up"
  (list (posn 1 1) (posn 1 2) (posn 1 3)))
 (list
  (goo (posn 1 0) 3)
  (goo (posn 5 8) 15)))
```

As you can see, we built the world in three steps. The first definition introduces a snake with three segments. The second one creates a list of two goos. And the third one combines these two in a pit.

6.3 The Main Function

Once you have figured out the data representations, the next task is to write the main function. Its purpose is to set up the initial game scenario and establish the event handlers. The goal of writing this function is to associate actions in the game with computer interaction modes.

For the Snake game, `start-snake` uses `big-bang` to set up and launch the game:

```
(define (start-snake)
  (big-bang (pit (snake "right" (list (posn 1 1)))
                 (list (fresh-goo)
                       (fresh-goo)
                       (fresh-goo)
                       (fresh-goo)
                       (fresh-goo)
                       (fresh-goo)))
            (on-tick next-pit TICK-RATE)
            (on-key direct-snake)
            (to-draw render-pit)
            (stop-when dead? render-end)))
```

The `big-bang` expression in this function consists of five parts. The first is the initial world, a snake pit. One important part is the `to-draw` clause. As implied by the name, `render-pit` renders the current world so that the player can see where the snake is and how to find the goo. The `on-tick` clause tells DrRacket to call `next-pit` every time the clock ticks. This function handles a number of actions: removing expired goo, checking if the snake can eat and grow, and making the snake slither. We also need a way to control the direction that the snake is moving in, so we hand `big-bang` the `direct-snake` function in the `on-key` spec. Finally, the game must stop when the snake dies, meaning we should supply a `stop-when` spec.

6.4 Clock Ticks

We could start anywhere with our discussion, but clock ticks mean action, and action is fun. The `on-tick` clause in `start-snake` tells DrRacket to call the `next-pit` function on every clock tick:

```
(define (next-pit w)
  (define snake (pit-snake w))
  (define goos (pit-goos w))
  (define goo-to-eat (can-eat snake goos))
  (if goo-to-eat
      (pit (grow snake) (age-goo (eat goos goo-to-eat)))
      (pit (slither snake) (age-goo goos))))
```

Like all clock tick handlers, this function consumes and produces a world. In this case, the function handles snake pits: making the snake longer when it has eaten, moving the snake, and handling the aging and renewing of goo.

The actual work proceeds in two steps. First, the internal definition goo-to-eat uses can-eat on the world's snake and the world's list of goo. This function returns #f or a goo within reach of the snake's head. Second, if goo-to-eat produces a goo, then the snake eats the nearby goo and grows, and the goo ages. Otherwise, the snake slithers and the goo ages.

Also note the first two local definitions. They extract the pieces from the given structure. Doing so is common because it makes it easier to read the rest of the function.

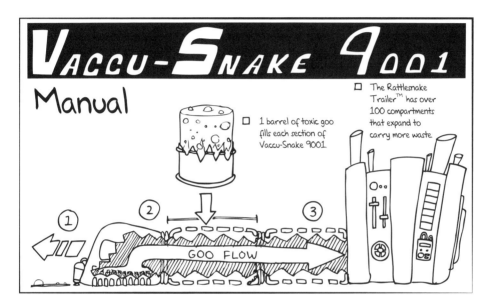

Eating and Growing

In order for us to determine when the snake needs to grow, we need to know when it can eat. We define the function can-eat to determine if there is a nearby goo that the snake's head can grab. If so, the function produces the piece that is to be eaten:

```
(define (can-eat snake goos)
  (cond [(empty? goos) #f]
        [else (if (close? (snake-head snake) (first goos))
                  (first goos)
                  (can-eat snake (rest goos)))]))
```

This function takes a snake and a list of goo. It then acts as a list-eater of the latter and determines if the snake's head, which is the first segment in its list of segments, is close to any of the goo items in the list of goo.

Like all list-eating functions, can-eat checks if the list of goo is an empty list. If it is, then the snake cannot eat because there is no goo. Otherwise, there is at least one goo in the list, so we use `close?` to ask if the head is close to the first `goo`. If it is, we've found a `goo` to eat, so we return it. If it isn't, we continue searching by recurring on the rest of the goos.

For the purposes of our simplistic game, the `close?` predicate just returns true when the given segment has the same location as the given `goo`:

```
(define (close? s g)
  (posn=? s (goo-loc g)))
```

But you can probably imagine how to change this definition for other interesting modes of play.

While we call `can-eat` a predicate, you should note that it doesn't just return Boolean values. Like `member`, `can-eat` produces `#f` if the snake cannot eat any of the goo. And also like `member`, it produces a real value, namely, the `goo` that the snake can eat. The `next-pit` function exploits this fact when it calls `eat` to tell that function which specific `goo` is to be absorbed.

Next, `eat` removes the `goo` and replaces it with a new `goo` item:

```
(define (eat goos goo-to-eat)
  (cons (fresh-goo) (remove goo-to-eat goos)))
```

The `eat` function consumes a list of `goo` and a `goo-to-eat`. The assumption is that `goo-to-eat` is in the list, so we remove it and `cons` on a fresh `goo` to the front of the list.

All we need now is the function `grow`, which actually makes the snake longer:

```
(define (grow sn)
  (snake (snake-dir sn)
         (cons (next-head sn) (snake-segs sn))))
```

This function creates a new snake that is one segment longer than the given one. It does so by calling `next-head` on the snake and by consing the resulting new head to the existing snake. While this trick may surprise you, the head is really just a `posn` to the function, just like all the tail segments.

Slithering

Our snake can eat and grow, so now we need to make it move when it is not eating. To do so, we create a new `snake` by adding a new head for the `snake` and removing the last element of the current `segs` list:

```
(define (slither sn)
  (snake (snake-dir sn)
         (cons (next-head sn) (all-but-last (snake-segs sn)))))
```

Like `grow`, the `slither` function calls the function `next-head` to move the head. But the end of the snake needs to advance as well, which we accomplish by consing on the new head and removing the last segment using `all-but-last`.

Here's the `all-but-last` function, which returns the given list of segments without its last one:

```
(define (all-but-last segs)
  (cond [(empty? (rest segs)) empty]
        [else (cons (first segs) (all-but-last (rest segs)))]))
```

Unlike the other list-eating functions we have seen so far, the `all-but-last` function works only on non-empty lists, because the snake always has a head. If the rest of the list is empty, meaning that there is one element in the list, then it returns `empty`. Otherwise, the function uses `cons` on the first element of the given list and recurs by calling `all-but-last` on the rest. As you probably guessed, this call retrieves all but the last segment of the rest of the list.

Now it's time to look at the often-used `next-head` function:

```
(define (next-head sn)
  (define head (snake-head sn))
  (define dir  (snake-dir sn))
  (cond [(string=? dir "up") (posn-move head 0 -1)]
        [(string=? dir "down") (posn-move head 0 1)]
        [(string=? dir "left") (posn-move head -1 0)]
        [(string=? dir "right") (posn-move head 1 0)]))
```

The `next-head` function contains two internal definitions: one for the snake's head and one for the snake's direction. We use a `cond` to create the new head. The function returns a new segment based on the given direction of the snake and where the head is currently located. It employs `posn-move` to determine the new location of the head:

```
(define (posn-move p dx dy)
  (posn (+ (posn-x p) dx)
        (+ (posn-y p) dy)))
```

This function takes a posn and two numbers: dx and dy. It adds dx to the x coordinate of the posn and adds dy to the y coordinate of the posn. It thus allows us to move a posn by a certain number of points along the x-axis and y-axis of a plane.

Rotting Goo

Finally, we make the goo rot and replace expired goo with new goo. We start by defining age-goo, which appears in the next-pit function:

```
(define (age-goo goos)
  (rot (renew goos)))
```

The age-goo function consumes and produces a list of goo. Since its purpose is to rot each of the goos and replace any totally rotten goos with fresh ones, age-goo is defined as the composition of two helper functions: rot and renew. The rot function's job is to decay each goo, so it just passes over the list, calling decay on each element:

```
(define (rot goos)
  (cond [(empty? goos) empty]
        [else (cons (decay (first goos)) (rot (rest goos)))]))
```

The renew function is a similar list-eater but uses rotten?:

```
(define (renew goos)
  (cond [(empty? goos) empty]
        [(rotten? (first goos))
         (cons (fresh-goo) (renew (rest goos)))]
        [else
         (cons (first goos) (renew (rest goos)))]))
```

Here's rotten?, which is used to detect goo that should be replaced with fresh goo:

```
(define (rotten? g)
  (zero? (goo-expire g)))
```

We still need to create the fresh-goo function, which randomly creates new goo structures:

```
(define (fresh-goo)
  (goo (posn (add1 (random (sub1 SIZE)))
             (add1 (random (sub1 SIZE))))
       EXPIRATION-TIME))
```

The fresh-goo function creates a new piece of goo with its loc field set to be a random posn within the boundaries of the pit. The x and y fields of the posn are random numbers chosen from the range 1 to the constant SIZE. The goo's expire field is set to be the constant value of EXPIRATION-TIME.

```
#|
```
NOTE: When we designed this game, we discussed the timing a lot. You may find a game with `(add1 (random EXPIRATION-TIME))` more appealing. Why do we need add1 here?
```
|#
```

And that is all there is to handling clock ticks. Now we can turn our attention to other aspects of the game, such as player input and game-rendering functions.

6.5 Key-Events

As mentioned at the beginning of this chapter, the player will use the arrow keys to direct the snake. Let's look at the `direct-snake` function that we saw in `start-snake`, because it deals with key-events:

```
(define (direct-snake w ke)
  (cond [(dir? ke) (world-change-dir w ke)]
        [else w]))
```

A key-handler such as this function takes two arguments: the current snake pit and a key-event. If that key-event is a direction, then we may want to change the direction of the snake in the pit; otherwise, we want to return the current world.

The `dir?` function checks whether the player has pressed an arrow key:

```
(define (dir? x)
  (or (key=? x "up")
      (key=? x "down")
      (key=? x "left")
      (key=? x "right")))
```

Next, we need a function that will change the direction of the snake in response to the player's keystroke:

```
(define (world-change-dir w d)
  (define the-snake (pit-snake w))
  (cond [(and (opposite-dir? (snake-dir the-snake) d)
              ;; consists of the head and at least one segment
              (cons? (rest (snake-segs the-snake))))
         (stop-with w)]
        [else
         (pit (snake-change-dir the-snake d) (pit-goos w))]))
```

The function `world-change-dir` consumes two arguments: a snake pit and a direction. It extracts the snake from the pit and then checks whether the direction d is the opposite of the snake's current direction. If this is true and the snake consists of more than just a head, the function returns the given world wrapped in `stop-with`. Remember that an instance of the `stop-with` struct tells `big-bang` to act as if the game has come to an end. And why does the function say so? Because a snake that flips its head runs into itself.

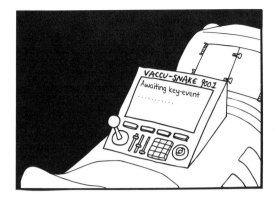

If the key-event d is acceptable or the snake consists of just a head, then it is time to create a new pit with a snake going in the chosen direction and the old goo. That's the purpose of calling `snake-change-dir`. You can actually experiment with `world-change-dir` in the interactions panel. You start by building up a snake and then you include this snake in a simple world:

```
> (define snake-going-left (snake "left" (list (posn 2 18))))
> (define plain-world (pit snake-going-left empty))
```

Note that `plain-world` comes without `goo`s, but that is okay for experiments. And then you apply the function to this world and a key-event, which you can do because a key-event is just a string:

```
> (world-change-dir plain-world "right")
(pit (snake "right" (list (posn 2 18))) '())
```

While `plain-world` contains a snake that is going left, the resulting `pit` contains a snake going right, which is precisely what you want. Before you read on, you may wish to open the source of the game in DrRacket and make up an experiment with snakes that contain some additional segments.

In order to complete the `world-change-dir` function, we need to define the helper function, `opposite-dir?`:

```
(define (opposite-dir? d1 d2)
  (cond [(string=? d1 "up") (string=? d2 "down")]
        [(string=? d1 "down") (string=? d2 "up")]
        [(string=? d1 "left") (string=? d2 "right")]
        [(string=? d1 "right") (string=? d2 "left")]))
```

The `opposite-dir?` function compares two direction values to check whether they point in opposite directions.

6.6 Rendering

Recall that the representation of the pit assumes that all pieces of the game are single points. This is convenient and makes it trivial to check whether the snake can eat a piece of goo, whether the snake has run into itself, and a few other things.

In an image, a snake's head takes up many pixels, and so does a radioactive piece of goo. To achieve this kind of scale-up, we create images of the same size for all basic pieces of the game: the snake head, `HEAD-IMG`; the snake segments, `SEG-IMG`; and the goo, `GOO-IMG`. Our rendering function then composes these images into a complete scene. This all works smoothly because every point in the representation is scaled up to the size of a basic image, and all basic images are of the same size.

Now consider the main rendering function that appears in the `big-bang` expression:

```
(define (render-pit w)
  (snake+scene (pit-snake w)
               (goo-list+scene (pit-goos w) MT-SCENE)))
```

The `render-pit` function calls two functions in order to render the game: `snake+scene` and `goo-list+scene`. Both functions operate exactly as implied by their names. The `snake+scene` function draws the snake into a given scene, and the `goo-list+scene` function draws the list of goo into the scene. And as you can see, it all starts with an empty scene. In order to make `render-pit` work, we need to define these functions.

We start with the `snake+scene` function:

```
(define (snake+scene snake scene)
  (define snake-body-scene
    (img-list+scene  (snake-body snake) SEG-IMG scene))
  (define dir (snake-dir snake))
  (img+scene (snake-head snake)
             (cond [(string=? "up" dir) HEAD-UP-IMG]
                   [(string=? "down" dir) HEAD-DOWN-IMG]
                   [(string=? "left" dir) HEAD-LEFT-IMG]
                   [(string=? "right" dir) HEAD-RIGHT-IMG])
             snake-body-scene))
```

The process to render the snake onto the given scene consists of three steps. First, `snake+scene` adds the body of the snake to the scene using the helper function `img-list+scene`. This function adds one `SEG-IMG` at each position of the body; if the list is empty, it returns the given scene. Second, the function extracts the snake's direction. Finally, `snake+scene` adds the image of the snake's head to the composite scene it has so far. The image used for the head is chosen based on the direction of the snake.

Now let's look at the `img-list+scene` helper function. It takes a list of `posns`, an image, and a `scene`:

```
(define (img-list+scene posns img scene)
  (cond [(empty? posns) scene]
        [else (img+scene
                (first posns)
                img
                (img-list+scene (rest posns) img scene))]))
```

As you can see, it is a standard list-eating function. It renders the given image at the positions specified by the given list of `posns` on top of the given `scene`. If the list is empty, then the function returns the given `scene`. Otherwise, it calls `img+scene`, which draws the given image at the first `posn` onto the scene that we get by calling `img-list+scene` again on the rest of the list of `posns`.

Here is the `img+scene` function:

```
(define (img+scene posn img scene)
  (place-image img
                (* (posn-x posn) SEG-SIZE)
                (* (posn-y posn) SEG-SIZE)
                scene))
```

It takes an image, a `posn`, and a `scene`. Using `place-image`, it places the given image at the x and y coordinates of the `posn`—multiplied by our agreed-upon size per image segment—onto the given scene.

All that is left to do as far as rendering is concerned is to draw the `goo`:

```
(define (goo-list+scene goos scene)
  (define (get-posns-from-goo goos)
    (cond [(empty? goos) empty]
          [else (cons (goo-loc (first goos))
                      (get-posns-from-goo (rest goos)))]))
  (img-list+scene (get-posns-from-goo goos) GOO-IMG scene))
```

Similar to the `snake+scene` function, `goo-list+scene` employs `img-list+scene` to render `goos`. The only difference is that we pass different arguments to the `img-list+scene` function. Instead of using the `SEG-IMG` constant, we use `GOO-IMG` for the image of a piece of goo.

We do need to define the `get-posns-from-goo` function in order to obtain the `posns` of each `goo` in the list of `goo`. Once again, this function uses the power of list recursion to create a list of `posns` from the list of `goo` that we provide the function. If the list is empty, then the function returns `empty`. Otherwise, the function uses `goo-loc` to access the `loc` field of the first piece of `goo`. We then use `cons` to attach this value to the recursion on the rest of the list of `goo`.

6.7 End Game

Now that we have completed the functions that help us handle the player's key input and render the game, we need to define some functions that determine when the game ends. There are two conditions that determine whether the game is over: the snake collides with either itself or the surrounding walls.

Let's consider the `dead?` function that appears in the `start-snake` function:

```
(define (dead? w)
  (define snake (pit-snake w))
  (or (self-colliding? snake) (wall-colliding? snake)))
```

This function returns `#t` if the `snake` from the world has collided with a wall or has collided with itself. If either is the case, then the `stop-when` clause in `big-bang` will be triggered and the game will end.

We should also produce an image for the `stop-when` clause, so that it is obvious when the game is over:

```
(define (render-end w)
  (overlay (text "Game Over" ENDGAME-TEXT-SIZE "black")
           (render-snake-world w)))
```

The `render-end` function overlays an image of "Game Over" on the last scene of the game. If you can think of something better, modify the code.

Next we look at the functions that determine if the snake collides with itself or the wall. First, we define `self-colliding?`:

```
(define (self-colliding? snake)
  (cons? (member (snake-head snake) (snake-body snake))))
```

The `self-colliding?` function consumes a `snake` and calls the built-in function `member`, which will check whether the head of the `snake` is the same as one of the segments in the rest of the snake's body. That's all there is to it because segments are just points.

All that remains for checking collision is to check against the walls of the pit:

```
(define (wall-colliding? snake)
  (define x (posn-x (snake-head snake)))
  (define y (posn-y (snake-head snake)))
  (or (= 0 x) (= x SIZE)
      (= 0 y) (= y SIZE)))
```

We start wall-colliding? by defining the x and y positions of the snake's head. Then, we check if its x or y coordinate is equal to any of the boundaries of the pit. If none of these four conditions is true, then the snake has not collided with the wall.

6.8 Auxiliary Functions

We are almost finished with the Snake game, but we need to define two helper functions that have been used in various parts of our code. First, we need the posn=? function, which determines whether two posns have the same x field and the same y field:

```
(define (posn=? p1 p2)
  (and (= (posn-x p1) (posn-x p2))
       (= (posn-y p1) (posn-y p2))))
```

This function compares the fields of two posns for equality. Yes, we could use equal? but you should know why we don't.

Beyond this equality function, we need four functions that manipulate the snake:

```
(define (snake-head sn)
  (first (snake-segs sn)))

(define (snake-body sn)
  (rest (snake-segs sn)))

(define (snake-tail sn)
  (last (snake-segs sn)))

(define (snake-change-dir sn d)
  (snake d (snake-segs sn)))
```

If you had bought a serious book on programming, it would explain these functions in gory detail. But this is a cheap book, and you get what you pay for.

`Return`—**Chapter Checkpoint**

In this chapter, we created the Snake game, which made heavy use of lists and recursive functions:

- We processed lists using a variety of list-eating functions.
- We gained a lot of experience with the `2htdp/image` library to visually render a game.

Chapter Challenges

● **Easy**   Change the program so that the final image displays the number of pieces of goo that have been eaten.

● **Easy**   Alter the game so that it has a randomly varying number of goos.

■ **Medium**   Add another type of goo that makes the snake grow two segments longer instead of one segment longer.

■ **Medium**   Add obstacles to the game. If the snake touches the obstacles, the game is over.

■ **Medium**   Once you have obstacles, make them move around at certain intervals.

♦ **Difficult**   Add a second snake that is controlled by the "w," "a," "s," and "d" keys. You may want to look in the docs for `on-pad`, another kind of `big-bang` clause. Then find a friend to play against you.

;; Chapter 7
(Land of Lambda)

```
#|
Are you tired of writing the same kind of functions over and over
again? Is the list empty? Do this. Is the list non-empty? Do that.
Don't forget to recur. In this chapter, we will show you how to
abstract and use lambda, something you probably didn't see in
your introductory programming courses. Al—whom you surely remem-
ber from the introduction—invented it in the 1930s, and Lisp has
had it for 50 years or more. This chapter is all about lambda and
its tricks.
|#
```

7.1 Functions as Values

Before we can begin to work with lambda, we need to discuss one key concept about functions in Racket. Functions in Racket are values, just like numbers, strings, and images. Let's look at an example:

```
> add1
#<procedure:add1>
```

When we enter add1 into the interactions panel without applying it to anything, DrRacket replies with #<procedure:add1>. But how can this be useful? Well, since functions are treated as values, we can pass them into other functions as arguments. Indeed, we can also return a function from a function. A function that consumes or produces another function is called a **higher-order function**, and it can compute all kinds of nifty things.

Here is a simple example called my-map:

```
(define (my-map func lst)
  (cond [(empty? lst) empty]
        [else (cons (func (first lst))
                    (my-map func (rest lst)))]))
```

This function takes two arguments: a function of one argument, called func, and a list. It applies func to each element of the list and then collects the results in a list. Let's see how we can apply this function:

```
> (my-map add1 '(1 2 3 4))
'(2 3 4 5)
```

In this example, we call my-map on the add1 function and a list of numbers. The add1 function is applied to each element of the list. As you can see from the output, each element of the original list increments by 1.

You may wonder how this could be useful. You shouldn't be surprised to read that it could have been handy in writing the Snake game. Recall the internal definition of `get-posns-from-goo` in the `goo-list+scene` function:

```
(define (get-posns-from-goo goos)
  (cond [(empty? goos) empty]
        [else (cons (goo-loc (first goos))
                    (get-posns-from-goo (rest goos)))]))
```

Here is the same function written with `my-map`:

```
(define (get-posns-from-goo goos)
  (my-map goo-loc goos))
```

The second version is much shorter and clearer. It directly communicates that `get-posns-from-goo` calls `goo-loc` on each element in the list and that it returns a list of the locations of each `goo` item from the original list.

Let's try another example:

```
(define (rot goos)
  (my-map decay goos))
```

This function is a rewriting of the `rot` function, but it uses `my-map` now. We call `my-map` using `decay` and `goos` to decrement the expiration date of each `goo`. This function performs the same task as the old version, but it relays the idea in a concise fashion.

7.2 Lambda

By now, you can appreciate functions as values, but you may find it a major hassle to create a named function that is used only once. This is where `lambda` comes in. With `lambda`, we can create nameless functions on the fly whenever we need them.

Let's illustrate the idea with a third version of `rot`:

```
(define (rot goos)
  (my-map (lambda (f)
            (goo (goo-loc f) (sub1 (goo-expire f))))
          goos))
```

Here, we create a function with `lambda`. It takes in one piece of goo, called `f`, and returns a different piece of goo. It is the same function as `decay` from the previous example, but it has no name.

Let's look at two ways to make the sub2 function. The old way requires define:

```
> (define (sub2 num)
    (- num 2))
> (sub2 5)
3
```

The new way uses lambda:

```
> (lambda (num)(- num 2))
#<procedure>
```

When using lambda, we write a number of parameters in parentheses, just as with a regular function definition, which will stand for the arguments of the function we create. We then add the body of the function and close it off with a parenthesis. That is all it takes to create a function with lambda, but as is, the function doesn't do anything. To get a function to compute, you need to apply it:

```
> ((lambda (num) (- num 2)) 5)
3
```

In this case, we apply the function to 5 and it returns 3.

7.3 Higher-Order Fun

Now that we have seen lambda and my-map, let's look at some other higher-order functions. We will start by defining a function called my-filter:

```
(define (my-filter pred lst)
  (cond [(empty? lst) empty]
        [(pred (first lst))
         (cons (first lst) (my-filter (rest lst)))]
        [else (my-filter (rest lst))]))
```

The my-filter function is applied to a predicate and a list. In turn, it applies the given predicate to every element in the list. If the result is true, then my-filter keeps the value in the list. Otherwise, the value is removed from the list. Essentially, it will appear as though the function has filtered out the elements that we do not want, according to the predicate.

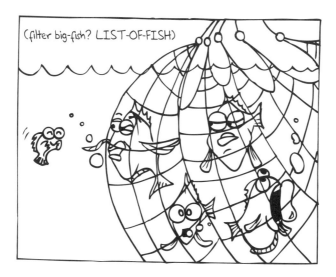

Let's look at another example from the Snake game:

```
(define (renew goos)
  (my-filter (lambda (f) (not (rotten? f))) goos))
```

The `renew` function has to remove any goo that has expired. Here, we use `my-filter` to accomplish the task. We create a `lambda` function that applies `not` to the call to the `rotten?` function on a piece of goo `f`. This predicate returns true if the goo is not rotten. In other words, we use `my-filter` to keep all of the goo that is not rotten. While this revised version of `renew` is not quite the original, it demonstrates nicely how `my-filter` works and how easy it is to use.

Another pair of higher-order functions plays an important role in Racket, and they use predicates too: `my-andmap` and `my-ormap`. We start with `my-ormap`:

```
(define (my-ormap pred lst)
  (cond [(empty? lst) #f]
        [else (or (pred (first lst))
                  (my-ormap pred (rest lst)))]))
```

The idea behind `my-ormap` is to determine whether any of the elements in the list return true when the predicate is applied to them. If the list is empty, then nothing in the list can match the criteria, so `ormap` returns #f. Otherwise, `ormap` applies the predicate to the first element in `lst` and uses `or` on it and the recursion of `my-ormap`. If any element of the list returns true, the function will return this result.

```
> (andmap produce-sound? PIANO-KEYS)
#t
```

The my-andmap function is similar, but it checks if all of the elements in the list return true when the predicate is applied:

```
(define (my-andmap pred lst)
  (cond [(empty? lst) #t]
        [else (and (pred (first lst))
                   (my-andmap pred (rest lst)))]))
```

This function differs from my-ormap in two ways. First, if the list is empty, then the function returns #t. Second, instead of combining the recursion and analysis of the first element with or, the function uses and.

Now that we have seen these two functions, let's see how they work:

```
> (my-andmap number? empty)
#t
> (my-ormap number? empty)
#f
```

Here, we apply my-andmap and my-ormap to the number? function. For my-andmap, this case always returns #t. The other function, my-ormap, returns #f in this case. The next two examples provide more insight:

```
> (my-andmap number? '(1 2 3 "a"))
#f
> (my-ormap number? '(1 2 3 "a"))
#t
```

The first example calls my-andmap on number? and a list. This means that if *all* the elements in the list are numbers, then the function returns #t. As not all of the elements are numbers, the function returns #f. The second example checks whether *any* of the elements in the list are numbers. If one is a number, then the function returns #t. Since there are numbers in this list, the function returns #t.

```
> (ormap home-key?
         HOUSE-KEYS)
#t
```

Let's look at one last example of my-ormap that shows how my-ormap would have been helpful in the Snake game:

```
(define (can-eat snake goos)
  (define head (snake-head snake))
  (my-ormap (lambda (g) (and (close? head g) g)) goos))
```

Here, we redefine the can-eat function to use my-ormap. We first extract the snake's head and give it a local name. Then we create a lambda function that takes in a goo structure and returns it if the snake's head is close. Finally, we use my-ormap to apply this function to every piece of goo on goos. And that is all we need to check whether the snake can eat any of the pieces of goo.

Another higher-order function that would be helpful in writing Snake is my-foldr:

```
(define (my-foldr f base lst)
  (cond [(empty? lst) base]
        [else (f (first lst) (my-foldr f base (rest lst)))]))
```

The my-foldr function takes three arguments: a function of two arguments, a base value, and a list. It returns base if the given list is empty. Otherwise, the given function is used to combine the first element of the list and the recursion on the rest of the list.

The `my-foldr` function can be especially useful for combining all of the elements of a list into a single result.

```
> (my-foldr + 0 '(1 2 3))
6
> (my-foldr beside empty-image (list 👽 ❤ ❗))
👽 ❤ ❗
```

In the first example of `my-foldr`, we use the + function on a list of numbers and a base value of 0. This function adds all of the numbers in the list together. The second function folds the list of images into a single image by aligning them horizontally with `beside`. Guess what would happen if we used `above` instead?

How to make a conventional burger :

And it should not come as a surprise that `my-foldr` would have come in handy with the Snake game:

```
(define (img-list+scene posns img scene)
  (my-foldr (lambda (p s) (img+scene p img s)) scene posns))
```

Here, we redefine the `img-list+scene` function to use `my-foldr`. We create a `lambda` function that takes in a `posn` and a `scene`. It calls `img+scene` to create the image. Because we are using `my-foldr`, the `lambda` function is called on all of the `posns` in the list. The function creates one scene out of the list of `posns`.

By now, you may have figured out that all these higher-order functions are built into Racket. They are called `map`, `filter`, `ormap`, `andmap`, and `foldr`. Their definitions are pretty much the way we defined them here, and you can use them freely.

7.4 Two More Higher-Order Functions

There are more higher-order functions worth mentioning. One is `foldl`. The difference between `foldl` and `foldr` is the last letter. In case you didn't guess, `l` stands for left-to-right, and `r` means the opposite.

```
(define (my-foldl f base lst)
  (cond [(empty? lst) base]
        [else (my-foldl f (f (first lst) base) (rest lst))]))
```

Put differently, `foldl` works in a similar fashion to `foldr` in that it also combines all the elements of a list. However, when `my-foldl` recurs, it starts by applying the function to the first element of the list and the base value. It passes this new value along and uses it as the new base value. Once the list is empty, it returns the accumulated value.

Let's look at some examples of `my-foldl`:

```
> (my-foldl cons empty '(a b c))
'(c b a)
> (my-foldr cons empty '(a b c))
'(a b c)
> (my-foldl + 0 '(1 2 3))
6
```

The first example shows that the order of processing is different from that of `my-foldr`. The outcome is the reverse of the given list. The second interaction shows that `my-foldr` proceeds in the opposite order. The last example shows that `my-foldl` can also combine lists like `my-foldr`. If we replaced the `my-foldl` call with `my-foldr` here, we would get the same result because in Racket it doesn't matter in which order you add up integers and rationals. Again, Racket's name for `my-foldl` is `foldl`.

How to make a lopsided burger :

The second function we need to look at is `my-build-list`. This function takes in a natural number n and a function `f`. It builds a list that has a length equal to n. The elements of the list are created by `f`:

```
(define (my-build-list n f)
  (define (builder k)
    (cond [(= n k) empty]
          [else (cons (f k) (builder (add1 k)))]))
  (builder 0))
```

In order to define this function, we start with an internal function `builder`, which also consumes a natural number. If the number given to `builder` is equal to the natural number given to `my-build-list`, then the function returns `empty`. Otherwise, it applies the given function to `k` and uses `cons` to attach the result to the recursion on the `builder` function. After we define `builder`, we call it with `0` so that we can recur up to the given natural number.

Let's look at two examples of `my-build-list`:

```
> (my-build-list 5 add1)
'(1 2 3 4 5)
> (my-build-list 10 (lambda (n) (* n 2)))
'(0 2 4 6 8 10 12 14 16 18)
```

The first uses the `add1` function. In this instance, `my-build-list` builds a list of length five and its elements are the numbers 1 through 5. Instead of using `my-build-list` in all of your programs, you can use the `build-list` function in Racket.

7.5 Derive This!

Before we close the chapter, let's take a second look at `lambda`. We will show you how to write a function that computes the derivative of some given function. If you haven't taken calculus, you might want to look on the Web for the basic concept of a derivative. The idea is that the derivative of a function `f` computes the approximate slopes of `f`.

It turns out that in Racket you can write a function that computes the derivative of another function:

```
(define (d/dx fun)
  (define ∂ (/ 1 100000))
  (lambda (x)
    (/ (- (fun (+ x ∂)) (fun (- x ∂))) 2 ∂)))
```

The derivative function starts off with an internal definition of the ∂ constant, which we will need for estimating the slope of the function at a given point. We then use `lambda` to create a function. Since we are working in a one-dimensional space right now, we need only one input for our function, but we can, in principle, deal with multi-dimensional math as well. Here, we just use the approximate slope of a line as the change in *y* over the change in *x*:

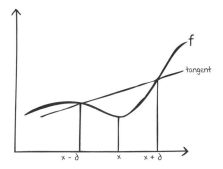

$$(f(x+∂)-f(x-∂))/(2*∂)$$

So we can see that our `d/dx` function takes in a function and outputs a function.

Finally, we can test our function by taking the derivative of functions that have simple derivatives:

```
> (define two (d/dx (lambda (x) (* 2 x))))
> (two 17)
2
> (map two '(2 -1 0 1 24))
'(2 2 2 2 2)
> (define newcos (d/dx sin))
> (newcos 0)
0.9999999983333334
> (map newcos (list (/ pi 2) pi))
'(-49999.4999975 -9.398762286028442e-12)
```

First, we differentiate a function that doubles its input, which in math you might write as $y = 2x$. Its derivative, as we can see when it is supplied as an argument to map, always produces the value 2, which is the slope at every point on the line y. Second, we can also differentiate the sine function, which is known to produce the cosine function. A quick test proves that applying our d/dx function to the sine function produces a function that acts approximately like cosine.

7.6 apply

There is one last higher-order function to discuss before we return to making games. The function is called apply, and it allows for some interesting tricks. The apply function takes a function and a list and applies the given procedure to the elements of the list:

```
> (define (sum lon) (apply + lon))
> (sum '(1 2 3 4 5 6))
21
```

This gives you the sum of a list of numbers.

Similarly, we can use apply to determine the maximum value in a list:

```
> (define (highest lon) (apply max lon))
> (highest '(58 64 77 77 22 94 93 78))
94
```

The function highest takes a list of numbers and uses apply to determine the largest one. We give apply the function max, which compares two numbers and returns the larger one.

The apply function does not work only on numbers. We can use it to manipulate other types of data, such as images:

```
(define (row lop) (apply beside (map frame lop)))
```

This function takes in a list of images and produces one image. It starts by using map to place a frame around each image with the frame function. It then calls apply with the beside function. Recall that the beside function comes with 2htdp/image and that it places all of the images beside each other.

—**Chapter Checkpoint**

In this chapter, we showed you that Racket programmers can abstract over list-eating functions, and we discussed how `lambda` makes this easy:

- Functions are values, just like numbers, strings, images, and any of the other kinds of values we've seen so far.

- You can write functions that abbreviate a lot of processing, and Racket provides a bunch: `andmap`, `apply`, `build-list`, `filter`, `foldl`, `foldr`, `map`, and `ormap`. It is as if you could write your own looping constructs in C# or Java.

- We saw that `lambda` is good for making simple functions; `lambda` is also good for creating some not-so-simple functions. You will see more of `lambda` soon.

ORC BATTLE

;; Chapter 8
(Mutant Structs)

```
#|
At this point, you've seen structures and lists. You've learned
how to write list-processing functions, and you know you can do
so concisely. In this chapter, we'll put that knowledge to good
use when we write the Orc Battle game. In the process, we'll show
you a convenient way of dealing with changes to structures.
|#
```

8.1 Chad's First Battle

Chad has managed to find himself stuck in an underground coliseum. All around him are monsters, ready for battle. Grabbing a sword, a shield, and some armor, he braces himself for the onslaught. For Chad to have any hope of escaping from his impending doom, you must help him defend himself.

Naturally, it's all just a game, and to us, it's all just software. But the Orc Battle is a good training ground to reinforce your list-processing skills and to add a few new ones concerning structs.

8.2 Orc Battle

Orc Battle is a basic turn-based fighting game in which
the player fends off some ravenous monsters. The player
starts with a certain amount of health, strength, and
agility. When the surviving monsters have their turn,
they attack the player, damage her health, weaken her
strength, or reduce her agility. When it is the player's
turn, she gets some number of attacks and must try to
kill as many monsters as possible; the only good monster
is a dead monster.

Agility determines the number of attacks the player
can perform. The player can attack in two different ways:
stab a specific monster or flail, hitting several monsters
at the same time. The effectiveness of each kind of attack
depends on the player's strength. As the player's health
dwindles, she can trade an attack for a healing action.
While a single healing action doesn't restore her health,
it will extend her life somewhat.

Monsters come in several flavors, yet they all have properties in common. Like the
player, every monster has a health status, which determines whether it is alive and the
effectiveness of its attack. Each monster, however, attacks the player in its own special way.
Orcs, the title characters, hit the player with their clubs. Hydras slice the player, but the
ferocity of their attack depends on their health. The slime creature is poisonous. Its attacks
slow down the player, meaning they reduce the player's agility, and it is intent on inflict-
ing some damage to her health. Finally, the brigand is the brains of the horde. It damages
the player in random, spur-of-the-moment ways. Depending on its mood, it may inflict
damage to the player's health, decrease her agility, or weaken her strength.

In this chapter, we will show you how to create such a game in Racket. But that's not
all. The real purpose of this chapter is to deepen your understanding of how to program
with lists that contain structs, which already contain lists. And that will expand your
knowledge of structs.

8.3 Setting Up the World, a First Step

As always, we start with a data structure that represents the world. The Orc game needs
a world with several "moving" parts: a player, who has several changing attributes; a
bunch of monsters, which have some common attributes (e.g., their health) and some
unique ones; and at least one turn-specific attribute, namely how many attacks the player
has left during the current turn.

All of this suggests that we should keep track of the orc world in a three-field struct:

```
(struct orc-world (player lom attack#))
```

The `player` field describes the player's attributes. The second field is a list of monsters. And the third field counts how many attacks the player may execute.

Next, we should figure out a representation for the player. The player has three changing attributes, so another struct with three fields looks like a good first step:

```
(struct player (health agility strength))
```

Each of the three fields will contain a natural number, such as 0, 1, 2, and so on. Here are some constants that describe the range of numbers you might find in a `player` struct:

```
(define MAX-HEALTH 35)
(define MAX-AGILITY 35)
(define MAX-STRENGTH 35)
```

Do you know what this means? As always, we encourage you to open the code in the IDE and experiment. There you will find many more constant definitions, and we hope that all their names explain their meaning as clearly as the three preceding definitions.

You know what lists are, and you should be able to imagine a list of monsters. But what are monsters? Given what we have shown you so far, you could define four struct definitions for the four kinds of monsters:

```
(struct orc (health club))
(struct hydra (health))
(struct slime (health sliminess))
(struct brigand (health))
```

All monsters have one property in common: `health`. Orcs also carry clubs, which come in different strengths; that explains the `club` field in the `orc` struct. The `sliminess` field in the `slime` struct is similar.

Now let's make a list of monsters:

```
> (list (orc MONSTER-HEALTH0 (add1 (random CLUB-STRENGTH))))
(list (orc 9 3))
```

This is a boring list with just one monster, but it is a list. You could even make an `orc-world` with this list:

```
> (orc-world
    (player MAX-HEALTH MAX-AGILITY MAX-STRENGTH)
    (list (orc MONSTER-HEALTH0 (add1 (random CLUB-STRENGTH))))
    0)
(orc-world (player 35 35 35) (list (orc 9 6)) 0)
```

This world has a player at maximal health, agility, and strength; it contains a list with a single monster; and it says the player has no attacks left. Surely, you can make complex worlds this way, but we find the struct definitions for monsters annoying, and you should, too.

To begin with, they don't say that these four structs describe a monster. Also, they don't say that all monsters have a common `health` field. That's fixable, and the fix is one of the two ideas we want to introduce in this chapter.

The first idea is called **struct inheritance.** As it turns out, in Racket you can define a struct as the "child" of another struct. In the context of our game, we can therefore define a `monster` struct like this:

```
(struct monster (health))
```

It says that all `monsters` have a `health` field that tells us how healthy a monster is. Next, you can say that all the monsters are like `monster`:

```
(struct orc monster (club))
(struct hydra monster ())
(struct slime monster (sliminess))
(struct brigand monster ())
```

The Grizzly Details of Inheritance

```
(struct bear (size))
```

= (bear 'small)

```
(struct hat-bear bear (hat))
```

= (hat-bear 'small 🎩)

```
(struct tie-bear bear (tie))
```

= (tie-bear 'small 🎀)

```
(struct sports-bear hat-bear (jersey))
```

= (sports-bear 'small 🎩 👕)

And this means that `orc`, `hydra`, `slime`, and `brigand` structs are like `monster` structs. They have a `health` field, and two of them have additional fields. So when you create an orc, keep in mind that it still has two fields:

```
> (orc MONSTER-HEALTH0 (add1 (random CLUB-STRENGTH)))
(orc 9 4)
```

If your functions ever need to select the `health` field from an `orc`, they do so with the `monster-health` function:

```
> (define my-orc (orc MONSTER-HEALTH0 2))
> (monster-health my-orc)
9
> (orc-club my-orc)
2
```

For the `club`, however, you will continue using `orc-club`. Okay? We will show you more examples as we build the game, and you can always practice with the code in DrRacket.

8.4 Action: How Structs Really Work

The second new idea in this chapter concerns what the player's actions do to our data. We told you that the handler functions in `big-bang` take the state of the world and return a new one. But there are two distinct ways of getting a new state. We have seen the first one twice now. With this one, the handler functions create *new* states. So imagine you're playing the game and you wish to stab an orc:

```
(define (stab-orc.v1 an-orc)
  (orc (- (monster-health an-orc) DAMAGE) (orc-club an-orc)))
```

Well, this function isn't enough. Because the `orc` struct is somewhere in the middle of the list of monsters, you also need a function that goes through the list, changes the one monster, and re-creates the entire list of monsters. And that isn't quite enough either because the list of monsters is inside the `orc-world` struct. You should be able to see what we are getting at. All of this can easily become a mess of code.

The second way to change a world avoids this extensive unzipping and zipping of lists and structs. Instead of creating new worlds, we *change* some part of the world or, as Lispers say, we **mutate** the struct. This alternative simplifies `stab-orc` a lot:

```
(define (stab-orc.v2 an-orc)
  (set-monster-health! an-orc (- (monster-health an-orc) DAMAGE)))
```

And `stab-orc.v2` is really all you need. In particular, you don't need to destructure the list, create a new one, restructure the list, and do all of this to `orc-world`. Mutation eliminates all these computations.

To make this work, we need to say that the `health` field in an `orc` struct is mutable:

```
(struct monster ([health #:mutable]))
```

With this small addition, the struct definition gives you one more function: the `set-monster-health!` **mutator**. Its purpose is to change the value of the orc's `health` field. With mutators, just one step lets every other function in the game know that something changed.

The monsters' health isn't the only attribute that changes over the course of the game. When it is the monsters' turn, they can affect all three of the player's attributes. Again, it is easiest to accommodate such changes by making the entire `player` struct mutable, like this:

```
(struct player (health agility strength) #:mutable)
```

By adding the `#:mutable` key to the struct definition, we ask Racket to supply one mutator for every field, giving us the `set-player-health!`, `set-player-agility!`, and `set-player-strength!` functions. Again, these mutators are created in addition to the constructor, the predicate, and the accessors.

Each of these mutators consumes an instance of the `player` struct and a value. It returns nothing and changes the value of a field. By the way, here is how you say "return nothing" in Racket:

```
> (void)
>
```

You see, `void` is a function that produces nothing, and this "nothing" isn't even worth printing in the interactions panel.

Let's experiment with `player` structures in DrRacket, and we will keep encouraging you to do so as well:

```
> (define player1 (player 1 2 3))
> (set-player-health! player1 33)
>
```

Nothing seems to have happened. The first line creates an instance of `player` called `player1`, and the second line seems to accomplish nothing. Did we say that these mutators return nothing? And did we also mention that instead they change their given struct?

```
> player1
(player 33 2 3)
```

Sure enough, player1's health field is now 33. Okay, take a look at these interactions:

```
> (define player2 (player 10 20 30))
> (set-player-health! player2 66)
> player2
(player 66 20 30)
> player1
(player 33 2 3)
```

We did it all over again. And just so you see that nothing but player2 changes this time around, we also looked at player1.

Here are some more interactions:

```
> (define player3 player1)
> (set-player-agility! player3 666)
> player1
(player 33 666 3)
```

The first line gives the value of player1 another name: player3. With the second line, we change player3, and this affects player1, too, as the last line shows. We can also do this when such structs are embedded in lists:

```
> (define players (list player1 player2 player3))
```

Here, we created a list of three players, though by now you can probably see that the first and the third players refer to the same struct. To test such a conjecture, use the eq? function:

```
> (eq? (first players) (third players))
#t
```

Recall from chapter 4 the difference between eq? and equal?. If not, now would be a good time to reread that section.

Next, we set the second player's strength field to a large number:

```
> (set-player-strength! (second players) 999)
> player2
(player 66 20 999)
> (second players)
(player 66 20 999)
```

And no matter how we refer to this player—by its name or by its position in some list—its strength is now 999.

It's time to use our new powers: mutators mixed with `lambda`. For every field, our game will need functions that add numbers to the player's attributes. Here is the function definition for changing the health of a player:

```
(define (player-health+ player delta)
  (define nih (interval+ (player-health player) delta HEALTH))
  (set-player-health! player nih))
```

The function first computes the new internal health value, `nih`, using interval addition, `interval+`. This function adds two numbers but makes sure the sum is between `0` and `HEALTH`. If the result is larger than the desired maximum, `internal+` produces the maximum. If the result drops below `0`, the function produces `0`. In short, you can beat a dead horse, but it won't get any deader.

In many languages, you would have to repeat this definition three times for `health`, `agility`, and `strength`. Racket, however, gives you more power. It gives you `lambda`. In this instance, we use `lambda` to abstract over the essence of the attribute manipulation and create as many of the concrete functions as you want:

```
(define (player-update! setter selector mx)
  (lambda (player delta)
    (setter player (interval+ (selector player) delta mx))))
```

This function consumes a `setter`, a `selector`, and an `mx`. It produces a nameless function using `lambda`, but boy, this nameless function can do a lot:

- It consumes a player and a number.
- It accesses the player's old attribute value, with the help of `selector`.
- It computes a new attribute value limiting the interval with the given `mx`, and then it sets the player's attribute to this new value with the help of the given `setter`.

Amazingly, with `player-update!`, the required three functions become one-liners. Here is one of them:

```
(define player-health+
  (player-update! set-player-health! player-health MAX-HEALTH))
```

You can go ahead and define the others, or look them up in the source code.

Mutators are confusing and can really mess with a program if used incorrectly. Make sure that you experiment thoroughly to get a grasp on them before putting them to use.

The dangers of mutation also require us to be more careful with our tests than ever before. If you need to test a function that changes values without returning them, you should have an expression that creates a new instance of the struct, then performs the mutation, and returns the struct. In Racket, we use `let` expressions for this purpose:

```
> (let ((p (player 1 2 3)))
    (player-strength+ p -3)
    p)
(player 1 2 0)
```

A `let` sets up local definitions. Here, p stands for `(player 1 2 3)`. The inner part of a `let` expression is called a `let` body, which includes a sequence of expressions. It is a sequence of actions, as in functions and `cond`s. The first few expressions are evaluated, and their results, if any, are discarded. That's why the result of this `let` expression is the modified struct `(player 1 2 0)`. Therefore, in order to formulate a test, we write this:

```
(check-equal? (let ((p (player 1 2 3)))
                (player-strength+ p -3)
                p)
              (player 1 2 0))
```

The first argument to `check-equal?` is a `let` expression that creates a player and mutates it, using `player-strength+`. The second argument is a struct that specifies the three desired attributes, and as you can see, its `strength` field is 0 instead of 3, the strength of the original player.

In summary, mutators make programming complex. We use them because they are powerful; they make changes to structs look concise. But this power is also difficult to control. Testing is no longer a question of calling a function and writing down the expected result. You need to test the *effect* that a function has by carefully setting up a new struct, returning the modified struct, and describing the expected results. Worse, you don't know whether the function had other effects. In principle, you should test that nothing else changed unintentionally. Mutators also make it difficult to see which other computations are affected, because the effect of changing a field is visible everywhere—wherever the struct is visible. That is dangerous! Observe how we use mutable structs and fields, and you will learn how to deal with the effects of mutation, too.

8.5 More Actions, Setting Up the World for Good

When you first have an idea of how to keep track of the state of a game, you should figure out which actions the player can perform. With `big-bang`, your game players can use the keyboard or the mouse. Keep in mind, clock ticks can change the state of the game.

For the battle with orcs, let's stick to keyboard actions. They are fast and furious. The "s" key signals stabbing, "f" is for flailing, and an "h" heals the player a bit. What else does attacking mean for the program? It means that at any point in time, some monster is selected as the focus of a potential attack. Since this kind of information is a part of the game state, we equip the orc-world struct with an additional field:

```
(struct orc-world (player lom attack# target) #:mutable))
```

We make the struct mutable because the values of the attack# and target fields change during a turn. And we pick arrow keys as a way to change the target.

Next, we need to figure out what kind of values to use with the target field. It tells us which of the monsters in lom is currently targeted. To connect the two fields, we stick a natural number into the target field and use this number to look up the currently targeted monster in lom:

```
> (define lom (list (orc 9 3) (orc 9 4) (orc 9 1)))
> (list-ref lom 0)
(orc 9 3)
> (define ow1 (orc-world 'some-player lom 2 0))
> (list-ref (orc-world-lom ow1) 2)
(orc 9 1)
```

So 0 in the target field of an orc-world indicates the first monster on the list, and 2 refers to the third one. All set?

8.6 Ready, Set, big-bang

It is time to get started:

```
(define (start)
  (big-bang (initialize-orc-world)
            (on-key player-acts-on-monsters)
            (to-draw render-orc-battle)
            (stop-when end-of-orc-battle? render-the-end)))
```

This function starts the Orc Battle game. Naturally, it uses big-bang. Let's look at all the parts. The initialize-orc-world function creates an initial state of the world, and doing so is pretty straightforward:

```
(define (initialize-orc-world)
  (define player0 (initialize-player))
  (define lom0 (initialize-monsters))
  (orc-world player0 lom0 (random-number-of-attacks player0) 0))
```

This combines a player, some monsters, a random number of attacks, and an initial target that points to the first monster on the list into an `orc-world`.

The remaining three clauses of `big-bang` in `start` describe how the world is transformed when the player presses a key during her turn, how to render the current state of the world as an image, and how to check whether the battle is over. The last clause also says that `big-bang` should use `render-the-end` when the battle is over, because we need to announce who won.

Let's look at these functions one at a time, starting with `end-of-orc-battle?`:

```
(define (end-of-orc-battle? w)
  (or (win? w) (lose? w)))
```

The battle is over when the player wins or loses. We'll look at these two helpers later.

Rendering the battle or the end of the battle is also easy:

```
(define (render-orc-battle w)
  (render-orc-world w (orc-world-target w) (instructions w)))

(define (render-the-end w)
  (render-orc-world w #f (message (if (lose? w) LOSE WIN))))
```

In both cases, we use `render-orc-world`, which consumes three arguments: the current state of the world, the current target or `#f` if there is no target anymore, and a message to the player. No matter what, `render-orc-world` must display three pieces of information: the player's status, the monsters, and some additional information. While the player is engaged in battle, the additional information consists of the game instructions, which mention some properties of the current state of the world. At the end of the game, the information tells the player who has won.

Before we move on, let's sketch out the rendering process just enough to see how a player experiences the game. The key is that the rendering function must display a list of monsters. We don't know how long the list is, but we do know we want to break it up into several rows so that the player can navigate easily among the monsters. So we pick a constant PER-ROW and say that this many monsters appear on each row. Put differently, if the game is launched with MONSTER#, then the display shows (quotient MONSTER# PER-ROW) rows of monsters, with PER-ROW monsters on each row. Here is what it might look like if you render the game with 12 monsters, 4 to a row:

```
> (render-orc-battle (initialize-orc-world))
```

In DrRacket, you don't need to launch a game to render a game state. You just call the rendering functions on the same game state, and you see what the player may see. She sees an image of her status on the left, the monsters arranged in a rectangular grid on the right, and the instructions below. Also note how the first monster is marked by a circle; it is the current target of the player. Remember that to change the target, the player uses the arrow keys to move around the grid of monsters.

And that brings us to the last function, the one that deals with key strokes:

```
(define (player-acts-on-monsters w k)
  (cond
    [(zero? (orc-world-attack# w)) (void)]
    [(key=? "s" k) (stab w)]
    [(key=? "h" k) (heal w)]
    [(key=? "f" k) (flail w)]
    [(key=? "e" k) (end-turn w)]
    [(key=? "n" k) (initialize-orc-world)]
    [(key=? "right" k) (move-target w +1)]
    [(key=? "left" k)  (move-target w -1)]
    [(key=? "down" k)  (move-target w (+ PER-ROW))]
    [(key=? "up" k)    (move-target w (- PER-ROW))])
  (give-monster-turn-if-attack#=0 w)
  w)
```

This function looks more like the first version of Guess My Number than anything else you have seen in this book. So far, you have seen functions that consist of a header, which lists the name of the function and the names of the arguments, and a body, which is usually just one expression that computes the result of the function. Now with `player-acts-on-monsters`, you see a function whose body consists of three expressions: a conditional, a function call to `give-monster-turn-if-attack#=0`, and the variable `w`.

When the function is called, the first expression is evaluated and its result is thrown away. The second expression is evaluated, and the result is thrown away again. Finally, the last expression is evaluated, and its value becomes the result of the whole function.

You may now think that `player-acts-on-monsters` is a really strange function. According to our explanation, it always returns `w`, the world that it is given when the player presses the "k" key. So here is the catch. With the introduction of mutators, the evaluation of an expression doesn't just produce a value—it may also affect the evaluation of *other expressions*.

The conditional in the body of `player-acts-on-monsters` determines whether and how to change `w` in response to the player's action on the keyboard. The function call to `give-monster-turn-if-attack#=0` checks whether the monsters can change `w`. Both expressions return nothing. In the end, `player-acts-on-monsters` evaluates the expression `w`, which has dramatically changed because of the first two expressions.

Now let's look in detail at the three steps. The conditional first checks whether the player may still attack. If not, the conditional uses `void` to perform no action. You may want to figure out why it would have been acceptable to write 42 instead of (void). If the player can still attack, the function checks which of the nine keys the player may have pressed. The first three keys trigger calls to functions that change the player or the monsters in the world. The next two are about ending the player's turn or starting over.

The final four `cond` clauses correspond to navigation actions; each calls `move-target` to change the index in the `target` field. The responses to the "←" and "→" keys seem obvious: they ask `move-target` to change the current target by adding +1 or -1 to the current target. The responses to "↓" and "↑" use the PER-ROW constant. Remember that the list of monsters is rendered as a grid with PER-ROW monsters in each row. Thus, if the player presses "↑", the key event tells the program, "Go up one row in the display." Similarly, if the player presses "↓", it means, "Go down one row in the display." Because all monsters are arranged in a linear list, and the current target monster is just an index into this list, `move-target` adds or subtracts PER-ROW monsters to this index and keeps the index in range.

Once the conditional is finished checking all conditions, the player may have used up all of her attacks. In that case, it is time to let the monsters loose. All live monsters will attack the player at once. When the monsters' attack is over, it's time to hand control back to `big-bang` by returning the modified world `w`. Doing so allows the player to take her next turn—unless of course the game is over.

8.7 Initializing the Orc World

Our initialization process relies on three functions. Two are simple:

```
(define (initialize-player)
  (player MAX-HEALTH MAX-AGILITY MAX-STRENGTH))

(define (random-number-of-attacks p)
  (random-quotient (player-agility p) ATTACKS#))
```

The first creates a player with maximal health, agility, and strength. The second picks a random number of attacks, like this:

```
(define (random-quotient x y)
  (define div (quotient x y))
  (if (> 0 div) 0 (random+ (add1 div))))

(define (random+ n)
  (add1 (random n)))
```

This `random-quotient` function picks a random number between 1 and `(quotient x y)` via `random+` unless the quotient is 0. In our specific case, this means that the number of attacks is determined as a random fraction of the player's agility. Naturally, we define `random-quotient` and `random+` as separate functions because we will use them again. If you can think of another way to determine a random number of attacks, try it. The code is all yours.

The third initialization function creates a list of monsters:

```
(define (initialize-monsters)
  (build-list
    MONSTER#
    (lambda (_)
      (define health (random+ MONSTER-HEALTH0))
      (case (random 4)
        [(0) (orc ORC-IMAGE health (random+ CLUB-STRENGTH))]
        [(1) (hydra HYDRA-IMAGE health)]
        [(2) (slime SLIME-IMAGE health (random+ SLIMINESS))]
        [(3) (brigand BRIGAND-IMAGE health)]))))
```

And voilà, you see `lambda` and `build-list` in action, and `case` is thrown in there, too. Since the goal is to create a list, the function uses `build-list`, which consumes the number of monsters we wish to start with and a function. We use `lambda` to make this function because it is used only here, it isn't recursive, and it is straightforward. After picking a random health, a random number is used to return one of four possible monsters.

We are almost finished, except for two little things. First, lambda uses _ as a parameter. In Racket, _ is just a plain old variable name, pronounced "underscore." Racketeers, by convention, use it to indicate that a function ignores this parameter. Remember that build-list applies this function to all numbers between 0 and MONSTER#. Since we don't need this number for anything in our world of orcs, the lambda function throws it away.

Second, if you look closely at all four constructors, you'll notice that they take one more argument than we've admitted: an image. Because we want to visualize the monsters at some point, we might as well stick their images into the monster structure once and for all:

```
(struct monster (image [health #:mutable]))
```

With the revision of this definition, all monster structs have two fields: image, which never changes, and health, which may change over the course of the game. Every substructure inherits these two fields. Because of inheritance, we needed to make only a single change to the program: the definition of the monster struct. Later on, when our program must render the monsters, it can use monster-image to pull out the images from the monsters.

8.8 Rendering the Orc World

The basic world setup mentions two small functions that render the instructions and the win and lose messages:

```
(define (instructions w)
  (define na (number->string (orc-world-attack# w)))
  (define ra (string-append REMAINING na))
  (define txt (text ra INSTRUCTION-TEXT-SIZE ATTACK-COLOR))
  (above txt INSTRUCTION-TEXT))

(define (message str)
  (text str MESSAGES-SIZE MESSAGE-COLOR))
```

The instructions are always the same, except for the number of remaining attacks. To show the remaining attacks, we convert the number into a string, stick it into an appropriate sentence, and convert the string to an image of the text. Otherwise, instructions assembles the two text images into one. The message function is even simpler than instructions. It merely turns the given string into text using an appropriate size and color.

The real workhorse of the rendering section is render-orc-world, a function that consumes three arguments and produces an image of the current world:

```
(define (render-orc-world w t additional-text)
  (define i-player  (render-player (orc-world-player w)))
  (define i-monster (render-monsters (orc-world-lom w) t))
  (above V-SPACER
         (beside H-SPACER
                 i-player
                 H-SPACER H-SPACER H-SPACER
                 (above i-monster
                        V-SPACER V-SPACER V-SPACER
                        additional-text)
                 H-SPACER)
         V-SPACER))
```

You should recall that render-orc-world is used in two different ways: during the game and after the game is over. For the former situation, it is called with the current state of the world, an index that specifies the target in the list of monsters, and instructions for the player. For the latter situation, the function is also applied to the state of the world—or #f if there is no live target left—and a termination message. In short, the second argument is either a number or a Boolean value, and you need to keep this in mind.

As you would expect, the function takes apart the given world struct and uses helper functions to render the two important pieces: the player and the monsters. Once it has images for these, it is simply a question of assembling them into the right layout.

You can imagine that we didn't arrive at this format without some experimentation. Once we had defined render-player and render-monsters, here is how we started experimenting in the interactions panel:

```
> (beside (render-player (initialize-player))
          (above (render-monsters (initialize-monsters))
                 (message "You win"))))
```

We didn't like how everything was squeezed together. So we played around. We added vertical and horizontal spacers, which are just a constant rectangles with a funny x or y dimension:

```
(define V-SPACER (rectangle 0 10 "solid" "white"))
(define H-SPACER (rectangle 10 0 "solid" "white"))
```

Moving on, here is the function that creates an image for the player:

```
(define (render-player p)
  (define s (player-strength p))
  (define a (player-agility p))
  (define h (player-health p))
  (above/align
    "left"
    (status-bar s MAX-STRENGTH STRENGTH-COLOR STRENGTH)
    V-SPACER
    (status-bar a MAX-AGILITY AGILITY-COLOR AGILITY)
    V-SPACER
    (status-bar h MAX-HEALTH HEALTH-COLOR HEALTH)
    V-SPACER V-SPACER V-SPACER
    PLAYER-IMAGE))
```

By now, you know the routine for this kind of function. The argument is a player struct. The function takes it apart, extracting the three pieces: strength, agility, and health. Then it uses one auxiliary function to create the pieces of the final image: status bars for health, agility, and strength. Guess what above/align does? It jams together a bunch of images, one above the other, and the first argument—a string—tells it how to align these images.

Let's take a look at the auxiliary function, `status-bar`:

```
(define (status-bar v-current v-max color label)
  (define w (* (/ v-current v-max) HEALTH-BAR-WIDTH))
  (define f (rectangle w HEALTH-BAR-HEIGHT 'solid color))
  (define b (rectangle HEALTH-BAR-WIDTH HEALTH-BAR-HEIGHT ...))
  (define bar (overlay/align "left" "top" f b))
  (beside bar H-SPACER (text label HEALTH-SIZE color)))
```

It consumes the current value, the maximal value, the desired color, and a string label to attach to the bar. The function first computes the width of the health bar: `(* (/ v-current v-max) HEALTH-BAR-WIDTH)`. If `v-max` should be displayed as `HEALTH-BAR-WIDTH`, then `(/ v-current v-max)` is the ratio of this number that determines how `v-current` should be displayed. Once it has this number, the function creates a filled and framed rectangle to create the bar. The final expression attaches `label` as a text image.

And that leaves us with rendering all the monsters, the trickiest function of the bunch. It consumes a list of monsters and an argument that indicates which of them is the current target, if any:

```
(define (render-monsters lom with-target)
  ;; the currently targeted monster (if needed)
  (define target
    (if (number? with-target)
        (list-ref lom with-target)
        'a-silly-symbol-that-cannot-be-eq-to-an-orc))

  (define (render-one-monster m)
    (define image
      (if (eq? m target)
          (overlay TARGET (monster-image m))
          (monster-image m)))
    (define health (monster-health m))
    (define health-bar
      (if (= health 0)
          (overlay DEAD-TEXT (status-bar 0 1 'white ""))
          (status-bar health MONSTER-HEALTH0 MONSTER-COLOR "")))
    (above health-bar image))

  (arrange (map render-one-monster lom)))
```

YOU WIN

Now you need to remember the images of the monsters. Clearly, `render-monster` must turn all monsters into images. With `map`, that's easy. All we need is `(map render-one-monster lom)` because this applies `render-one-monster` to every monster on the `lom` list and you have a list of images. If you arrange them properly, you get the full scene of all monsters, but for now, let's postpone the discussion of `arrange` and focus on the images of the monsters.

At this point, it is time to exploit the `with-target` argument. It is either a number or `#f`. If it is a number, the function must mark the current target. If it is false, there is no current target, and the game is over. The first definition inside of `render-monsters` turns `with-target` into one of the monsters from the list, using `list-ref`, or a symbol. The `render-one-monster` uses this value to determine whether the given monster is the current target.

To get an image of one monster, `render-one-monster` extracts the image from the given monster struct and adds the target marker, if the monster is `eq?` to the target. The rest of the function creates a health bar for the monster. Two things stand out, though. First, look how we use `eq?` to compare `render-one-monster`'s argument with the `target`. We really want this specific struct on the `lom` list, not a struct with the same content—that is, `equal?` would be wrong. That's what `eq?` is for. Second, the `health-bar` calculation looks complex because we want the graphics to look good when monsters die. Experiment with the code to see what happens when you simplify the first branch of the `if` expression that computes the `health-bar` image. Then figure out what a health bar looks like if it has a current value of 0, a maximum value of 1, white color, and an empty label. It is just an invisible rectangle. So this three-line calculation in render-one-monster just ensures that the rectangle is exactly as tall as an empty health bar.

Here is the final function needed for rendering a world, arrange:

```
(define (arrange lom)
  (cond
    [(empty? lom) empty-image]
    [else (define r (apply beside (take lom PER-ROW)))
          (above r (arrange (drop lom PER-ROW)))]))
```

This is a recursive function, though it only superficially looks like the kinds of list-eating functions we have seen before. After making sure that the list isn't empty, arrange retrieves the first PER-ROW images with take, which is one of those general-purpose built-in list functions you just have to know:

```
> (take '(a b c d e f) 2)
'(a b)
> (drop '(a b c d e f) 2)
'(c d e f)
```

With (apply beside ...), the arrange function creates the image of a row, and with (above r ...), it layers this row above the remaining ones. To remove the first PER-ROW images, arrange uses drop, which, like take, comes with Racket. So yes, arrange is recursive, but it doesn't eat the list on a one-by-one basis. Read it again.

8.9 The End of the World

When does the world come to an end? Well, it's over when all the monsters are dead or one of the player's attributes sinks to 0:

```
(define (win? w)
  (all-dead? (orc-world-lom w)))

(define (lose? w)
  (player-dead? (orc-world-player w)))

(define (player-dead? p)
  (or (= (player-health p) 0)
      (= (player-agility p) 0)
      (= (player-strength p) 0)))
```

```
(define (all-dead? lom)
  (not (ormap monster-alive? lom)))

(define (monster-alive? m)
  (> (monster-health m) 0))
```

And that's all it takes. The only interesting function is `all-dead?`, which uses `ormap` to determine whether any of the monsters are alive. Are you wondering why `monster-alive?` is defined separately? We could have just made it a `lambda` within the `all-dead?` function, but `monster-alive?` is also useful when it comes to executing actions.

8.10 Actions, A Final Look

We've kept the game actions for last. All actions consume the current state of the world and mutate it. The player has five actions, all triggered in response to certain keystrokes: `stab`, `heal`, `flail`, `end-turn`, and `move-target`. The monsters have one action, aptly called `give-monster-turn-if-attack#=0`, because its name tells us that it runs a monster turn if the player has no attacks left.

With that in mind, let's tackle the implementation of actions. One function has a trivial definition:

```
(define (end-turn w)
  (set-orc-world-attack#! w 0))
```

If the player really wishes to end her turn prematurely, just set the number of remaining attacks to 0. Then, `give-monster-turn-if-attack#=0` takes over and gives the monsters their turn.

Like `end-turn`, the definition of `heal` is obvious:

```
(define (heal w)
  (decrease-attack# w)
  (player-health+ (orc-world-player w) HEALING))
```

A player can trade one attack for one healing action. So `heal` pays for the action and then calls a function that increases the player's health by some constant factor.

The definition of `heal` suggests a pattern for other actions, namely, to first call `decrease-attack#` to pay for the attack and then to execute some action. And yes, we see this pattern again in the definition of `stab`:

```
(define (stab w)
  (decrease-attack# w)
```

```
(define target
  (list-ref (orc-world-lom w) (orc-world-target w))))
(define damage
  (random-quotient (player-strength (orc-world-player w))
                   STAB-DAMAGE))
(damage-monster target damage))
```

In addition, stab immediately extracts the targeted monster from the world. As for the stabbing, stab picks a random damage value based on the player's current strength and a constant dubbed STAB-DAMAGE. Then it calls a function that inflicts the chosen damage on the chosen monster. That's all. Yes, we owe you a little helper function, damage-monster, but as you will see later, it is really straightforward.

Our player's most complicated form of attack is flail. Recall that its purpose is to attack a whole bunch of live monsters, starting from the chosen target:

```
(define (flail w)
  (decrease-attack# w)
  (define target (current-target w))
  (define alive (filter monster-alive? (orc-world-lom w)))
  (define pick#
    (min
     (random-quotient (player-strength (orc-world-player w))
                      FLAIL-DAMAGE)
     (length alive)))
  (define getem (cons target (take alive pick#)))
  (for-each (lambda (m) (damage-monster m 1)) getem))
```

Like stab, flail also pays for the attack and picks the current target. Then it filters the living monsters from the dead ones and chooses the number of monsters that can be attacked, a number that depends on the player's strength and the global constant FLAIL-DAMAGE. Finally, flail will cons the current target on to the list of chosen monsters so that it can attack them all—a little bit. Notice that this may damage the currently targeted monster twice, but so it goes when you flail wildly.

We have yet to define the three helper functions that the player's actions rely on. They aren't complicated, and we aren't hiding anything. The names of the functions tell you what they do, and their definitions are one-liners:

```
(define (decrease-attack# w)
  (set-orc-world-attack#! w (sub1 (orc-world-attack# w))))
```

```
(define (damage-monster m delta)
  (set-monster-health! m (interval- (monster-health m) delta)))

(define (current-target w)
  (list-ref (orc-world-lom w) (orc-world-target w)))
```

The first one, decrease-attack#, subtracts one from the attack# field in the given
world w. The second one performs interval arithmetic on the monster's health—the same
kind we used for manipulating the player's attributes. And the third one extracts the currently targeted monster from the list.

If you are at all confused here, take a breath. Open the code in the chapter directory. Play with some of the functions. Make up a world. Call the function on the world.
Interact with the world.

Time to tackle the last function that player-acts-on-monsters demands:

```
(define (move-target w delta)
  (define new (+ (orc-world-target w) delta))
  (set-orc-world-target! w (modulo new MONSTER#)))
```

Not surprisingly, move-target adds the given delta to the current target index. But
this addition may produce a number that is too large or too small, a number that goes
beyond the end of the list or before its beginning. So before we store this new target number into the target field of w, we use the modulo function to find the appropriate number
between 0 and the actual number of monsters.

It may have been a while since your teacher tormented you with the modulo function, so let's experiment. First, we set up the world:

```
> (define p (player 3 4 5))
> (define lom (list (monster 0 2) (monster 1 3)))
> (define a-world (orc-world p lom 1 0))
```

Next, we call move-target on a-world:

```
> (move-target a-world 1)
> a-world
(orc-world (player 5 5 5) (list (monster 0 2) (monster 1 3)) 1 1)
```

As you can see, move-target has no result, but it has an effect on a-world. So we check
to find out what happened to it.

Now it's your turn. Try move-target on some of the numbers we used here, like +1,
-1, (+ PER-ROW), (- PER-ROW). Watch what happens in various situations.

Of course, it's actually the monsters' turn. We still need to create all the functionality to make our fearsome monsters attack, suffer, and retreat. The first function we need to define is `give-monster-turn-if-attack#=0`:

```
(define (give-monster-turn-if-attack#=0 w)
  (when (zero? (orc-world-attack# w))
    (define player (orc-world-player w))
    (all-monsters-attack-player player (orc-world-lom w))
    (set-orc-world-attack#! w (random-number-of-attacks player))))
```

We know the function consumes a world. Its name tells us *what* it does, and its definition shows *how* it accomplishes all this. Remember that `when` is like a `cond` expression with just one branch. This one branch may contain a series of definitions and expressions, just like a function body. In this particular case, the `when` expression checks whether the player has any attacks left for this turn. If the player has no attacks left, the function extracts the player from the given world and gives the monsters their due. Once they are finished damaging the player, `give-monster-turn-if-attack#=0` sets the number of attacks for the next player's turn. Put differently, the all-important line in this function is the second one in the `when` expression, which calls `all-monsters-attack-player` with the player and the list of monsters.

And what do you think `all-monsters-attack-player` does? It does exactly what its name says: it allows each live monster to attack the player in its orcish, hydranous, slime-a-licious, or brigandy way:

```
(define (all-monsters-attack-player player lom)
  (define (one-monster-attacks-player m)
    (cond
      [(orc? m)
       (player-health+ player (random- (orc-club m)))]
      [(hydra? m)
       (player-health+ player (random- (monster-health m)))]
      [(slime? m)
       (player-health+ player -1)
       (player-agility+ player
                        (random- (slime-sliminess monster)))]
      [(brigand? m)
       (case (random 3)
         [(0) (player-health+ player HEALTH-DAMAGE)]
         [(1) (player-agility+ player AGILITY-DAMAGE)]
         [(2) (player-strength+ player STRENGTH-DAMAGE)])]))
  (define live-monsters (filter monster-alive? lom))
  (for-each one-monster-attacks-player live-monsters))
```

When someone explains a function and says, "Every actor executes some action," you want to use `for-each` to code it up. It is kind of like `map`, but it doesn't collect any results. And when someone says, "All items on this list that are good," you use `filter` to extract the good items from this list. And that explains `all-monsters-attack-player` almost completely. The only point left to explain is what each monster actually does to the player, but as you can see, that's also spelled out in one single, locally defined function: `one-monster-attacks-player`. It consumes a monster, determines which kind of monster it is, and from there, it's all downhill for the player. Go read the definition of this last remaining function and explain to yourself what each monster does.

Then fight the monsters and save Chad. Good luck!

`Throw`—**Chapter Checkpoint**

In this chapter, we used structures to model the world:

- Structures are good for representing objects with a fixed number of parts.

- A structure definition also defines several new functions for you. One is for making new instances of the structure, which is called a constructor. Another is for determining if a value is an instance of the structure, called a predicate. Finally, you get one function for accessing each part of a structure, called an accessor.

- Entire structures or individual fields can be declared mutable. If so, the structure definition defines mutators. The best use for a mutator is to change a structure deeply embedded in either lists or other structures.

- With mutable structures, `eq?` becomes critically important.

Chapter Challenges

- **Easy**   Add actions that allow the player to regain strength and agility.

- **Medium**   Equip the player with an `armor` property. Then create an action called `block` that adds to the player's armor. A player's armor can absorb some of the damage from creatures, but each of the creature's attacks reduces the `armor` value.

- **Medium**   Create a monster that ignores the player's armor when it attacks.

;; Chapter 9
(The Values of Loops)

```
#|
Lists are a central data type in Racket. We started off manipu-
lating them manually. Then we learned about lambda and functions
like map and foldl. Now we will introduce a third and even more
powerful way of managing lists: for loops.
|#
```

9.1 FOR Loops

If you have taken a run-of-the-mill course on programming or read one of those standard introductory books, you know about `for` loops. Racketeers have a special relationship with loops, and therefore Racket has many kinds of `for` loops. Each has its own uses and purposes. Anything you can do with `map`, `foldl`, `foldr`, `filter`, `andmap`, `ormap`, and so on, you can do with `for` loops.

The basic **for loop** looks and acts like the one you may already know:

```
> (for ([i '(1 2 3 4 5)])
    (display i))
12345
```

The clause immediately after the for keyword sets up **variable bindings** for the body of the loop. A binding consists of a variable paired with an expression that evaluates to a list. In this example, the variable is i and the expression is '(1 2 3 4 5). Racket sets the variable to each element of the list and for each one evaluates the body of the for loop—in this case, (display i). Here, the for loop iterates across the list '(1 2 3 4 5) and uses the display function to print each value.

The basic for loop is for effect only. Like for-each, it returns nothing. The preceding for loop example is equivalent to (for-each display '(1 2 3 4 5)). If we want to mimic map, which involves building or running over a list, we use a different kind of for loop:

```
> (for/list ([i '(1 2 3 4 5)])
    (/ 1 i))
'(1 1/2 1/3 1/4 1/5)
```

This for/list loop acts like for, but it takes the last value of each iteration and collects these values in a list. You could think of it as follows:

```
> (map (lambda (x) (/ 1 x)) '(1 2 3 4 5))
'(1 1/2 1/3 1/4 1/5)
```

One of the most powerful loops is for/fold. This loop accumulates a value much like foldr and foldl:

```
> (for/fold ([sqrs 0])
            ([i '(1 2 3 4 5 6 7 8 9 10)])
    (+ (sqr i) sqrs))
385
```

The value returned in each iteration is bound to `sqrs`, which is initialized to 0. In essence, what we wrote above is equivalent to this expression:

```
> (foldl (lambda (i sqrs) (+ (sqr i) sqrs))
         0
         '(1 2 3 4 5 6 7 8 9 10))
```

But let's say we also wanted to keep track of the number of squares over 50. We could do it like this:

```
> (for/fold ([sqrs 0]
             [count 0])
            ([i '(1 2 3 4 5 6 7 8 9 10)])
    (values (+ (sqr i) sqrs)
            (if (> (sqr i) 50)
                (add1 count)
                count))))
385
3
```

Wait! Look over this example again because it is complicated. Actually, it isn't just complicated—it uses a feature of Racket that you have never seen before: an expression that produces *multiple* values. This is so new that it deserves its own section.

9.2 Multiple Values

The `values` function returns whatever you pass to it:

```
> (values 42)
42
```

It may seem silly to have a function that just returns what it is given. But the `values` function can take anything and any number of values, and it returns them all at *once*:

```
> (values 'this 'and-this 'and-that)
'this
'and-this
'and-that
```

These values can be caught with `define-values`, another way to define variables:

```
> (define-values (one two three) (values 'three 'two 'one))
> one
'three
> two
'two
> three
'one
```

Like `values`, `define-values` can work with any number of arguments. Like `define`, `define-values` gives names to values. As the example explains, `define-values` comes with a sequence of identifiers between parentheses. It expects its right-hand side to deliver that many values. When it gets the values, it gives them the specified names.

Here is an example with a more complicated right-hand side:

```
> (define-values (x y)
    (if (string=? (today) "tuesday")
        (values 10 20)
        (values 42 55)))
> x
```

We will let you figure out what the value of x is because we don't know on what day of the week you are reading this book.

9.3 Back to FOR/FOLD

Let's look at the `for/fold` example from section 9.1 again:

```
> (for/fold ([sqrs 0]
             [count 0])
            ([i '(1 2 3 4 5 6 7 8 9 10)])
    (values (+ (sqr i) sqrs)
            (if (> (sqr i) 50)
                (add1 count)
                count)))
385
3
```

On closer observation, `for/fold` is a bit like both `define-values` and `values`. It sets up two sets of bindings. The first one determines how many values each loop iteration with the loop body must return and how many values the loop itself returns. As you may have guessed, the body of the `for/fold` loop may refer to these names. Here, the loop sets up two such bindings, initializing both to 0 and giving them the names `sqrs` and `count`. The loop body consists of a `values` expression that produces two values. For each iteration, the first value is the square of `i` added to `sqrs`, and the second value is `count` or (`add1 count`), depending on how large the square of `i` is. In the end, the loop produces 385 and 3. Do you understand why?

9.4 More on Loops

All `for` loops come with the ability to skip some iterations. In the part of the `for` loop where we specify the lists we are using, we can put in a `#:when` clause. Each `#:when` clause comes with an expression that is evaluated for every iteration. The iteration is performed only if the expression following `#:when` evaluates to true:

```
> (for/list ([i '(1 2 3 4 5)]
             #:when (odd? i))
    i)
'(1 3 5)
> (for/fold ([sum 0])
            ([i '(1 2 3 4 5)]
             #:when (even? i))
    (+ sum i))
6
```

In this manner, `#:when` clauses make `for` loops act like `filter`.

Why should you use Racket's `for` loops? You should not use `for` loops just because you are familiar with their impoverished cousins from pedestrian languages. You should get to know Racket's `for` loops because they are far more powerful than what you may have encountered. Racketeers are keenly aware of the advantages of `lambda`, `map`, `andmap`, `filter`, and friends, and therefore Racket provides many more kinds of `for` loops than you have ever seen. If you can wrap your head around them, you will write compact yet highly readable code.

One major benefit of `for` loops is that they easily run through a lot of lists at once. All you need to do is add more `for` clauses, and the `for` loop binds all of those expressions simultaneously and iterates over all of them in parallel. The loop ends as soon as the shortest list is exhausted:

```
> (for/list ([i '(1 2 3 4 5)]
             [j '(1 2 3 4)]
             [k '(5 4 3 2 1)])
    (list i j k))
'((1 1 5) (2 2 4) (3 3 3) (4 4 2))
```

Here, we bind `i`, `j`, and `k` to the elements of three separate lists. Because the shortest list—bound to `j`—has only four elements, while the others have five, the loop runs four times, ignoring the last elements of the lists bound to `i` and `k`.

Take a look at this example:

```
> (for/list ([i '(1 2 3 4 5)]
             [s '("a" "b" "c" "d" "e")]
             #:when (and (even? i) (string=? s "d")))
    i)
'(4)
```

As you can see, it evaluates the loop body, `i`, only when `i` is 4 and `s` is the string "d".

Something else you can do with `for` loops is nest them. Instead of writing . . .

```
(for ([i '(1 2 3)])
  (for ([j '(1 2 3)])
    (for ([k '(1 2 3)])
      (displayln (list i j k)))))
```

. . . Racketeers would write the much more concise

```
(for* ([i '(1 2 3)]
       [j '(1 2 3)]
       [k '(1 2 3)])
  (displayln (list i j k)))
```

Every kind of `for` loop comes with this `for*` variety: `for*/list`, `for*/fold`, and so on. Note that `for*/list` is equivalent to a nested `for` loop but with all values collected into one list:

```
> (for*/list ([i '(1 2 3)]
              [j '(4 5 6)])
    (+ i j))
'(5 6 7 6 7 8 7 8 9)
> (for/list ([i '(1 2 3)])
    (for/list ([j '(4 5 6)])
      (+ i j)))
'((5 6 7) (6 7 8) (7 8 9))
```

The sublists in a `for*` are evaluated just as they would be in a nested `for` loop—every time a level runs, the corresponding list is evaluated. That allows us to compute values like this:

```
> (for*/list ([k '((1 2) (3 4) (5 6) (7 8))]
              [n k])
    n)
'(1 2 3 4 5 6 7 8)
```

Here, we flatten a list of lists—turn it into a single list of numbers—by binding each element in the superlist to `k`, binding each element of those lists to `n`, and returning those values. We can do this because every time we change elements in the list bound to `k`, the initial value for `n` is recomputed.

There is one more piece of `for` loop magic: `in-range`. We can use it to iterate across ranges of numbers or to perform an action a set number of times. The `in-range` function accepts one to three arguments and returns something a `for` loop can iterate over:

```
> (for/list ([i (in-range 10)])
    i)
'(0 1 2 3 4 5 6 7 8 9)
> (for/list ([i (in-range 5 10)])
    i)
'(5 6 7 8 9)
> (for/list ([i (in-range 0 10 2)])
    i)
'(0 2 4 6 8)
```

When given n as an argument, `in-range` returns a sequence containing the numbers from 0 to n minus 1. Given two arguments, it returns a sequence from the first argument to one less than the second. If it is given a third argument, it increments each element of the sequence by the third argument until it reaches the second argument. Try it out.

Now, `in-range` is different from all the other Racket functions we have seen before:

```
> (in-range 10)
#<stream>
```

It returns a **stream**, which is a special kind of **sequence**.

As it turns out, `for` loops can iterate across many different kinds of sequences—even strings. There is not enough room in this book to cover all of them, but if you're interested, look up "sequences" in the Racket documentation.

The following table describes a few other loops. There are more; if you're interested, you know where to look.

Loop	Purpose	Example	Value
`for/and`	Joins all the results with `and`.	`(for/and ([i '(1 2 #f)]) i)`	`#f`
`for/or`	Joins all the results with `or`.	`(for/or ([i '(1 2 #f)]) i)`	`1`
`for/first`	Like `for` but it returns the first result.	`(for/first ([i '(1 2 3)]) i)`	`1`
`for/last`	Like `for` but it returns the last result.	`(for/last ([i '(1 2 3)]) i)`	`3`

`Waitpid`—Chapter Checkpoint

In this chapter, we saw an alternative way of writing loops:

- There are several variants of `for` loops. Each combines its results in a different way.
- The `for*` loop is convenient shorthand for writing nested loops.
- A `for` loop iterates over a sequence of values. You can make a sequence using lists, strings, `in-range`, `in-list`, vectors, and many other values.

Dice of Doom

Excuse me, but what is behind those doors and how do I get in?

I am Dicetromonom!

Behind me are the upper dungeons. If you want to get in, you have to beat me in a game of...
DICE OF DOOM!!!

Hmm, okay. How bad can it be?

243
LOSSES
LATER
. . .

Oh...

;; Chapter 10
(Dice of Doom)

```
#|
We are finally ready to create a truly sophisticated and fun pro-
gram. In this chapter, we'll develop Dice of Doom, a game full of
chance and strategy. What you'll learn in this chapter isn't suf-
ficient, however, to make the implementation run fast enough for
large games. Therefore, the next couple of chapters will show you
how to refine this game's implementation.
|#
```

10.1 The Game Tree

While wandering the expanses of DrRacket's dungeons, Chad comes across a massive door guarded by a humongous machine known as Dicetromonom. When he asks the guard where the door leads, it replies, "Behind me are the upper dungeons. If you want to get in, you have to beat me in a game of . . . DICE OF DOOM!!!" Hoping to get closer to an exit, Chad challenges the guard. Game after game after game, Dicetromonom obliterates Chad. Dejected, Chad gives up and begins to wander the dungeons once more, looking for a way out. After a while, he stumbles across the mythical game tree, which grants Chad the ability to defeat Dicetromonom. Can Chad master the art of the game tree? It is your job to help him, and this chapter shows you how.

10.2 Dice of Doom, The Game

Dice of Doom is a turn-based strategy game played by two or more players. Each player controls territories on the board, and each territory contains a few dice. On each turn, the current player may attack an adjacent enemy territory but only if the attacker's territory contains more than one dice.

When two neighboring territories are engaged in combat, the two players roll the dice from their respective territories. If the attacker's sum is greater than the defender's sum, all of the dice are removed from the targeted territory and all but one of the attacker's dice will invade it. The attacking player now occupies that targeted territory. On the other hand, if the sum of the defender's dice is greater than that of the attacker, all but one of the dice are removed from the territory that launched the attack. The game is over when one player controls all the territories.

During a turn, a player may attack as many times as possible or pass at any time. When a player passes, some number of dice are added to all of the current player's territories depending on the specific rules on which the players agree. In our case, it depends on how the game is implemented.

10.3 Designing Dice of Doom: Take One

Weeks of programming can save you hours of planning. Realistically, you cannot implement a game until you have figured out the details. In addition, you may wish to simplify the game for the first implementation and then add complexities later on. Also, you must decide how players interact with the software. Doing so often guides the rest of the design.

Filling in the Blanks

The basic game description leaves two aspects open to interpretation: a territory's appearance and the distribution of dice at the end of a player's turn.

The typical game board for a Dice of Doom game consists of hexagons. As illustrated in the image to the right, each hexagon is one territory, meaning each territory can have up to six adjacent territories. Keep in mind a player may attack and take over any neighbor.

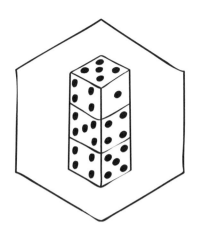

As for the supply of dice, we assume a global pool of spare dice. When a player ends her turn, one dice is moved from the pool to each of her territories. When the pool is empty, no player will receive any more reinforcements.

Simplifying the Rules

We want to show you how to program using a game tree, which is a piece of data that contains every possible move for a game. Therefore, we are going to make three simplifications to the rules to better align the game with our purpose.

The first simplification concerns how the game ends. Some snarky player may just pass on her turn forever. To eliminate this possibility, we will make it illegal for a player to pass on the first move of her turn, thus guaranteeing that the number of dice decreases on each turn. Following this logic, the game will reach a state when no attacks can be launched because there aren't enough dice on the territories. Alternatively, the game ends when a player has conquered all territories. The first simplification ensures that there is only a finite number of moves in every game, and therefore we can represent an entire game as one piece of data.

The second simplification is to make attacks nonrandom. In our simplified version of the game, the attacking territory must have more dice than the defending territory, and the attacking territory always wins because it is stronger.

The third simplification introduces the constraint that only two human players interact with the implementation. When the game starts up, one player takes control of the keyboard and plays a turn. To pass means to let the implementation know that the turn is done *and* to hand the keyboard to the other player. We know that this sounds a bit clumsy, but even this goal is ambitious right now. In chapter 12, we will show you how the game itself can play the role of the second player and why our implementation makes this addition simple.

End of Game

The revised game is over when a player cannot make any first move, other than pass. The winner is the player who owns the most territories.

Controlling the Game

A human player may perform five actions in our version of the game. The first is to consider a territory either as a launch pad for an attack or as a target. Let's have the left and right arrow keys control tile consideration so we can simply cycle through territories. The second action is to mark a territory as the source or destination of an attack. For that, we assign the "Enter" key. We choose that the player first marks the source and then the destination. The invasion starts at the very moment a player marks the destination of an attack. The fourth action is to unmark the source territory, which allows a player to change her mind. We allocate the "d" key for this purpose. Finally, there must be a way for the player to pass on her turn *after* she has attacked at least once. For this, we reserve the "p" key.

In summary:

- A player can pass only when she has made at least one attack.
- In order to attack, the attacking territory must have more dice than the defending territory.
- Two human players will play this game.
- The "←" and "→" keys are for cycling through the tiles.
- The "Enter" key is for marking a territory.
- The "d" key is for unmarking a territory.
- The "p" key is for passing a turn.

10.4 How Game Trees Work

As we mentioned earlier, this implementation of the game will use a game tree, which is a chart of all possible states of the game board. These states are linked to the players' moves because states of the board change depending on what moves have been made by the players. At every point in the game, we will maintain only the part of the tree whose root is the current state. This means we will always know our current state and a list of possible moves. When a player makes a move, that move will be used to find the next state from the list of links. Then we set that state to be the current state. By doing so, many old parts of the game tree are thrown away, thus diminishing the game tree.

The game tree gives us a central point of control for our game and its rules because every bit of information needed to play a game is saved in one data structure. In the next two chapters, we will show you how to create a more efficient representation of the game tree and how it can be used to create an artificial intelligence that can play this game. All of this is pretty abstract, so let's look at a concrete and simple example.

Tic-tac-toe is a simple, finite game. The first level of the game tree consists of an empty board and nine possible moves for player X. The tree attached to each of the resulting game states has eight moves, representing player O's possibilities. On the third level, we see seven branches, each representing the next level of X's game, and so on all the way to game states in which the game has ended. The sketch shows how you should imagine a game tree for tic-tac-toe.

 GAME TREE

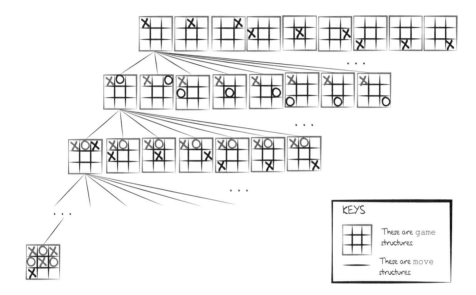

Now we use this tree to play a game of tic-tac-toe. Player X starts out with nine possible moves. She chooses to place her X in the upper-left corner. As a result, we focus only on the leftmost branch of the tree, leaving player O with eight possibilities. Say player O then marks the spot directly next to the X. This in turn means we again choose the leftmost branch. We keep pruning the tree like this until the game is over, which happens when one player wins or all fields are marked.

Generating the tic-tac-toe tree is reasonably straightforward. Suppose we have a data representation for the two players, X and O, and we represent the tree itself with `ttt` nodes:

```
(struct ttt (board moves))
```

Each such node contains the current state of the board and the list of possible moves. Each move is a two-element list that combines an action with the resulting game tree, where an action is just another structure:

```
(struct action (player position))
```

It records the player that takes the action and her chosen token placement.

The tree-generating function consumes the two players and produces a complete game tree starting from an empty board:

```
(define (generate-ttt-tree player1 player2)
  (define (generate-tree board player opponent)
    (ttt board (generate-moves board player opponent)))
  (define (generate-moves board0 player opponent)
    (define free-fields (board-find-free-fields board0))
    (for/list ((f free-fields))
        (define actnow (action player f))
        (define board1 (board-take-field board0 player f))
        (list actnow (generate-tree board1 opponent player))))
;; -- start here --
  (generate-tree the-empty-board player1 player2))
```

As you can see, the function introduces two auxiliary functions: `generate-tree` and `generate-moves`. The first one generates a tree node from the current state of the board and two players, assuming the first player takes an action. The second function generates the list of possible moves from the current board and the two players, still assuming that the first player is the active one.

From the definition, you can see that `generate-tree` is straightforward. It creates the node from the current board and generates the possible moves with the second function. In contrast, the `generate-moves` function must iterate over all free fields, which it finds with `board-find-free-fields`, a function not shown here. For each of the free fields, the loop creates an action for the current player and the free field. Then it computes with `board-take-field` the effect of the action on the current board. The result of an iteration is a two-element list that pairs the action with the resulting tree, which is determined via a recursive call to `generate-tree`. When the loop has finished, `generate-moves` returns an entire list of such two-element lists.

With the two functions in place, it is easy to see how to launch the tree-generating process. We call `generate-tree` on the empty board and pass along the two players. It takes a while to generate the entire tree, and if you wish to display it, be prepared to take a coffee break. But really, that's all there is to game trees. The details are a bit tedious, but improving the tree operations' efficiency is fun, and you'll see that in the next two chapters.

10.5 Game States and Game Trees for Dice of Doom

Tic-tac-toe is a bit simple for using game trees, but it is a good model for our data design. For Dice of Doom, we need three pieces of data to represent a game state:

```
(struct dice-world (src board gt))
```

The first field, `src`, designates the territory that a player has marked as the source of her attack. It is an index label for one of the territories or `#f` if no territory has been marked yet. The second field, `board`, contains a list of all territories. The first element of this list is the territory that the player is focused on. Recall that this means that the player is contemplating it for a move. When she presses the "Enter" key and `src` is still `#f`, the in-focus territory becomes the marked one. The third field, `gt`, is the game tree for the current state of the board.

The definition of `dice-world` requires two more kinds of data. The first is a territory:

```
(struct territory (index player dice x y))
```

The first field, `index`, is the label that simultaneously describes the territory's location relative to other territories and acts as a unique identifier. The second field, `player`, identifies the player who currently owns this territory. In this game, the players are represented by natural numbers. This allows us to cycle through players by adding one to the current player index instead of cycling through a list of names. The third field, `dice`, is the number of dice on this territory. We include the last two fields, x and y, as the coordinates for drawing this territory. Strictly speaking, these last two fields aren't necessary, but they tremendously simplify the rendering process.

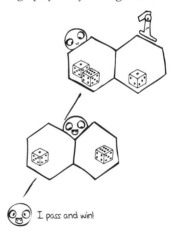

I pass and win!

The second definition we need for `dice-world` is the game tree, which is a little tricky. We need two pieces of data: one representing an entire game tree and the other representing a move. Plus, we need to keep track of whose turn it is. So the game tree needs three pieces:

```
(struct game (board player moves))
```

The first field, `board`, is the state of the board, which, as you may recall, is a list of territories. The second field, `player`, identifies the player whose turn it is. The third field, `moves`, is a list of all possible moves starting at this state of the game. If a player cannot make a move, this list is empty. We refer to such a game tree as the empty game tree, which indicates that the game has ended.

To represent a move, we use two pieces of data:

```
(struct move (action gt))
```

The first field, `action`, describes the attack that a player is going to perform. It is either `empty`, representing a pass, or a list of two numbers, representing an attack from the first territory against the second territory. The second field, `gt`, is the game tree that results from executing this move on the current board.

Remember that you can relate this idea to the tree image of tic-tac-toe in section 10.4. Each node in the tree represents a game, and a connection between two nodes represents a move. A `game` represents each of the nodes on that tree, whereas a `move` represents one of the between-node connections.

Let's build a small game tree for a simplistic Dice of Doom game on a 2×1 board. To start, we'll look at the total game tree. For a graphical view, see the diagram on page 173.

The board consists of two territories, owned by players 0 and 1. The game begins with player 0's turn. Because it is her first move and there is only one other territory on the board, her only option is to attack that territory. After this attack, there are no other territories on the board she can attack, so she must pass. Once she passes, it is player 1's turn. Our rules state that a player's first move must be an attack, but that's impossible because player 1 has no more territories. With no possible moves left, the game concludes.

According to our description of the gameplay, there are three possible states of the board:

```
(define b0 (list (territory 0 0 2 'x 'y) (territory 1 1 1 'a 'b)))
(define b1 (list (territory 0 0 1 'x 'y) (territory 1 0 1 'a 'b)))
(define b2 (list (territory 1 0 1 'a 'b) (territory 0 0 1 'x 'y)))
```

The states of the board are listed in consecutive order of gameplay. In b0, player 0 owns a territory with two dice and player 1 owns a territory with only one dice. In b1 and b2, player 0 owns both territories that each contain one dice. Note that the only difference between b1 and b2 is the ordering of the territories in the list. Do you remember when the ordering plays a role?

To build any game tree manually, we must start at the bottom. In this case, it is the game tree with the final board:

```
(define gt2 (game b2 1 '()))
```

In this bottommost game tree, it is player 1's turn and both territories are owned by player 0. Therefore, her list of moves is empty.

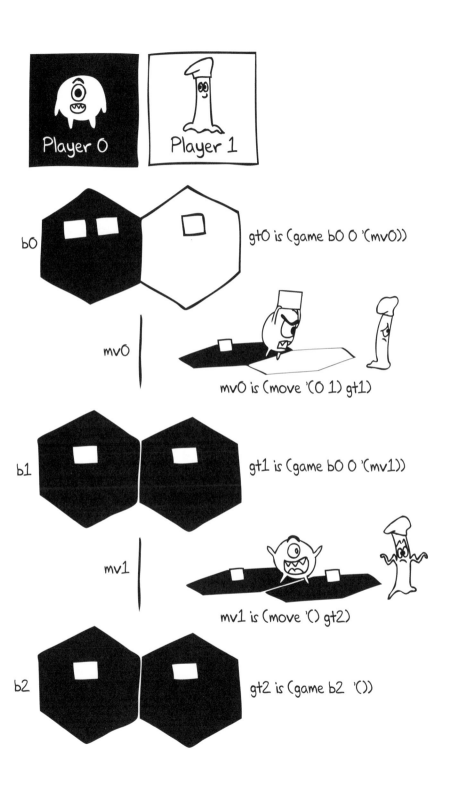

Player 0

Player 1

b0   gt0 is (game b0 0 '(mv0))

mv0   mv0 is (move '(0 1) gt1)

b1   gt1 is (game b0 0 '(mv1))

mv1   mv1 is (move '() gt2)

b2   gt2 is (game b2 '())

The move in the game tree gt2 starts from b2, where player 0 owns both territories. Hence, the move can be only a pass by player 0:

```
(define mv1 (move '() gt2))
(define gt1 (game b2 0 (list mv1)))
```

Since a pass cannot be player 0's first move, player 0 has to make a move that leads to gt1:

```
(define mv0 (move '(0 1) gt1))
(define gt0 (game b0 0 (list mv0)))
```

This move represents an attack from territory 0 on 1 and contains gt1, which is the result of the attack. Game tree gt0 contains the starting board, which is the ultimate game tree that we are trying to build. The diagram on page 173 graphically explains the game tree. A picture is worth a thousand words.

10.6 Roll the Dice

Now we can finally start making the game:

```
(define (roll-the-dice)
  (big-bang (create-world-of-dice-and-doom)
            (on-key interact-with-board)
            (on-draw draw-dice-world)
            (stop-when no-more-moves-in-world?
                       draw-end-of-dice-world)))
```

This function launches the game. It uses the same kind of big-bang expression you have seen throughout the book. The function first creates a random world with create-world-of-dice-and-doom:

```
(define (create-world-of-dice-and-doom)
  (define board (territory-build))
  (define gamet (game-tree board INIT-PLAYER INIT-SPARE-DICE))
  (define new-world (dice-world #f board gamet))
  (if (no-more-moves-in-world? new-world)
      (create-world-of-dice-and-doom)
      new-world))
```

The function creates a random board and uses it to create a world with a game tree. If the generated game has no moves for the first player, it will immediately end the game, which we don't want, so the function tries again. Otherwise, we accept the world as it is.

The rest of the big-bang clauses specify how to handle events, draw the world, determine whether the game is over, and if so, draw an image for the end of the game.

The simplest of these clauses is the ending condition, which we also used in the world creation function:

```
(define (no-more-moves-in-world? w)
  (define tree (dice-world-gt w))
  (define board (dice-world-board w))
  (define player (game-player tree))
  (or (no-more-moves? tree)
      (for/and ((t board)) (= (territory-player t) player))))
```

This function checks whether a world's list of moves is empty or the current player has conquered all territories. In either case, the game is over.

Rendering the final state of the game is also straightforward:

```
(define (draw-end-of-dice-world w)
  (define board (dice-world-board w))
  (define message (text (won board) TEXT-SIZE TEXT-COLOR))
  (define background (add-board-to-scene w (PLAIN)))
  (overlay message background))
```

At the end of the game, we generate a string using the function won that overlays the text on the background scene. The text either announces the winning player or acknowledges a tie.

Drawing the game in play is slightly more involved:

```
(define (draw-dice-world w)
  (add-player-info
   (game-player (dice-world-gt w))
   (add-board-to-scene w (ISCENE))))
```

The add-player-info function draws information about whose turn it is on a scene. Both add-player-info and add-board consume a scene on which they draw their images.

The remaining big-bang clause specifies the key-handler:

```
(define (interact-with-board w k)
  (cond [(key=? "left" k)
         (refocus-board w left)]
        [(key=? "right" k)
         (refocus-board w right)]
        [(key=? "p" k)
         (pass w)]
        [(key=? "\r" k)
         (mark w)]
        [(key=? "d" k)
         (unmark w)]
        [else w]))
```

The first two clauses handle the player changing focus. They call `refocus-board`, which uses the current world and the direction to rotate the board. The third clause deals with the passing action. It calls `pass` on the world, which switches the current player and prunes the game tree to the pass move. The fourth case marks a territory. It invokes `mark`, which will either change the `src` field of the world to the in-focus territory, if the source for an attack has yet to be selected, or change the `src` to #f and initiate the attack. Doing so prunes the game tree and switches the `board` of the world to the `board` of the new game tree. The fifth clause deals with unmarking a territory. This action switches the `src` field to #f. The final case says to ignore all other keystrokes.

10.7 Rendering the Dice World

Drawing Dice of Doom requires two functions: `draw-dice-world` and `draw-end-of-dice-world`. Both are used in the main function. In turn, the two require three auxiliary functions: `add-player-info`, `add-board`, and `won`. The first two add imagery to a given scene; the last constructs text from the current state of the game, which is then added to the background.

The `add-player-info` function is simple:

```
(define (add-player-info player s)
  (define str (whose-turn player))
  (define txt (text str TEXT-SIZE TEXT-COLOR))
  (place-image txt (- WIDTH INFO-X-OFFSET) INFO-Y-OFFSET s))
```

First, it decides whose turn it is, using an uninteresting auxiliary function, and records this information as a string. Second, it converts this string to a text image, which is finally added to the bottom of the background scene.

The second function, `add-board`, is much more complicated than `add-player-info`:

```
(define (add-board-to-scene w s)
  (define board   (dice-world-board w))
  (define player  (game-player (dice-world-gt w)))
  (define focus?  (dice-world-src w))
  (define trtry1  (first board))
  (define p-focus (territory-player trtry1))
  (define t-image (draw-territory trtry1))
  (define image (draw-focus focus? p-focus player t-image))
  (define base-s  (add-territory trtry1 image s))
  (for/fold ([s base-s]) ([t (rest board)])
    (add-territory t (draw-territory t) s)))
```

```
(define (draw-focus marked? p-in-focus p t-image)
  (if (or (and (not marked?) (= p-in-focus p))
          (and marked? (not (= p-in-focus p))))
      (overlay FOCUS t-image)
      t-image))
```

It consumes a world and a scene. From this data, it constructs an image that contains the board and informs the player whose turn it is. The first five internal definitions extract the relevant pieces from the given data. The local definition of image highlights the in-focus tile under certain conditions, using a simple auxiliary function. Specifically, the function overlays the basic image with the FOCUS frame if the currently acting player has used the arrow keys to focus on either a launching pad for an attack or a target. This special first territory on the board is then used to create the base image. The rest of the result is created by folding over the board with draw-territory.

The function draw-territory consumes a territory and returns the image for that hexagon with all of its dice:

```
(define (add-territory t image scene)
  (place-image image (territory-x t) (territory-y t) scene))

(define (draw-territory t)
  (define color (color-chooser (territory-player t)))
  (overlay (hexagon color) (draw-dice (territory-dice t))))
```

The image of the territory is created by overlaying a semi-opaque hexagon of the player's color onto an image of the dice that occupy this territory. That way, the dice will have the same color as their territory.

The choice of color deserves some attention:

```
(define (color-chooser n)
  (list-ref COLORS n))
```

The all-caps variable name COLORS tells you that our code contains a constant definition, and this definition introduces COLORS as a list of colors. The color-chooser takes the nth value in it and calls it the nth player's color.

Our list of COLORS differs from the way we have made colors before. In order to change the opacity of a color, we cannot use strings such as "red" because that's 100% opaque. Instead, we use make-color, which takes four numbers between 0 and 255 to create a color. Respectively, these numbers represent the red, green, blue, and transparency values of a color. This means that the first three arguments define what shade the color will have: 0, 0, and 0 would give you black; 255, 0, 0 would give you red; 255, 255, 255, would give you white; and so on. The transparency specifies how opaque the color is, where 0 is transparent and 255 is completely opaque.

Drawing the dice requires the number of dice to draw:

```
(define (draw-dice n)
  (define first-dice  (get-dice-image 0))
  (define height-dice (image-height first-dice))
  (for/fold ([s first-dice]) ([i (- n 1)])
    (define dice-image (get-dice-image (+ i 1)))
    (define y-offset   (* height-dice (+ .5 (* i .25))))
    (overlay/offset s 0 y-offset dice-image)))
```

Since each territory must be occupied by at least one dice, `draw-dice` creates one image of a dice and uses it to place all others atop.

The `draw-dice` function then folds across the remaining dice, adding dice to the base dice. For this, we must stack the dice using an increasingly larger offset in the vertical direction, as the size of the accumulated image is increased.

We can get the dice image the same way we got the color for a hexagon—by using and looking up some image in a list of images:

```
(define (get-dice-img i)
  (list-ref IMG-LIST (modulo i (length IMG-LIST))))
```

When you design image-creating functions, it is always good to experiment in the interactions panel:

```
> (define (draw-dice dice)
    (define first-dice  (get-dice-image 0))
    (define height-dice (image-height first-dice))
    (for/fold ([s first-dice]) ([i (- n 1)])
      (define dice-image (get-dice-image (+ i 1)))
      (define y-offset   (* height-dice (+ .5 (* i .25))))
      (overlay/offset s 0 y-offset dice-image)))
> (draw-dice 3)
```

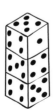

As you can imagine, we experimented quite a bit before we got this image just right.

10.8 Input Handling

Our player uses the keyboard to interact with the Dice of Doom game. As you may recall, she can perform four kinds of actions: switching focus from one territory to another, passing her turn, marking a territory, and unmarking a territory. Hence, handling keyboard inputs requires four functions: `refocus-board`, `pass`, `mark`, and `unmark`.

The `refocus-board` function takes in the world and a function that rotates a list either `left` or `right`. Its purpose is to rotate the board so that the newly focused territory is on the head of the list that represents the board.

```
(define (refocus-board w direction)
  (define source (dice-world-src w))
  (define board  (dice-world-board w))
  (define tree   (dice-world-gt w))
  (define player (game-player tree))
  (define (owner? tid)
    (if source (not (= tid player)) (= tid player)))
  (define new-board (rotate-until owner? board direction))
  (dice-world source new-board tree))
```

To accomplish its purpose, the function rebuilds the world, rotating the `board` field to the left or right. It uses two auxiliary functions: the locally defined `owner?` and `rotate-until`. Depending on the value of the `src` field, the rotation must look for either a territory of the active player or a territory of one of her opponents. The `owner?` function implements this comparison process, using a reference to the `player` from the current game tree.

The `rotate-until` function works as follows:

```
(define (rotate-until owned-by board rotate)
  (define next-list (rotate board))
  (if (owned-by (territory-player (first next-list)))
      next-list
      (rotate-until owned-by next-list rotate)))
```

It consumes a function, a board, and another function. With the `owned-by` function, `rotate-until` checks whether the first territory in `board` is owned by the desired player. With the `rotate` function, `rotate-until` executes the actual rotation on a step-by-step basis. Here, rotation can mean only one of two things: rotate left or rotate right.

We rotate the list to the left by `append`ing the `first` of it to the end:

```
(define (left l)
  (append (rest l) (list (first l))))
```

Rotating to the right uses a silly trick:

```
(define (right l)
  (reverse (left (reverse l))))
```

It reverses the given list, shifts left, and reverses again. We leave it to you to explore these two functions in the interactions panel and to confirm that they work properly for any non-empty list. As you play the game, you will notice that the game is perfectly responsive, even though this trick looks slow.

The key-handler also processes pass moves. This is done with pass, which consumes a dice-world and uses the game tree to create a new dice-world.

```
(define (pass w)
  (define m (find-move (game-moves (dice-world-gt w)) '()))
  (cond [(not m) w]
        [else (dice-world #f (game-board m) m)]))
```

Using find-move, pass tries to find the desired passing move in the list of moves of the game tree. If it is found, the matching game tree is returned; otherwise, find-move produces #f, possibly because passing is disallowed during the first move of a player's turn. If there is a move, the src field is changed to false, and the rest of the new game state is drawn from the game tree that results from choosing the passing move.

Finding the move is easy. All we need is the list of moves and the list that represents the action to be taken:

```
(define (find-move moves action)
  (define m
    (findf (lambda (m) (equal? (move-action m) action)) moves))
  (and m (move gt m)))
```

The function uses findf to drive the process. So if findf finds a move, the and expression extracts the corresponding game tree. Otherwise, the function returns #f.

The findf function is another one of those nice higher-order, list-eating functions. This one produces the first element of the list for which the given predicate returns true, or it returns false if nothing is found.

The last actions needed are functions that mark and unmark territories. The function mark consumes the world and either marks the in-focus territory or initiates an attack against the selected territory from the src territory:

```
(define (mark w)
  (define tree   (dice-world-gt w))
  (define board  (dice-world-board w))
  (define source (dice-world-src w))
  (define focus  (territory-index (first board)))
```

```
(if source
    (attacking w source focus)
    (dice-world focus board tree)))
```

First, `mark` deconstructs the given world into its pieces. Second, if the `src` field of this world is `#f`, the selected territory is marked. Otherwise, `mark` attacks by delegating to a helper:

```
(define (attacking w source target)
  (define feasible (game-moves (dice-world-gt w)))
  (define attack   (list source target))
  (define next     (find-move feasible attack))
  (if next (dice-world #f (game-board next) next) w))
```

The `attacking` function makes an attack and compares it against the list of feasible moves. If `execute` is not in the `feasible` list, the attempted move is illegal, and the world remains the same. But if the attack is valid, `attacking` creates a new world from the corresponding game tree and changes the `src` field to `#f` so that the player can launch another attack.

The final function in the key-handler deals with unmark requests:

```
(define (unmark w)
  (dice-world #f (dice-world-board w) (dice-world-gt w)))
```

The purpose of `unmark` is to change `src` to `#f` so that no territory is the source of an attack.

10.9 Creating a Game Tree

Now that we know how to manipulate the world, let's build the world. The major element of our world is the game tree, and building the game tree relies heavily on the board representation. We therefore start with the function that creates boards:

```
(define (territory-build)
  (for/list ([n (in-range GRID)])
    (territory n (modulo n PLAYER#) (dice) (get-x n) (get-y n))))
```

The `territory-build` function uses `for/list` to create the territories. For each territory index, the `for` loop creates one territory. The structure is assigned to some player, equipped with a random number of dice, and allocated to a particular point on the GUI grid.

Here are the three auxiliary functions:

```
(define (dice)
  (add1 (random DICE#)))

(define (get-x n)
  (+ OFFSET0
     (if (odd? (get-row n)) 0 (/ X-OFFSET 2))
     (* X-OFFSET (modulo n BOARD))))

(define (get-y n)
  (+ OFFSET0 (* Y-OFFSET (get-row n))))
```

The functions get-x and get-y probably look a little weird to you, but that's just because drawing hexagons is weird in the first place. Both of these functions use get-row to determine in which row the territory with index n is located.

```
(define (get-row pos)
  (quotient pos BOARD))
```

The Game Tree

With territory-build under your belt, we can explain how to generate a game tree from a given board. Recall that a game tree contains every possible state and move. Its root starts with the given board and explores all possible moves for the current player. When she passes, the tree starts with the board for the next player and explores all possible moves from here. This process continues until it reaches boards that represent a win, loss, or tie.

Generating all possible moves, even in a game as simple as Dice of Doom, is a somewhat tricky task. It's one of those situations where functional programming excels. Indeed, it is flat-out superior to traditional assignment-based programming, but it is still the most complex code you will find in this book.

What's tricky is that we need to generate all feasible attacks, followed by one passing move for each turn; everything else is illegal. With functional programming, we can compute all these possibilities because generating one branch of the game tree does not affect any other branch. The following code accomplishes this feat, so bear with us as we explain its complexities.

Since Dice of Doom comes with two kinds of moves, game-tree relies on two locally defined functions: attacks and passes. The first generates a list of trees, each starting with an attack. The second generates a tree that starts with a pass. In both cases, the subsequent moves in the tree are generated by recursively calling game-tree, but in the case of passes, the players' roles are switched. Now that you know this much, read the code:

```
(define (game-tree board player dice)
  ;; create tree of attacks from this position; add passing move
  (define (attacks board)
    (for*/list ([src board]
                [dst (neighbors (territory-index src))]
                #:when (attackable? board player src dst))
      (define from (territory-index src))
      (define dice (territory-dice src))
      (define newb (execute board player from dst dice))
      (define more (cons (passes newb) (attacks newb)))
      (move (list from dst) (game newb player more))))
  ;; create a passing move and the rest of the game tree
  (define (passes board)
    (define-values (new-dice newb) (distribute board player dice))
    (move '() (game-tree newb (switch player) new-dice)))
  ;; -- START: --
  (game board player (attacks board)))
```

Look at the line below the comment that says START. Given the current board, player, and number of dice left in the pool, game-tree begins by building a game structure including the list of all possible moves generated by attacks. Thus, this line implements the restriction that the first move of each turn must be an attack, because we know that attacks does not generate an initial passing move.

The attacks function is the workhorse of game-tree. Using for*/list, it traverses the territories of the board. For each src territory, it looks at each neighbor, dst, as a potential target. If an attack from src to dst is feasible, attacks builds a move structure. To do so, attacks uses the execute function to create the board resulting from a single attack. Having attacked, it's now possible to pass, so we cons a passing move onto the list of attacks for that branch of the game tree.

The passes function is simpler than attacks. It calls distribute and gets back the reduced number of dice in the pool and the updated board. Using those, it creates the passing move by applying game-tree to the new board, the other player, and the remaining number of dice.

To make passes work in the way we just explained, we need to design the functions switch and distribute. The shorter of these is switch, which changes to the next player:

```
(define (switch player)
  (modulo (add1 player) PLAYER#))
```

Because we represent players as numbers, we can use the `modulo` function to switch players.

The `distribute` function is more complex than `switch`. It consumes three values: the current board, the player whose territories get additional dice, and the number of spare dice left in the pool:

```
(define (distribute board player spare-dice)
  (for/fold ([dice spare-dice] [new-board '()]) ([t board])
    (if (and (= (territory-player t) player)
             (< (territory-dice t) DICE#)
             (not (zero? dice)))
        (values (- dice 1) (cons (add-dice-to t) new-board))
        (values dice (cons t new-board)))))
```

This function folds across the current board, modifying the `player`'s instances of `territory` and the dice pool. Specifically, the loop checks whether each territory is owned by the `player`, whether it has fewer than the maximum number of dice, and whether there are spare dice left to distribute. If these three conditions are met, it subtracts one dice from the pool of spare dice and adds it to the current `territory` using this function:

```
(define (add-dice-to t)
  (territory-set-dice t (add1 (territory-dice t))))
```

As you can see, this function adds 1 to the number of dice on the territory. Even though we don't define `territory-set-dice` here, you can imagine that it creates a new `territory` from the old values, except for the `dice` field, which receives the given value.

Why does `territory-set-dice` create a new territory? In other contexts, we have used mutation to change one field of a structure if all others stay the same. The program can't mutate `territory` here because doing so would modify this structure throughout the entire game tree—something we definitely do not want. All that needs to be changed is this particular `territory` in the current tree node.

Neighbors

The definition of `attacks`, within `game-tree`, requires us to implement two functions: `neighbors` and `attackable?`. The `neighbors` function consumes the unique index of a `territory` and returns a list of indices for the territories that border it. This function gets a little tricky because there are two kinds of hexagons we need to worry about here: the ones on even rows and the ones on odd rows. In order to get the hexagons to fit together, we shift every other row to the left. Accordingly, there are two kinds of calculations needed or, actually, one calculation adjusted for the shift in rows.

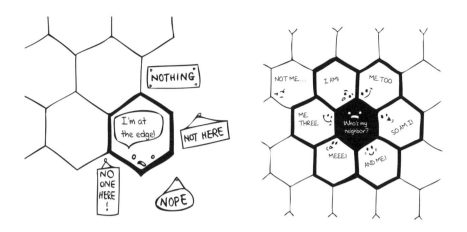

n on an odd-numbered row

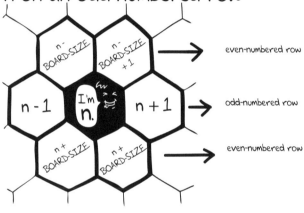

n on an even-numbered row

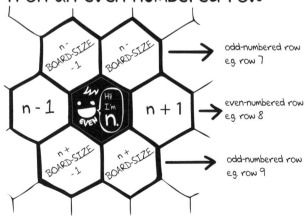

Every hexagon has maximally six neighbors: two above, two below, and one on either side. Pictorially, the calculations proceed according to the diagrams on page 184. But there is one more thing to consider. If a hexagon borders any of the four edges, it doesn't have neighbors on some sides, so the math shown will return meaningless results.

Now let's think about how the `neighbors` function might create the list of indicies. If it weren't for border cases, the function would produce a list of six numbers. Hence, this looks like a good first sketch:

```
(define (neighbors n)
  (list  upper-right
         bottom-right
         upper-left
         lower-left
         right
         left))
```

As discussed earlier, some of these numbers are added only when certain conditions hold. An easy way to choose whether or not to add something to a list is to define another function:

```
(define (add b x)
  (if b empty (list x)))
```

It takes a Boolean and a value and returns either the `empty` list or the list with just that value. Using `add`, you can then append as many of these values together as you wish, and the resulting list contains just the right number of elements.

At this point, our `neighbors` function becomes fairly straightforward:

```
(define (neighbors pos)
  (define top?       (< pos BOARD))
  (define bottom?    (= (get-row pos) (sub1 BOARD)))
  (define even-row? (zero? (modulo (get-row pos) 2)))
  (define right?     (zero? (modulo (add1 pos) BOARD)))
  (define left?      (zero? (modulo pos BOARD)))
  (if even-row?
      (even-row pos top? bottom? right? left?)
      (odd-row  pos top? bottom? right? left?)))
```

The algorithms for handling even and odd rows are nearly identical:

```
(define (even-row pos top? bottom? right? left?)
  (append (add (or top? right?)    (add1 (- pos BOARD)))
          (add (or bottom? right?) (add1 (+ pos BOARD)))
          (add top?                (- pos BOARD))
          (add bottom?             (+ pos BOARD))
          (add right?              (add1 pos))
          (add left?               (sub1 pos)))))
```

Look up the odd-row function—you know where it is.

As you can see, these functions use the row and edge information to append and add lists together to create a list of neighbors. In order, each of the expressions corresponds to upper right, bottom right, upper left, lower left, right, and left.

Attacks

Recall from the discussions of game-tree that we have to show you two more functions: attackable? and execute. The attackable? function checks the validity of an attack using the board, the current player, the source territory, and the index of the destination territory:

```
(define (attackable? board player src dst)
  (define dst-t
    (findf (lambda (t) (= (territory-index t) dst)) board))
  (and dst-t
       (= (territory-player src) player)
       (not (= (territory-player dst-t) player))
       (> (territory-dice src) (territory-dice dst-t)))))
```

We use this function to determine whether dst has an owner who is not the current player and whether src has more dice than dst.

Before we check all of these conditions, though, we ensure that the dst index actually points to a valid territory on the board. Doing so simplifies the for loop in game-tree and allows us to iterate through all possible indices, regardless of the shape of the board.

The `execute` function consumes the board, the current player, the `src` index, the `dst` index, and the number of dice on the `src`. From this data, it builds the board resulting from an attack of `src` on `dst`:

```
(define (execute board player src dst dice)
  (for/list ([t board])
    (define idx (territory-index t))
    (cond [(= idx src) (territory-set-dice t 1)]
          [(= idx dst)
           (define s (territory-set-dice t (- dice 1)))
           (territory-set-player s player)]
          [else t])))
```

The function traverses the board and re-creates the `territory` structs for the `src` and `dst` of the attack. The former now has one dice, and the latter has changed owners. It also transfers dice so that `dst` receives all but one of the dice from `src`. The function `territory-set-player` is just like `territory-set-dice` in that it changes the `player` field of the struct.

10.10 The End Game

Naturally, we saved the end of the game for last. As you might remember, the draw-end-of-dice-world function uses won, which takes in the board and constructs text describing the final state of the board:

```
(define (won board)
  (define-values (best-score w) (winners board))
  (if (cons? (rest w)) "It's a tie." "You won.")))
```

We use the winners function to fetch two values: the most territories owned by anyone and the list of players who own that many territories. If there are more than two winners in the list, the game ends in a tie. Otherwise, it constructs a string describing who won.

Calculating the winners from the board works like this:

```
(define (winners board)
  (for/fold ([best 0][winners '()]) ([p PLAYER#])
    (define p-score (sum-territory board p))
    (cond [(> p-score best) (values p-score (list p))]
          [(< p-score best) (values best winners)]
          [(= p-score best) (values best (cons p winners))])))
```

Here, we use for/fold to traverse the list of players. For each player, we get the number of occupied territories. When best is below p-score, the next loop iteration uses p-score as the winning score, and its list of winners contains only p, the unique identifier for the current player. When best is above p-score, nothing changes. Finally, when the two scores are identical, the loop adds p to the list of current winners. Since there are no other possibilities, the loop body covers all cases.

The very last function we need is sum-territory. It consumes a board and a player's index, and it calculates the number of territories that the player owns:

```
(define (sum-territory board player)
  (for/fold ([result 0]) ([t board])
    (if (= (territory-player t) player) (+ result 1) result)))
```

This function is a simple for/fold that runs through the board and adds 1 to its return value every time it finds a territory that is owned by player.

Using this knowledge, Chad can finally beat Dicetromonom and proceed to the next level of DrRacket's dungeons!

`Kill`—Chapter Checkpoint

In this chapter, you encountered a new technique for manipulating a game using a game tree as a point of control.

- Creating a game tree produces a data structure that contains all legal moves from any state.
- Running a game becomes a mere matter of making sure turns are played according to the data in the game tree.

Chapter Challenges

■ **Medium**   Change our version of Dice of Doom so that the dice are rolled for an attack. Have both the attacker and defender roll the number of dice on their respective territories. If the attacker wins, she takes the territory. If the defender wins, the attacker loses all but one dice on her territory. You may want to get the random numbers from a third-party site, such as `www.random.org`. Here's some code for retrieving a bunch of random numbers:

```
(define (get-random-numbers)
 (define n 1000)
 (define src
   (string-append
    "http://www.random.org/integers/?num="
    (number->string n)
    "&min=1&max=6&col=5&base=10&format=plain&rnd=new"))
 (define ip (get-pure-port (string->url src)))
 ;; -- go get them --
 (for/list ((i n)) (read ip)))
```

■ **Medium**   After implementing the previous suggestion, create a display that tells you the probability of winning an attack on the selected enemy territory.

;; Chapter 11
(Power to the Lazy)

```
#|
As every college student knows, being lazy is on occasion a
remarkably effective way to get work done. What we mean, of
course, is that some work just goes away if you wait long
enough. In this chapter, we'll show how these virtues of
laziness carry over to the world of computation.
|#
```

11.1 Doomsday

Dice of Doom is fun, but the board is a little small. Try setting the board size so you get a 3×3 board and run the game. Did you notice that the generation of the game tree seems to just hang? It hangs because the time it takes to process the number of possible moves for a 3×3 board is massive compared to the time it takes for a 2×2 board. But think about it: do we really need to consider all possible moves at each step? The program should inspect only

one move at a time, and many moves in the tree are never used. If there were some way to delay the generation of those subtrees that may not be needed immediately, we could make headway. There is a way, and it's called lazy evaluation.

11.2 Lazy Evaluation

Lazy evaluation allows your program to delay computations until absolutely necessary. By doing so, it avoids a bunch of work that isn't needed in the first place. So moves in our lazy game tree won't be generated until the program asks for them. When it does ask for the moves, each subtree will undergo the same process, and it won't be generated until it's needed.

Another way to think about lazy evaluation is to imagine that the computation is being placed in a little box. We don't know anything about the content of the box until we open it. Racketeers call this "box" a **suspended computation** or a **thunk**.

The simplest way to make a suspended computation is by wrapping a no-arguments `lambda` around an expression:

```
> (define lazy+ (lambda () (apply + (build-list 5000000 values))))
> lazy+
#<procedure:lazy+>
```

To obtain the value of the suspended computation, you just call the function:

```
> (lazy+)
12499997500000
```

Given the time it takes to compute the sum of a list of 5 million numbers, it's easy to see why we would want to suspend the computation until we need its result, especially if we might never need it. But what if we end up needing that value again and again and again? Hold that thought. Let's first look at some advantages of delaying computations.

The key advantage is that a program does not have to use all elements in a list of suspended computations. To illustrate this point, let's define a function that creates suspended computations such as `lazy+`:

```
(define (make-lazy+ i)
  (lambda ()
    (apply + (build-list (* 500 i) values))))
```

This function consumes a natural number `i`, builds a list from `0` to `(* 500 i)`, and then returns the sum of the list. But really it doesn't. Instead, `make-lazy+` wraps a `(lambda () ...)` around this expression, meaning it doesn't immediately produce a sum. Rather, it produces a suspended computation that must be run to return the sum. If you apply this function to `10000`, you get `lazy+` back, but just getting `lazy+` back is boring. It would be better to build a list that consists of 5000 such suspended computations:

```
(define long-big-list (build-list 5000 make-lazy+))
```

At this point, you should be scared because computing all these sums might take an eternity—or a bit longer.

But we don't have to compute all the elements in the list. We can easily write a function that computes only every 1000th element in the list:

```
(define (compute-every-1000th l)
  (for/list ([thunk l] [i (in-naturals)]
             #:when (zero? (remainder i 1000)))
    (thunk)))
```

Clearly, this `for` loop is run to create a list—the `/list` part says so. The second clause uses a novel element, `(in-naturals)`, though you can probably guess that it is a sequence of *all* natural numbers. So this loop runs over the given list and all natural numbers in parallel. Recall that this kind of loop stops when either of the two sequences is exhausted. Finally, the `#:when` clause makes sure that the body of the loop is run only when we have a natural number that is divisible by `1000`. The body itself is almost trivial; `thunk` refers to one element of `l`, and this element is a suspended computation. With `(thunk)` we retrieve its value.

Now consider this little program and guess what it will return when you run it in DrRacket:

```
> (compute-every-1000th long-big-list)
```

Do you get it? Don't read on until you figure out the *shape* of the result. Once you hit the "Enter" key behind this expression in the interactions panel, DrRacket computes and returns a list of five numbers:

```
'(0 124999750000 499999500000 1124999250000 1999999000000)
```

Everyone can figure out the 0; the remaining numbers require serious calculating. The key point, however, is that we never computed the vast majority of sums embedded in long-big-list.

11.3 Memoized Computations

It is time to return to the delayed question concerning the reevaluation of suspended computations. What happens if we need the value of a suspended computation time and again? Naively, it looks like we have to recompute the value as often as it is needed. Since recomputing the value is clearly time-consuming, Racketeers use memoization. But they do so only when a suspended computation doesn't use effects, such as set! and friends.

   Memoization is the technique of saving the result of a suspended computation in a hidden variable. If the result is needed again, it is enough to look at this hidden variable instead of rerunning the computation. Here is a first attempt:

```
(define (memoize suspended-c)
  (define hidden #f)
  (define run? #f)
  (lambda ()
    (cond [run? hidden]
          [else (set! hidden (suspended-c))
                (set! run? #t)
                hidden])))
```

This function returns a function that serves as a replacement for the suspended computation. When this replacement function is called, it checks whether it has been run before. If it hasn't been run, the `suspended-c` function is called, and the result is saved in `hidden`. The replacement function sets `run` to true and then remembers it has been run. The next time it's called, it can return the value of `hidden` without needing to run `suspended-c` again.

Now why does this work? Well, a `lambda` in Racket creates a **closure**, which captures all the bindings in the `lambda`'s context. This way, whenever a closure flows to a different scope, it can still reference all of its original bindings. Hence, the variables `hidden` and `run?` are enclosed with the returned computation. Any change to these variables affects how all copies of this computation run.

Memoization eliminates the need to call any time-consuming thunk more than once:

```
> (define lazy+ (lambda () (apply + (build-list 5000000 values))))
> (define mlazy+ (memoize lazy+))
> (mlazy+)
12499997500000
> (mlazy+)
12499997500000
```

Did you notice how little time the second evaluation of (mlazy+) took? That's what memoization is about.

Here is a second definition of `memoize` for those who truly understand `set!` and functions as values:

```
(define (memoize.v2 suspended-c)
  (define (hidden)
    (define the-value (suspended-c))
    (set! hidden (lambda () the-value))
    the-value)
  (lambda () (hidden)))
```

Like `memoize`, this function both consumes and returns a suspended computation. The returned computation calls the locally defined function `hidden`. When `hidden` is called for the first time, it evaluates `suspended-c` and then changes the definition of `hidden` to a new different thunk. Thus, when `hidden` is called a second or third or whatever time, it merely returns the value of `suspended-c` without rerunning it.

The essential point of this trick is the call to `hidden` inside the suspended computation that `memoize.v2` returns. A change to this variable affects all copies of the suspended computation. This would not hold if `memoize.v2` just returned `hidden`. Think about it.

11.4 Racket Can Be Lazy

Fortunately, Racket has two built-in mechanisms to make your program lazy without you needing to rewrite a lot of code. One of them is an entire language called Lazy Racket. To use it, change the `#lang racket` at the head of your program to `#lang lazy`. The idea behind `lazy` is that absolutely every computation is a lazy computation. Nothing is ever computed until it's needed, and everything is memoized. While we will not use Lazy Racket in this book, you can look it up in the documentation if you are interested.

The other mechanism is a library that gives us the ability to choose which part of the program is lazy. Unlike the `2htdp/image` and `2htdp/universe` libraries, the `#lang racket` line already imports this functionality because it is so important.

The most important forms in `racket/promise` are `delay` and `force`. The first one, `delay`, suspends a computation and returns a `promise`. A **promise** represents a suspended computation that can be evaluated at a later date with `force`. Let's use the previous example of lazy evaluation:

```
> (define lazy+ (delay (apply + (build-list 5000000 values))))
> lazy+
#<promise:lazy+>
> (force lazy+)
12499997500000
```

As you can see, calling `force` on `lazy+` is like applying a `lambda`. Now notice something else. If you force `lazy+` again, the output is printed immediately:

```
> (force lazy+)
12499997500000
```

A promise created with `delay` is memoized. With `racket/promise`, everything is simplified and streamlined, so lazy evaluation and memoization become easy. Now we're ready to create a version of Dice of Doom that can handle large boards via lazy game trees. And then we will use the leftover machine cycles to add an artificial intelligence.

Delay—Chapter Checkpoint

In this chapter, we introduced a powerful new programming idea that can save your programs from doing needless work:

- Laziness procrastinates work until necessary.
- Memoization remembers the value of computations to avoid recomputing them.
- The `force` and `delay` forms express memoized laziness in Racket programs.

#|
Author's Note:
The following comics contain the flame thrower-wielding squirrels that were introduced as Dicetromonom's head exploded in
chapter 10. We love these magnificent beasts and couldn't imagine
a book without them. To give them a bit more context and so that
we could keep them in the comics, we want to mention one more
thing about suspended computations. Remember how we described
lazy evaluation as a "boxed" computation? Well, imagine instead
that you put those computations into an old-school icebox. This
"frozen" evaluation is just another word for suspended computation. Now, what could fireball-throwing squirrels have to do with
frozen computations?
|#

;; Chapter 12
(Artificial Intelligence)

```
#|
Playing Dice of Doom against other people can be fun, but what
if you could play against the program itself? What if the pro-
gram were intelligent enough to win? We can make that happen with
artificial intelligence (AI), that is, techniques that make pro-
grams appear as smart as people in narrow domains. In this chap-
ter, we will make our implementation of Dice of Doom lazy and
create an AI player.
|#
```

12.1 An Intelligent Life-form

Chad has finally beaten DrRacket's Dicetromonom guard. In shock, Dicetromonom explodes, which gives Chad a chance to figure out what made Dicetromonom tick. He dissects Dicetromonom's head and finds a small hard drive.

Chad plugs the drive into his computer and begins to examine the robot's game software. He discovers a number of neat coding tricks. First, he notices that Dicetromonom can play on large game boards because it generates the game tree lazily. Second, he discovers Dicetromonom's way of planning a game strategy, and it is amazingly simple.

12.2 Lazy Games

Recall that all our discussions of Dice of Doom in chapter 10 involved 2×2 boards. If you tried to run the program on a larger board than that, it just wouldn't work, unless you had access to a really great supercomputer. With the lazy evaluation trick from chapter 11, we can easily improve the performance of our program. Laziness enables our program to play on large boards, and best of all, it saves some time.

Here's how we use `force` and `delay` in our Dice of Doom game. First, we add `delay` to the `game-tree` function:

```
(define (game-tree board p dice)
  ;; create tree of attacks from this position; add passing move
  (define (attacks board)
    (for*/list ([src board]
                [dst (neighbors (territory-index src))]
                #:when (attackable? board p src dst))
      (define from (territory-index src))
      (define dice (territory-dice src))
      (define newb (attack board p from dst dice))
      (define gt-attack
        (game newb p (delay (cons (passes newb) (attacks newb)))))
      (move (list from dst) gt-attack)))
  ;; create a passing move and the rest of the game tree
  (define (passes board)
    (define-values (new-dice newb) (distribute board p dice))
    (move '() (game-tree newb (switch p) new-dice)))
  ;; -- START: --
  (game board p (delay (attacks board))))
```

Here, we have wrapped the generation of moves in (`delay` ...) as indicated in two places with bold. These `delay`s postpone the generation of all possible moves in `game` structs. In particular, the `for` loop in `attacks` and all direct and indirect recursive calls become suspended computations.

You may think that all we have to do is find all uses of the `game-moves` function and wrap them with (`force` ...) so that we get lists and not just suspended computations. While find-and-insert is indeed one way to apply all the requisite calls to `force`, in Racket there's another way, and you will find the second one much more appropriate for this chapter. The second way is made for *lazy* programmers, that is, programmers who think hard and avoid manual typing on the keyboard until necessary.

The lazy way is to *redefine* the function `game-moves` once and for all. Doing so has a huge advantage: we don't need to change the rest of the code at all. Better still, when we add code to the game, we don't need to remember that `game-moves` retrieves a promise and that we need to use `force` to get the list from this promise. The forcing just happens automatically.

The following is the lazy way to define the `game` struct so that `game-moves` forces its field every time it is used:

```
(define-values (game game? game-board game-player game-moves)
  (let ()
    (struct game (board player delayed-moves))
    (values game
            game?
            game-board
            game-player
            (lambda (g) (force (game-delayed-moves g))))))
```

It is a mouthful of code, and it is complicated, but once you understand this trick, you will find that it is extremely useful in many situations. We will use it again in chapter 14.

The first line in this code snippet sets up a multiple-values definition. Specifically, it defines five functions: `game`, `game?`, `game-board`, `game-player`, and `game-moves`. If you squint just a bit, you see that these are precisely the functions introduced by this structure definition:

```
(struct game (board player moves))
```

The second line sets up a local scope of definitions, and the third line defines the expected `game` struct in that scope. The function definitions that it introduces are visible only inside of `(let ...)`. The trick is that the next expression is a `values` expression that bundles up `game`, `game?`, `game-board`, and `game-player`, plus one more function so that they match up with the variable names introduced by `define-values`.

As you can see, the last value in this bundle is a function that accepts a game tree, retrieves the delayed list of moves, and forces the promise to deliver the actual list. This function uses the locally defined `game-moves` and `force`. But because the whole bundle of values escapes the scope, this unnamed `lambda` function becomes the value of the *globally* defined name `game-moves`. When this function is used, it has access to the original selector, while the rest of the program accepts this `lambda` function as the selector. We can have our pie and eat it, too.

In short, we use the power of Racket to change a large program in two small ways to get a large change in behavior. You can mimic some aspects of laziness in other languages, but this isn't normally one of those ideas you see early on. With Racket, however, it can become a part of your first-year repertoire.

Now you may wonder why the call to `force` doesn't create the whole game tree, canceling all the benefits we get from suspending the game tree generation in the first place. To understand why it works, take a second look at `game-tree`. Once we `force` the list of moves, the next step is always to call the locally defined `attacks` function on `board`. This call will indeed create one complete level of the game—a complete list of moves—with a `delay`. Furthermore, because of the recursive nature of `game-tree`, the generation of the tree is suspended in each node attached to a move. Only the next call to `force` will unfold one more level passing of the game tree, but only for the moves the game needs to execute. And voilà, you have a lazy version of Dice of Doom.

Lazy Dice of Doom has two advantages over our first draft of the game. First, Lazy Dice of Doom no longer needs restrictions on the rules that make Dice of Doom a finite, terminating game. It is okay to play infinite games now, because the game tree is unfolded only as much as needed, and we never need more than a finite portion. Second, Lazy Dice of Doom is good not only for playing infinite games, but also for playing on large game boards.

Try it out. Play on a 3×3 or 5×5 board. But just playing the game by yourself is boring, even with a bigger board. Let's make the game interesting by adding AI.

12.3 Adding Artificial Intelligence

The strategy of search and evaluate is one idea behind John McCarthy's notion of AI. For games, this idea works amazingly well and truly invokes the perception of intelligence. Our game's AI will search the game tree, evaluate all moves, and determine the best one. To complete the evaluations, we will use something called the **minimax** algorithm.

The principle behind the minimax algorithm is "what is good for me is bad for my opponent," and vice versa. Hence, the algorithm minimizes the maximum damage an opponent can inflict during a turn. Roughly speaking, the algorithm proceeds in two steps. First, it assigns a value to each move in the tree, up to a certain level. Second, it determines the minimum of the maximal damage at each level of the tree, from the perspective of the current player. At the root of the game tree, the AI picks the move that results in the best possible outcome as far out as the algorithm can see.

To write the AI, we need a depth limit:

```
(define AI-DEPTH 4)
```

We do not want the AI to make an evaluation beyond a certain depth in the game tree. Otherwise, the AI forces every single level in the game tree, and we lose all the advantages of going lazy. For this game, we define the depth to be 4, so the AI will evaluate only four moves deep into the tree. The depth limit reduces the AI's intelligence but without it the program would run too slowly.

Next, we should write a function that limits the evaluation of the tree. This `prune-tree` function would take a game tree and the desired depth of evaluation. It would then create a `game` structure and recursively trim each branch via a `for` loop.

The process could stop when the desired depth reaches 0. But we don't write a separate tree-pruning function. Instead, we prune as we go. That is, the rating function evaluates the moves as it goes and stops evaluating when it reaches the specified depth.

As it turns out, we actually need a pair of rating functions: one for rating moves in the tree and one for rating positions. Here is the first one:

```
(define (rate-moves tree depth)
  (for/list ([move (game-moves tree)])
    (list move (rate-position (move-gt move) (- depth 1)))))
```

The `rate-moves` function consumes a tree and a depth. With a `for/list` loop, it produces a list that pairs each move with the rating of the position that results from this move. The latter is obtained via `rate-position`, the function that assigns a value to each tree:

```
(define (rate-position tree depth)
  (cond [(or (= depth 0) (no-more-moves? tree))
         (define-values (best w) (winners (game-board tree)))
         (if (member AI w) (/ 1 (length w)) 0)]
        [else
         (define ratings (rate-moves tree depth))
         (apply (if (= (game-player tree) AI) max min)
                (map second ratings))]))
```

The function generates a numeric point rating for a given branch of the game tree. If the function has reached the desired depth or the state has no further moves, we'll need to check who the winner is for the current position. If the current player isn't among the winners of this position, we can give the position the minimum rating of 0. Otherwise, we'll divide 1 by the number of winners to determine our rating. By doing this, we also give a meaningful rating for ties. If the player is the sole winner, the rating, according to this formula, will be the maximum value of 1. For a two-player tie, the rational result would be 1/2.

If, however, more moves are available, we'll need to look at all the subsequent moves to decide how to rate the current position. We accomplish this by calling our `rate-moves` function. As per the minimax principle, we will then pick either the `max` or `min` rating of all the follow-up moves, depending on whether the move being rated is for the AI player or its opponent.

Now we can bring all of these functions together into a single function that acts as an artificially intelligent player. In this role, `the-ai-plays` takes a game tree and determines the best possible moves at the given tree node:

```
(define (the-ai-plays tree)
  (define ratings  (rate-moves tree AI-DEPTH))
  (define the-move (first (argmax second ratings)))
  (define new-tree (move-gt the-move))
  (if (= (game-player new-tree) AI)
      (the-ai-plays new-tree)
      new-tree))
```

The function starts by rating all possible moves from the root of the given tree to some fixed depth. The best move is determined by Racket's higher-order `argmax` function, which finds the element of `ratings` that maximizes the output of `second`. So in this case, it returns the move that has the maximum rating, and then `the-ai-plays` creates a new game tree from it. If the current player after this move is still the AI player, then `the-ai-plays` continues to pick moves. Otherwise, it returns the new game tree.

All that's left to do is link the AI into Dice of Doom. To this end, we modify the `pass` function to allow the AI to take over the role of the players:

```
(define (pass w)
  (define m (find-move (game-moves (dice-world-gt w)) '()))
  (cond [(false? m) w]
        [(or (no-more-moves? m) (not (= (game-player m) AI)))
         (dice-world #f (game-board m) m)]
        [else
         (define ai (the-ai-plays m))
         (dice-world #f (game-board ai) ai)]))
```

This new version calls the AI when it is the AI's turn; otherwise, the function just passes the turn normally.

We now have a fully functional game that employs an AI. Try it out!

Stop-when—**Chapter Checkpoint**

In this chapter, we used lazy evaluation to improve Dice of Doom, and then we created an AI player so that you can play against the program:

- Lazy evaluation allows us to make the game more efficient so that it can handle larger game boards by ignoring branches of the game tree until they are absolutely needed.

- We used a simple minimax algorithm to create an AI player.

- Finally, you learned how to define structures that implement more than just the built-in constructors, accessors, and predicates.

Chapter Challenges

- ● **Easy**   Make the AI step through its moves. Right now, it executes all of its moves at lightning speed, leaving players slightly dazed by the crushing blows that it inflicts. It will be easier for the player to understand if the AI executes its moves step-by-step instead of all at once.

- ■ **Medium**   Create a hint feature. When you press a certain key, a good enemy territory will be highlighted as a suggested attack. Hint: This will require you to use some of the pieces of the AI for the human player.

- ♦ **Difficult**   Search the Web for other AI algorithms that an automated Dice of Doom player could employ against you. Then turn the new player loose on your friends.

;; Chapter 13
(The World Is Not Enough)

```
#|
In the beginning, you drew images, you built GUIs, you created
games, and you fabricated entire worlds. But that's not enough.
In this chapter, we will show you how to write programs that work
across multiple computers. We will show you how to construct com-
plete universes from your worlds in preparation for our greatest
creation: the best and most entertaining game ever.
|#
```

13.1 What Is a Distributed Game?

The games we've written so far have one major shortcoming: they run on one computer, which makes multiplayer games awkward. So far, our multiplayer games require players to crowd around one keyboard as they all take turns tapping on it. But many multiplayer games run on a network and allow players from all over the world to interact with each other. To create this kind of game, we need to introduce you to **distributed programming**.

In order to create a distributed game, we set up a **server** that acts as a central communication point for the game. The players' computers all act as clients that connect to this server and communicate with each other via messages routed through this server. Usually, the server will handle the logic of the game and enforce the rules, informing the clients about changes to the state of the game as needed. In contrast, the **clients** deal with players' inputs, draw the current game state, and notify the server of the players' actions.

Creating a server resembles creating a world. A server is basically a world that doesn't draw its state and that has the ability to accept multiple connections from client worlds anywhere on the Internet, even the very computer it runs on. The latter is important when you develop your games. It's only later that you really want people from anywhere in the world to connect to your game server.

Technically, the key differences between a server and a world are that the former uses a `universe` expression instead of `big-bang` and that a `universe` expression comes with different kinds of event-handling clauses than those of a `big-bang` expression. In addition, we need to tell you about new kinds of events and about a new way to write event handlers for worlds. So in this chapter we will go over the `universe` system and the new ways of writing `big-bang` expressions.

Let's look at the big picture first. When a server is available, worlds can register with a server. The act of registering with a server is an event for the universe, and it deals with these registration events in the same way that worlds deal with key-events. All the clients exist in their own realms, live on their own cycles, react to their own inputs, and so on. If an event handler in one world needs to communicate with the universe, it returns a new world state and a message to be sent to the server. The arrival of the message is also an event for the server, and some event handler takes care of it. One possible reaction is to send mail to other worlds. Naturally, the arrival of a message at a world is just another kind of event, and if a world is equipped with an event handler for messages, this event handler is applied to the current state of the world and the incoming message—just like a key-event handler is applied to the current state of the world and a key-event. But enough of the abstract picture. It's time for a concrete example.

13.2 The Data

Let's go over all the new items in detail, starting with messages.

Messages

In reality, messages aren't a new kind of data; they are any of the data introduced in chapter 3, and we call them messages because they are sent across the network. Put differently, a message is a number, symbol, string, Boolean, or nested list containing only messages. Following good old John McCarthy, we call this form of data an **S-expression**.

If the client or the server tries to send other forms of data, Racket will signal an error. The error message says, "`expected <S-expression> as argument`," and it means the data your program sent is not a message.

Previously Fabricated Structures

But this picture isn't quite complete. There is one more type of message that we need to mention: a previously fabricated structure, or **prefab**. Prefabs are a kind of structure designed for operations like network communication. They, too, can be sent across the network like any other kind of message, as long as they contain only messages, like lists or other prefabs. This becomes useful when a client and server need a similar structure type, like the representation of a player.

Prefabs also print a little differently than regular structures:

```
> (struct foo (bar) #:transparent)
> (foo 5)
(foo 5)
> (struct foo (bar) #:prefab)
> (foo 5)
'#s(foo 5)
```

This printing difference is related to why prefabs work for network communications, but that's not really important here. If you want to know more, you can look it up. What is important here is that when you see `'#s`, you're dealing with a prefab.

Packages

The first new kind of data is a **package**, built with the `make-package` function. A package combines two pieces of data: a world state and a message. In order to send a message to its server, a client's event handler returns a package to `big-bang` instead of just a world. The world state in the package becomes the new world, and the message in the package is sent to the server. And who does this sending? Why, `big-bang`, of course.

Bundles

A **bundle** is the `universe` equivalent of a package. All handlers in a `universe` expression construct it with the `make-bundle` function. A bundle wraps up all the data that the server needs to continue its operation: the new universe state, a list of messages to send to clients, and a list of clients to drop. Unlike packages, however, bundles are mandatory—every event handler in a `universe` expression must return a bundle.

Mail

The second argument of `make-bundle` is not just a simple list of messages; it's actually a list of **mail**, each piece created with `make-mail`. The mail we refer to here is like mail in real life. It contains two pieces of data: an address and a message in S-expression shape. When the universe encounters a `mail`, it sends the message to the client with that address.

iworld Structures

So what data do we use as addresses? Take another look at the comic on page 214. Not only is it funny, but it also illustrates how network connections work. To represent the addresses and the connections, `universe` uses `iworld`s. Most importantly, an `iworld` structure includes the wired connection between a client and the server. When a new client connects to your `universe` server, the `universe` creates an `iworld` for the client and hands it to the event handler for new connections. When a new message arrives, the handler for new messages is applied to the `iworld` that represents the sender. When messages need to be sent to a client, the server finds all the necessary information in the `iworld` struct inside mail. Hence, `iworld`s can serve as addresses.

If you read the documentation for `iworld`, you will notice that `iworld`s come without an `iworld` constructor. This gap is not an oversight in the design of `2htdp/universe`; it's a deliberate choice. Only `universe` can construct `iworld`s when clients sign up. Its event handlers may use, but not create, `iworld`s. Indeed, to make sure your programs don't make mistakes, the `iworld` structures are `#:opaque`. There is no way to look inside such a structure. For testing purposes, there is an `iworld=?` function and a few predefined `iworld`s: `iworld1`, `iworld2`, and `iworld3`.

13.3 The Network Postal Service

Roughly speaking, `universe` works like `big-bang`. It looks at the given clauses and uses them to decide how to react to events, such as the receipt of a new message, the request for a new connection to a world, or a clock tick.

The `universe` form comes with two mandatory clauses: `on-new` and `on-msg`. The `on-new` clause handles new connections. The function used for this clause takes in the current state of the `universe` and the `iworld` that represents the new connection. Like all `universe` functions, it must return a bundle. The `on-msg` clause deals with messages from already connected clients. Its corresponding handler function consumes the current state of the `universe`, the `iworld` representation of the client who sent the message, and the actual message. When it is finished, it returns a bundle.

In addition to `on-new` and `on-msg`, programmers may use several optional clauses to describe the workings of a `universe` server, such as `on-tick` and `connect` clauses. For more information, consult the Racket documentation. We will use only the mandatory clauses in this chapter.

The `big-bang` form gets two new clauses to enable network communications. The first of these is the `register` clause. Unlike the other clauses, it doesn't come with a handler function; rather, it gives the IP address of the server that `big-bang` should connect to, such as `"192.168.0.10"` or `"realmofracket.com"`. If the server happens to be running on the same machine, put the constant `LOCALHOST` here. This constant is provided by `2htdp/universe` and points the client to your computer.

The second new `big-bang` clause is `on-receive`. It does exactly as its name implies: it handles the receipt of a message from the server. Its handler function consumes the current state of the world and the message from the server. After some computing, it returns either a world or a package.

13.4 Organizing Your Universe

Writing distributed programs can get messy. Servers and clients often need to share code, but putting everything into one file would make our code confusing. Ideally, we should organize our code into three separate **modules**: one for the client, one for the server, and one for shared material. The purpose of a shared module is to allow the client and server to reuse its definitions. It is also a good place to document how the server and its clients communicate.

A Racket module is a file that starts with `#lang racket`. Getting definitions from another file is easy. In fact, we have done this in most of our programs. When we say `(require 2htdp/image)`, we're telling Racket to look in the main collection of libraries, called **collects**, go to the **2htdp** folder, and get the code from the **image.rkt** file. If we wanted to grab definitions from a file elsewhere, we would put in a string with the name of the file relative to the current module. For instance, `(require "source.rkt")` would retrieve the provided names from the **source.rkt** file in the directory where the current module is located.

We need to be careful when sharing code between modules. On occasion, we may wish to hide some functions in one module to prevent another module from using them incorrectly. Therefore, you must explicitly say what you're making visible outside your module with a `provide`. By specifying what can be accessed, the purpose of the module also becomes clearer, which makes the code easier to read.

Here is an example:

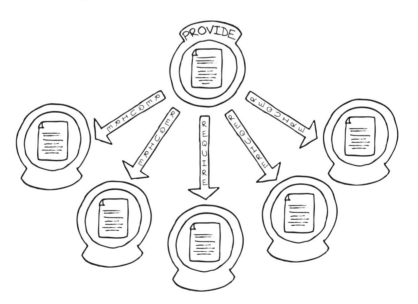

```
#lang racket
(provide foo addone)
(define foo 5)
(define (addone) (set! foo (addx 1)))
(define (addx x) (+ foo x))
```

This module allows access to `foo` and `addone`. A simple `(require "foobar.rkt")` is enough. However, it is impossible to access `addx`. It is also forbidden to use `set!` directly on `foo` in a `require`-ing module. Racket imposes this restriction to prevent client modules from interfering with your module's internal state. If you want a client module to modify a variable in your own module, you must provide a function such as `addone`.

For convenience, Racket gives us a way to provide every function declared by a structure so we don't have to type it all out ourselves. It's called `struct-out`:

```
#lang racket
(provide (struct-out bar) (struct-out baz))
(struct bar (a b))
(struct baz (a [b #:mutable]))
```

The `provide` statement here is the same as saying this:

```
(provide bar bar? bar-a bar-b baz baz? baz-a baz-b set-baz-b!)
```

As you can see, the first one is shorter and usually clearer. So use it!

13.5 Distributed Guess

Remember Guess My Number? We have already written two versions of this game, and now it's time to develop a third one. Using our knowledge of modules and `universe`, we'll develop a distributed variant of the game—one that runs on a network. As before, the player picks a number between 0 and 100. But now he creates a client, and the client connects to a central Guess My Number server—think something like www.guess-my-number.com—and it is this server that attempts to guess the number that the player has in mind. The server deals with one client only; if another client tries toconnect when a game is already in progress, the server just drops the connection.

As in our GUI version of Guess My Number, the player will respond to each guess with an "↑" or "↓" signal, where the former means the number is larger than the guess and the latter means the opposite. The player may press "=" at any time to signal that his number was found or "q" to quit the game.

From these rules, you can see that the client needs to send only two messages to the server: `"up"` and `"down"`. In turn, the server needs to react to just these two kinds of player responses, and it does so with a new guess. Since a guess is a number, we know that the server always sends a number to the client. When the server guesses the client's number correctly, it expects the player to admit defeat, which will close the connection on the client's side. Once a `universe` discovers that the client has disconnected, it reboots to its initial state. In our case, this means the server is ready for the next Guess My Number client.

After some thought, you may realize that the server can reuse many functions from the GUI version of the game. So all we really need to add is the communication software. But we're getting ahead of ourselves. Remember that after determining what kind of messages the server and the client(s) exchange, we need to figure out which portions of the distributed game go into which of its three modules. In this book, we use the file names **shared.rkt**, **client.rkt**, and **server.rkt**.

When you develop a distributed game, you always start with a **shared.rkt** file. Because of the simplicity of the Guess My Number game, the shared file consists of two constant definitions: the upper and lower bounds of the guesses. The client needs these limits to tell the player what range to pick a number from, and the server also needs these in order to guess an appropriate number.

Here is the complete file:

```racket
#lang racket
(provide UPPER LOWER)

#|
In the Distributed Guess My Number game, a player uses a client to
connect to the server. The server attempts to guess what number the
player is thinking of. Each time the server guesses, the player must
use the arrow keys to tell the server if it is too small or too large.

A StoCMessage, a server to client message, is any natural number
between LOWER and UPPER (inclusive). The numbers represent the guess.

A CtoSMessage, a client to server message, is one of the following
two strings:
-- "up"
-- "down"
with the obvious meaning.
|#

(define UPPER 100)
(define LOWER 0)
```

We also add a block comment that describes the purpose of the project and the messages that go from the server to the client and vice versa. So **shared.rkt** really contains all the information that represents common knowledge for both clients and servers—even if some of it has to be in comment form.

The State of the Client and the State of the Server

The second step is to figure out the state of the client and the state of the server. For Guess My Number, the client needs to keep track of the most recent guess it received from the server, as well as whether the server has even sent a guess yet. We choose strings to represent these states, which implies that the on-receive handler must convert guesses to strings on arrival. Let's start with the client's initial world state:

```racket
#lang racket
;; clientstate is a string
(define clientstate0 "none available")
```

The server's state is a little more complicated than the client's state. As mentioned, the server has the same logic as the second version of Guess My Number. It needs the interval for guessing appropriately, but it also needs to know whether it's connected to the client. As you can imagine, this calls for a state representation with two distinct cases:

server.rkt

```
#lang racket
;; GmNState is one of:
;; -(interval nat nat)
;; -#f
(struct interval (small big))
(define u0 (interval LOWER UPPER))
```

The `interval` structure is pulled right out of chapter 5, and naturally, the initial interval is bounded by LOWER and UPPER. When the universe state is `#f`, no client is connected to the server.

The Server

As always, we start the server module with the main function:

server.rkt

```
(define (launch-guess-server)
  (universe #f
            (on-new connect)
            (on-msg handle-msg)))
```

The initial universe has no client connected to it, so its state is `#f`. The only clauses that the server needs are `on-new` and `on-msg`.

When a client attempts to connect, the server can either accept the connection or ignore it. The `connect` function in our `on-new` clause decides whether to accept a new connection depending on whether the server is already connected to a client:

server.rkt

```
(define (connect u client)
  (if (false? u)
      (make-bundle u0 (list (make-mail client (guess u0))) '())
      (make-bundle u empty (list client))))
```

If the state is false, then no client has connected. So `connect` accepts the client, sets the initial state to u0, and sends a guess for u0. Otherwise, the server is busy and the new client is dropped. The drop is accomplished by returning a bundle of the current state of the `universe`, an empty list of mail, and a list containing the `iworld` of the client that is trying to connect.

The `handle-msg` function is also simple:

---

server.rkt

```
(define (handle-msg u client msg)
  (define w (next-interval u msg))
  (make-bundle w (list (make-mail client (guess w))) '()))
```

First, it determines the next interval based on the client's message. Second, it returns this interval as the state of the universe in a bundle, with a new guess for its client in the mail.

And that brings us to `next-interval`:

---

server.rkt

```
(define (next-interval u msg)
  (cond [(not (string? msg)) u]
        [(string=? "up" msg) (bigger u)]
        [(string=? "down" msg) (smaller u)]
        [else u]))
```

If the client's message is not a string, then the server will regard the message as junk and won't change anything. You may think that we don't need to check whether the message is a string, but you never know who connects what kind of code to the server, so we are better off protecting it. A computer scientist says that such a `cond` clause makes the server **fault tolerant**.

The next two clauses check the client's response. If the client tells the server that its guess was too big or small, then the server does the same thing as the program from chapter 5. It modifies its `interval` using either `smaller` or `bigger`.

The functions used on intervals—`smaller`, `bigger`, `guess`, and `single?`—are taken directly from the source of chapter 5. Just plop them into **server.rkt**.

As you may have guessed, the last `cond` clause is another one that we introduced for fault tolerance. Even if the client sends a string, you never know what kind of string you'll get. It's best to ignore bad strings explicitly.

The Client

The code for the distributed Guess My Number client is just as short as the code for the server. Once again, we start with a main function to launch `big-bang`:

```
                                                              client.rkt

(define (launch-guess-client n)
  (big-bang clientstate0
            (to-draw draw-guess)
            (on-key handle-keys)
            (name n)
            (register LOCALHOST)
            (on-receive handle-msg)))
```

The function consumes a string and spawns a world whose initial state is an informative string. This `big-bang` looks just like the ones we've written throughout the book, with the exception of three clauses: `name`, `register`, and `on-receive`. So let's first look at its function, `handle-msg`:

```
                                                              client.rkt

(define (handle-msg c msg)
  (number->string msg))
```

This function translates its message to a string, which becomes the current state.

Handling key-events is similar to what we've seen before:

```
                                                              client.rkt

(define (handle-keys w key)
  (cond [(key=? key "up")    (make-package w "up")]
        [(key=? key "down")  (make-package w "down")]
        [(key=? key "q")     (stop-with w)]
        [(key=? key "=")     (stop-with w)]
        [else w]))
```

If the player presses a valid arrow key, the handler sends that message to the server using `make-package`, and the world state in that package becomes the new world. When either the "q" or "=" key is pressed, `stop-with` ends the game, as you know from preceding chapters. Finally, if the player doesn't use any relevant keys, we just ignore the keystroke. It's simple.

The `to-draw` clause is nearly identical to the drawing function from chapter 5:

```
                                                              client.rkt

(define (draw-guess c)
  (overlay (text c SIZE COLOR) MT-SC))
```

Running the Game

That's it. You have now seen all the code that is needed for a distributed game. Although building the game brought up several new concepts, the code itself is simple. If this simplicity surprises you, keep in mind that 2htdp/universe hides some magic. Then again, this is what good languages do for you.

In principle, you could now copy the code onto two different computers, start the server, start the client, and play the game. This sounds cumbersome, and if you have a mistake in the code, you need to repeat this procedure again. And again. So it won't surprise you to find out that 2htdp/universe comes with a tool to explore distributed programs on one machine. The right way to do this is to create a fourth file—call it **run.rkt**. Here is the entire file:

run.rkt

```
#lang racket
(require 2htdp/universe "server.rkt" "client.rkt")
(define (run)
  (launch-many-worlds (launch-guess-client "Adam")
                      (launch-guess-server)))
```

It requires the client module, the server module, and 2htdp/universe. From the latter, it receives launch-many-worlds. The run function uses launch-many-worlds with two function calls:

```
(launch-guess-client "Adam")
(launch-guess-server)
```

As you may have guessed, the first is given a string and launches a client world; the second runs a server. Then the former connects to the latter, and the two work together.

Now go and play the game with a friend. You deserve it.

Error—**Chapter Checkpoint**

In this chapter, you have seen the basics of distributed game programming:

- The universe form and its on-new and on-msg clauses
- The representation of client worlds via iworld structs
- The server's event handlers and the bundles they return
- Prefab structs for network communication
- The on-receive clause for big-bang

- The packages that `big-bang` handlers may return
- Racket modules for organizing code

We know that this bombardment of ideas can be a bit overwhelming. Do experiment with the code for this chapter. And when you are ready, read on. Chapter 14 promises to introduce the best game yet.

Chapter Challenges

● **Easy**   Design a version of the distributed Guess My Number game in which two human players face off. The first player who connects to the server should set the number to be guessed, and the second player to connect must guess that number.

■ **Medium**   Try writing a simple chat client and server. When you finish, you can use it to talk to your friends in class, instead of paying attention to the professor. See *How to Design Programs, Second Edition* (www.ccs.neu.edu/home/matthias/HtDP2e/) for hints.

;; Chapter 14
(Hungry Henry)

```
#|
Guess My Number is good and all, but it's getting a little old.
Let's take everything we have shown you and create a distributed
game from scratch. Today, we feed Hungry Henry.
|#
```

14.1 King Henry the Hungry

After fleeing from the squirrels, Chad resumes his search for a way out of the dungeons. While exploring, Chad comes across an enormous man sitting on a golden throne. "Hail, traveler!" the man calls, "I am King Henry the Hungry!" Then he proclaims, "Come hither, I have a proposition for you!" As Chad approaches, the king begins to tell his story. "Long ago, I was just like you, boy, a prisoner in the dungeons of DrRacket. Starving, I created a program to gather food, and what better food to eat than cupcakes? I forgot the stop-when clause and have been happily eating cupcakes ever since."

The king continues, "I've had so much practice that I could beat anyone at a cupcake-eating competition, and now is the time to prove it. But I need your help to change my program so that the whole world can participate. If you help me, I will help you find a way out." Can you help Chad run Hungry Henry's tournament?

14.2 Hungry Henry, the Game

The goal of this chapter is to turn King Henry's eating competition into a distributed game. A server sets up a field of cupcakes and waits for players to sign up for a round of Hungry Henry. Once a player connects to the server, she is given her own avatar to control. The objective of the game is to navigate this avatar around the screen, getting to cupcakes before other players do. To navigate, the player sets waypoints on the screen by clicking the desired location. The avatar then travels to each of these waypoints in turn. But players must choose these waypoints carefully. Once one has been added, it may not be removed. Each time an avatar collides with a cupcake, the food is removed and the avatar increases in size. Of course, a growth in girth means the avatar slows down.

When all the food is gone, the game displays a table that lists the players and the number of cupcakes they ate. After a delay, the game restarts. If a player attempts to join while a game is in progress, she will be forced to watch. Once the game restarts, these spectators are assigned avatars, too.

14.3 Two United States

Before we show you how to implement the Hungry Henry game, we need to drill down on one more concept: the **state machine**. While all world games are state machine games, Hungry Henry makes explicit use of two distinct states in two different state machines.

Consider the ubiquitous soda machine. Initially, it is full. You put in a dollar bill, and the machine responds by dispensing a can of soda. The machine is now in a different state; it is partially empty. Eventually, it will dispense its last can and enter its final state, the empty state. Think of Hungry Henry's state machines like this, but with less liquid and more cupcakes.

In this chapter, the universe and all of its worlds are in one of two different kinds of states: **waiting** and **playing**. The universe starts in a waiting state. When it's time for the game to start, the universe switches to a playing state. Our program will thus need to understand how to handle events depending on the current state of the universe. Distinguishing these two states will significantly simplify our data and message protocol.

14.4 Henry's Universe

Our next step is to divvy up responsibilities between the server and the clients, and these responsibilities need to be carefully assigned. For example, if we let the client handle the movement of her avatar or the eating of cupcakes, who will enforce the rules of the game? You could easily imagine a player changing the client code to her own advantage. So our choices must prevent players from acting in this malicious manner.

The client will be responsible only for reporting a player's mouse clicks to the server and rendering the current state of the game. Essentially, the client will implement the on-mouse and on-draw specs for big-bang. The server, in contrast, does a lot more work. It is in charge of handling movement, collisions, eating, and ending the game. And, of course, whenever something changes, the server sends the new state of the universe to all the clients.

Message Data and Structures

So what kind of information is actually sent from client to server and vice versa? While the client needs to send only information about where the player clicked on the screen, the server needs to send back four kinds of messages: an ID to inform the player of her avatar's name, a fraction of the waiting period that has passed, the current state of the avatars and cupcakes, and the final scores.

To keep the protocol simple, the multipart messages are lists tagged with a symbol that identifies the type of message. Here is the only type of message the clients can send:

```
(list GOTO Number Number)
```

It is just a three-part list: a constant to identify the message type and the x-coordinate and y-coordinate of a mouse click.

Two of the server's messages are even simpler than that. When a client registers, the server responds with a new unique ID for the avatar. By defining an ID as a string, the server can make use of iworld-name to generate an easily recognizable ID.

The time message is just a number between 0 and 1, representing the percentage of wait time completed. While the server waits for enough players to sign up, the number gets closer to 1 but is never equal to 1.

The most complex message describes the state of the game:

```
(list SERIALIZE [Listof Player] [Listof Cupcake])
```

This message is a three-element list containing the constant SERIALIZE, a list of players, and a list of cupcakes.

Players are represented with prefab structures:

shared.rkt

```
#lang racket
(provide ...
         (struct-out player)
         (struct-out body)
         ...)

(struct player (id body waypoints) #:prefab)
```

Players need their own ID, which clients use to differentiate themselves from other players. The next field, body—think an astronomical body—is used to describe the location and size of a player. The last field, waypoints, is a list of waypoints from oldest to newest, the order in which the avatar will travel. Ordering points in this way is efficient because the program must look at the head of the list many times as the avatar moves incrementally along its path.

Both avatar bodies and cupcakes can be described as physical bodies:

shared.rkt

```
(struct body (size loc) #:prefab #:mutable)
```

The first field, size, is a positive integer that represents the radius of the body. The second field, loc, is a complex number that represents the actual location of the body. The structure is mutable to make it easy for the server to grow or move any object.

Finally, the score message contains just the expected table:

```
(list SCORE [Listof (list ID Number)])
```

At the end of the game, the server will send a list of two-element lists. The first element is a player's ID, and the second is the player's score.

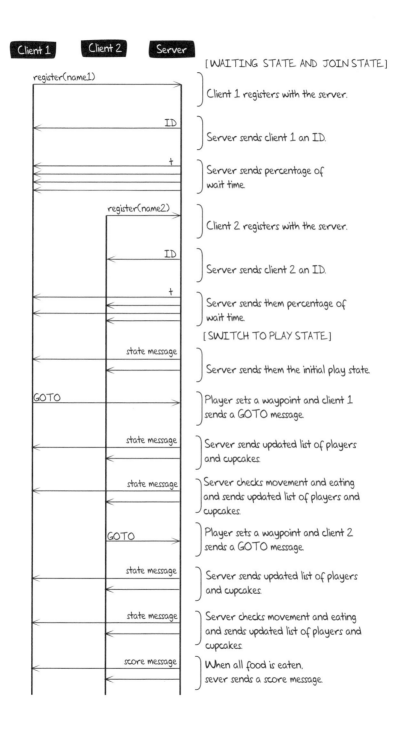

Client 1 **Client 2** **Server**

[WAITING STATE AND JOIN STATE]

register(name1)
Client 1 registers with the server.

ID
Server sends client 1 an ID.

t
Server sends percentage of wait time.

register(name2)
Client 2 registers with the server.

ID
Server sends client 2 an ID.

t
Server sends them percentage of wait time.

[SWITCH TO PLAY STATE]

state message
Server sends them the initial play state.

GOTO
Player sets a waypoint and client 1 sends a GOTO message.

state message
Server sends updated list of players and cupcakes.

state message
Server checks movement and eating and sends updated list of players and cupcakes.

GOTO
Player sets a waypoint and client 2 sends a GOTO message.

state message
Server sends updated list of players and cupcakes.

state message
Server checks movement and eating and sends updated list of players and cupcakes.

score message
When all food is eaten, sever sends a score message.

Complex Numbers Are Good Positions

Complex numbers, such as 3+2i, are convenient for representing coordinates, so we'll use them for waypoints. To model movements, we can use normal math operators, such as * and +. To access the *x*-coordinate of a complex number, we use the built-in function `real-part`, which gives us the real portion of the complex number. To access the *y*-coordinate, we use `imag-part`, which extracts the imaginary portion. If there is a need to construct an imaginary number from two real numbers, we use the `make-rectangular` function, which takes two real numbers and returns a complex number, where the real part is the first number and the imaginary part is the second number.

A Day in the Life of a Server

In the beginning, our server just ticks along, waiting for a client to join. When a client connects to the server, it is sent an ID. During this phase, the server continually keeps its clients up-to-date with the approximate time left until the game starts. Once time has run out and enough players have signed up, the server switches to a play state. From this point on, any new clients are considered spectators, and the server tells the players and spectators the location of all the food and avatars in the game. Once the players have eaten all of the food, the server tallies the scores and sends a SCORE message to the clients. Afterward, it resets to its `join` state, joining together all the players and spectators as the players for the next round.

A Day in the Life of a Client

The first action that any good client takes is to register with the server. In response, it gets an ID back and begins to receive time messages. Using these time messages, the client draws a progress bar and waits. When the client gets a message from the server that describes the state of the game, it means the game has started. The client switches to a play state and renders the state messages, which contain the location of all the food and players. Whenever the player clicks the mouse, the client must send a message to the server describing the location of the player's chosen waypoint. Eventually, the client gets a message that contains all score tallies, signaling the end of the current round of play.

14.5 State of the Union

Now that we know what our message protocol looks like and how the clients and server interact, let's turn to the data that is used within the client and the server. As we go along, keep in mind that our server and client are interacting state machines.

State of Henry

The client can be in one of two states: waiting or playing. Clearly, the client is in a waiting state until the server sends the first state message. Then it transitions to playing. Once a game ends, the client transitions back to waiting, giving that state a second purpose—to display the scores from the game.

With that in mind, let's call the first state an appetizer:

client.rkt

```
(struct app (id img countdown))
```

The app structure has three fields, which the client uses to render a waiting screen. The first field, id, names the player's assigned ID, which is later used in gameplay. During the waiting phase, it is #f. The next field, img, is the base image that displays messages to the screen. These messages include waiting text or the score table from the last game, if there was one. The last field, countdown, holds the time left until the game starts, and it is used to render a progress bar.

The second state, the playing state, is called entree because it follows an appetizer:

client.rkt

```
(struct entree (id players food))
```

As before, the first field is this player's id. The next two fields are lists of the current players and the available cupcakes.

State of the House

Like the client, the server has two states. The first state is a join state, representing the period during which players are allowed to join the server:

server.rkt

```
(struct join (clients [time #:mutable]))
```

The first field of join is a list of players who have joined. The second field holds the time that remains until the server intends to start the game.

The second server state is called play, and it represents the server while the game is in progress:

server.rkt

```
(struct play (players food spectators) #:mutable)
```

Like join, the first field of play stores a list of the players who are in the game. The second field, food, is a list of body structures that represent the remaining cupcakes. The last field keeps track of the current spectators. When the server transfers back to the join state, these spectators are appended to the list of current players.

You may have noticed that neither join states nor play states include information about the iworlds that represent clients and allow the server to communicate with clients. Well, the preceding data representation is a bit of a lie. Instead of plain prefab players, the server uses lists of *internal* player representations:

```
(define-values
  (ip ip? ip-id ip-iw ip-body ip-waypoints ip-player)
  (let ()
    (struct ip (id iw body waypoints player))
    (define (create iw id body waypoints)
      (ip id iw body waypoints (player id body waypoints)))
    (values
      create ip? ip-id ip-iw ip-body ip-waypoints ip-player)))
```

This definition is a mouthful, but look closely, and you'll see that it's similar to how we handled forcing moves in the lazy version of Dice of Doom. With this structure definition, we can construct internal players the same way we construct ordinary struct instances. But what really happens is that an ip adds a field, which contains the prefab player that would result from the arguments given to ip.

Now we can send a representation of players to clients simply by calling the ip-player function and sending that result to the iworld in ip. To clarify, an instance of ip is never sent across a network. It is used only by the server to hold all of its knowledge about a player.

14.6 Main, Take Client

Since the client is clearly simpler than the server, we will deal with the main function of the client first. It handles three actions: drawing, messaging waypoints to the server, and receiving messages in return.

```
(define (lets-eat label server)
  (big-bang INITIAL
            (to-draw render-the-meal)
            (on-mouse set-waypoint)
            (on-receive handle-server-messages)
            (register server)
            (name label)))
```

This function takes a name that the client wishes to use as her ID and the address of the server that the client wishes to join. These two pieces of data are used by the last two clauses of big-bang.

The functions in the other clauses all follow the same pattern; they dispatch the event to a different function based on the client's present state. For example, the drawing and message-handling functions look like this:

client.rkt

```
(define (render-the-meal meal)
  (cond [(app? meal)    (render-appetizer meal)]
        [(entree? meal) (render-entree meal)]))

(define (handle-server-messages meal msg)
  (cond [(app? meal)    (handle-appetizer-message meal msg)]
        [(entree? meal) (handle-entree-message meal msg)]))
```

Very little thought is required in writing these. Before anything can be done, we need to understand the context of our situation—that is, the current state—and then pass the current state to the appropriate helper function.

Handling mouse events proceeds in a similar fashion, but the handler must take into consideration another condition:

client.rkt

```
(define (set-waypoint meal x y me)
  (if (and (entree? meal) (mouse=? me "button-down"))
      (make-package meal (list GOTO x y))
      meal))
```

Because the rules state that a player's only action is to click the mouse during the game, the mouse event handler checks these two conditions first. If true, set-waypoint sends the appropriate message to the server. If not, the state is returned unchanged.

The Appetizer State

While the player is waiting for the server to start a game, the client is in the so-called app state. In this state, it displays any message that the server sends. The top-level function for rendering appetizer states draws a progress bar:

client.rkt

```
(define (render-appetizer app)
  (add-progress-bar (render-id+image app) (app-countdown app)))
```

The `render-appetizer` function adds the most recent message to the image in `app` by making a call to `render-id+image`. It then adds a progress bar on top of that image with a call to `add-progress-bar`. The `render-id+image` function takes the `app` structure and generates an image from the latest message the client received:

client.rkt

```
(define (render-id+image app)
  (define id (app-id app))
  (define base-image (app-img app))
  (overlay
   (cond
     [(boolean? id) base-image]
     [else (define s (string-append LOADING-OPEN-TEXT id))
           (above base-image (text s TEXT-SIZE TEXT-COLOR))])
   BASE))
```

This function renders the image as well as the player's ID if the server has sent it already. Adding a progress bar is so easy that we won't show it here.

The remaining events concern messages from the server:

client.rkt

```
(define (handle-appetizer-message s msg)
  (cond [(id? msg)    (app msg (app-img s) (app-countdown s))]
        [(time? msg)  (app (app-id s) (app-img s) msg)]
        [(state? msg) (switch-to-entree s msg)]
        [else s]))
```

As the protocol specifies, this function handles three messages. The first two cond clauses should be obvious. They just switch out one field with the newly arrived message. The third cond clause switches the client to the entree state. The last clause makes our message handling fault tolerant; it handles any violation of the agreed-upon protocol by ignoring the message and returning the current state. To make the program fault tolerant, the predicates that check our messages need to be programmed defensively. For example, here is the definition of time?:

```
(define (time? msg)
  (and (real? msg) (<= 0 msg 1)))
```

It doesn't just check whether the message is a number but also ensures that number is real and between 0 and 1.

There is only one more function to deal with the app state. The function switch-to-entree is called when the first state message arrives. It consumes the current state and the state message, and it returns an entree:

```
(define (switch-to-entree s m)
  (apply entree (app-id s) (rest m)))
```

Do you remember `apply`, the higher-order function introduced in chapter 7? Go back and reread that section if you don't. All `apply` does here is call the `entree` constructor on the current `id` and the remaining two elements of the state message, which just happen to make up the fields of an `entree`. Isn't that easy? Time to eat.

The Entree State

The `entree` state represents the client's playing state. In this state, the player may interact with the world by clicking the screen to direct the avatar. The client displays the player's avatar, all of the other avatars, and some information about each one in the rendering function `render-entree`:

client.rkt

```
(define (render-entree entree)
  (define id (entree-id entree))
  (define pl (entree-players entree))
  (define fd (entree-food entree))
  (add-path id pl (add-players id pl (add-food fd BASE)))))
```

This function starts by drawing all of the food and players onto the base scene. It then draws the path of this client's player. So let's look at how players are drawn:

```
(define (add-players id lof base-scene)
  (for/fold ([scn base-scene]) ([feaster lof])
    (place-image (render-avatar id feaster)
                 (feaster-x feaster) (feaster-y feaster)
                 scn)))
```

The `add-players` function consumes this client's `id`, a list of all the players in the game, and a scene to add images on. The function uses `for/fold` to create a single image from the list of players. The given scene is used as the base case, and the function iterates over the given list of players. The loop creates an image with `render-avatar` and places it on the scene.

The `render-avatar` function creates an image of an avatar based on the client's `id` and the `feaster` that represents the player to be drawn:

```
(define (render-avatar id player)
  (define size (body-size (player-body player)))
  (define color
    (if (id=? id (player-id player)) MY-COLOR PLAYER-COLOR))
  (above
   (render-text (player-id player))
   (overlay (render-player-score player)
            PLAYER-IMG
            (circle size 'outline color))))
```

This function decides what color the avatar's bounding circle should be, based on the given `id`. It then draws the bounding circle that has a radius based on the size of the given player. The actual avatar is placed at the center of the circle. By drawing the player's avatar in this way, we have an accurate view of how large the avatar is, but we avoid pixelating the image by stretching it. We will leave it to you to write the rendering function that displays scores. The list of food is rendered in a similar fashion.

The last rendering step in the client concerns the path for this client's avatar:

```
(define (add-path id players base-scene)
  (define player
    (findf (lambda (x) (id=? id (player-id x))) players))
  (if (boolean? player)
      base-scene
      (add-waypoint* player base-scene)))
```

This function takes an id, a list of players, and an image to which the path is added. The function checks if this client's id exists in the list of players. If it does not exist, then the id came from a spectator and no waypoints are drawn. Otherwise, it draws all the points for this client. This function is straightforward, so we leave it as an exercise for you.

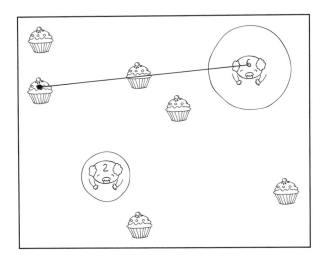

Finally, we deal with message handling for the entree state. The function for handling the messages in the entree state is similar to the message handler for the app state:

client.rkt

```
(define (handle-entree-message s msg)
  (cond [(state? msg) (update-entree s msg)]
        [(score? msg) (restart s msg)]
        [else s]))
```

In the case of a state message, the handler calls update-entree, which works like switch-to-entree. In the case of a score message, the game restarts:

client.rkt

```
(define (restart s end-msg)
  (define score-image (render-scores end-msg))
  (app (entree-id s) (above LOADING score-image) ZERO%))
```

This function builds an image that contains a table of all the scores and uses it as the base image for a new `app` structure. Building the table image is really easy as well:

client.rkt

```
(define (render-scores msg)
  (define scores (sort (second msg) < #:key second))
  (for/fold ([img empty-image]) ([name-score scores])
    (define txt (get-text name-score))
    (above (render-text txt) img)))
```

Here, we take the list of scores and sort it in ascending order based on the second value of each list. If you want more detail about #:key, look up "keyword arguments" in the documentation. The function then iterates across this sorted list with `for/fold` and builds an image with the name and score, sticking it above the previous rows. And there you go. That's the entire client.

14.7 Main, Take Server

Whenever we get to modules, we start with a main function, which is a `universe` function in the case of a game server:

server.rkt

```
(define (bon-appetit)
  (universe JOIN0
            (on-new connect)
            (on-tick tick-tock TICK)
            (on-msg handle-goto-message)
            (on-disconnect disconnect)))
```

The initial state of the universe is a `join` state with no clients and some initial time.
    The `on-new` clause deals with new connections:

server.rkt

```
(define (connect s iw)
  (cond [(join? s) (add-player s iw)]
        [(play? s) (add-spectator s iw)]))
```

Like all `on-new` handlers, this function takes the current universe and an `iworld`, a piece of data representing the new connection. Once again, this event handler dispatches to auxiliary functions depending on the current state `s` of the universe. All of the `universe` handlers employ a similar strategy.

The function `disconnect` does exactly what it sounds like. It handles dispatch for disconnections:

server.rkt

```
(define (disconnect s iw)
  (cond [(join? s) (drop-client s iw)]
        [(play? s) (drop-player s iw)]))
```

Just as before, this function determines the current state of the server and passes along its argument to the appropriate function.

Ticking works like this:

server.rkt

```
(define (tick-tock s)
  (cond [(join? s) (wait-or-play s)]
        [(play? s) (move-and-eat s)]))
```

In the `join` state, the function counts down and possibly transitions to the `play` state. In the `play` state, it moves all the players and lets them eat cupcakes. The `move-and-eat` function may also transition back to the `join` initial state if the last cupcake has been eaten.

The final universe clause we need to explain is `on-msg`. The `on-msg` handler clause is a little different from all of the others. Recall that the server accepts messages only when it is in the `play` state, and even then, there is only one kind of message that it accepts:

server.rkt

```
(define (handle-goto-message s iw msg)
  (cond [(and (play? s) (goto? msg)) (goto s iw msg)]
        [else                        (empty-bundle s)]))
```

If the server is in the `play` state, and the message is a valid GOTO message, we add the new waypoint to the given player's path. If not, then we do nothing, which in the case of a server, means we return a bundle with no messages, no dropped clients, and an unchanged state. It's a really short function:

server.rkt

```
(define (empty-bundle s)
  (make-bundle s empty empty))
```

The rest of the section explains how the server reacts to the network events and clock tick events, depending on which state it is in. Altogether, this makes four combinations. We start with a close look at how to handle network events while the server is in the `join` state.

The Join State and Network Events

One network event signals the arrival of a new client. Think about this event and how we might handle it in the `join` state. Now think about how we might handle it in the `play` state. In both states, we must create a new internal player, add it to the state, and send the client its new `id`. The difference is that in the `join` state, we add the new internal player to the list of players, and in the `play` state, we add it to the list of spectators.

So let's take advantage of these similarities with a little abstraction:

server.rkt
```
(define (make-connection adder)
  (lambda (u iw)
    (define player (named-player iw))
    (define mails   (list (make-mail iw (ip-id player))))
    (make-bundle (adder u player) mails empty)))
```

This function consumes `adder`, a function that takes a state and a player and returns a state. Using `adder`, `make-connection` creates another function. This newly created function consumes a universe state and an `iworld`. It builds a new player, and it constructs mail for the new client that contains the guaranteed unique ID created with the new player's name. The function returns this bundle.

This abstract function allows us to define the function to handle new clients for the `join` state in one line:

server.rkt
```
(define (join-add-player j new-p)
  (join (cons new-p (join-clients j)) (join-time j)))

(define add-player (make-connection join-add-player))
```

The other part of the `make-connection` function we need is `named-player`:

server.rkt
```
(define (named-player iw)
  (create-player iw (symbol->string (gensym (iworld-name iw)))))
```

It uses a fancy function, called `gensym`, to create a unique name that starts with the name of the client. Then it creates a player using `create-player`:

server.rkt
```
(define (create-player iw n)
  (ip iw n (create-a-body PLAYER-SIZE) empty))
```

This creates a player with all the specified information, a body with some initial size, and an empty list of waypoints. The body of the player is placed at some random point on the playing field.

```
#|
NOTE: The gensym function comes with all members of the Lisp family.
It's used to generate unique symbols that are not eq? to any other
symbol in the entire program. You will learn more about why this
facility is useful for writing programming languages in the next
chapter. Here, we just use it for making unique names.
|#
```

Other than the arrival of new players, the server must also deal with player disconnections:

server.rkt

```
(define (drop-client j iw)
  (empty-bundle (join-remove j iw)))
```

When a client is dropped, drop-client must find the player with the same iworld and remove it from the list of players. It does this using join-remove:

server.rkt

```
(define (join-remove j iw)
  (join (rip iw (join-clients j)) (join-time j)))
```

The rip function finds the player with the given iworld and removes it from the list of clients. To do so, it uses the remove function, which we know from chapter 6, but with a twist:

server.rkt

```
(define (rip iw players)
  (remove iw players (lambda (iw p) (iworld=? iw (ip-iw p)))))
```

As this definition shows, remove is actually a higher-order function that takes an optional third argument for equality testing. By default, this function is equal?, but here we define "equality" to mean "having the same iworld" instead of "being exactly the same." Why do you think we use iworld=? instead of the equal? function?

The Join State and Tick Events

Dealing with tick events requires a complex handler. It all starts with `wait-or-play`:

```
                                                                    server.rkt
(define (wait-or-play j)
  (cond [(keep-waiting? j) (keep-waiting j)]
        [else             (start-game j)]))
```

As the name says, this function either continues waiting or transitions into the `play` state. Checking whether or not to transition works as follows:

```
                                                                    server.rkt
(define (keep-waiting? j)
  (or (> PLAYER-LIMIT (length (join-clients j)))
      (> WAIT-TIME (join-time j))))
```

The server waits if there are not enough players for a good game or if the allotted wait time is not up. It's equally easy to define `keep-waiting`:

```
                                                                    server.rkt
(define (keep-waiting j)
  (set-join-time! j (+ (join-time j) 1))
  (time-broadcast j))
```

All that's necessary is to increment the time and send that new time to all clients, which the following function accomplishes:

```
                                                                    server.rkt
(define (time-broadcast j)
  (define iworlds (map ip-iw (join-clients j)))
  (define load% (min 1 (/ (join-time j) WAIT-TIME)))
  (make-bundle j (broadcast iworlds load%) empty))
```

The key is the call to `broadcast`. This helper will be used in a number of places to send a message to all clients. It takes a list of `iworlds` and the message to be sent, which in this case is a percentage of the current time. It returns a list of `mails`, one for each client.

Let's take a look at the broadcast function:

server.rkt

```
(define (broadcast iws msg)
  (map (lambda (iw) (make-mail iw msg)) iws))
```

With map, this function definition becomes downright trivial. We show it only because it is used in almost every function that sends a message from the server to the clients.

Now it is time to look at how the server starts a game:

server.rkt

```
(define (start-game j)
  (define clients (join-clients j))
  (define cupcakes (bake-cupcakes (length clients)))
  (broadcast-universe (play clients cupcakes empty)))
```

The start-game function takes a join state and creates a play state. This play universe starts with the list of players from the join universe, a list of food, and an empty list of spectators. Using broadcast-universe, we send this initial state to all of the clients. We generate a number of cupcakes that is directly proportional to the number of players:

server.rkt

```
(define (bake-cupcakes player#)
  (for/list ([i (in-range (* player# FOOD*PLAYERS))])
    (create-a-body CUPCAKE)))
```

We chose to generate cupcakes in this fashion, but you can define this function in whatever way you want. Take note that we use the create-a-body function.

Onwards to the broadcast-universe function:

server.rkt

```
(define (broadcast-universe p)
  (define mails (broadcast (get-iws p) (serialize-universe p)))
  (make-bundle p mails empty))
```

Here, we reuse the broadcast function to create a state message for each of the clients. As usual, this function returns a bundle with the universe and the list of mail that needs to be sent. While `get-iws` is another easy little function that you should be able to write yourself, `serialize-universe` is a little trickier:

server.rkt

```
(define (serialize-universe p)
  (define serialized-players (map ip-player (play-players p)))
  (list SERIALIZE serialized-players (play-food p)))
```

Remember that `ips` contain complete `players` and that these are represented with prefab structures. As planned, we can send those across the network, and that's what we do. With that, we are finished with the `join` state for the server.

The Play State and Network Events

Now our server can reach the `play` state. It is time to think about how the `play` state should handle network events. As with the `join` state, we start with handling new connections, which are added as spectators. Recall that we have already dealt with new connections for `join` states and that we created an abstraction for dealing with them.

You're late, kid
Go join the spectators
and I'll let you play the
next game.

Having said that, here is `play-add-spectator`, which `conses` the new client onto the list of spectators.

```
(define (play-add-spectator pu new-s)
  (define players (play-players pu))
  (define spectators (play-spectators pu))
  (play players (play-food pu) (cons new-s spectators)))

(define add-spectator (make-connection play-add-spectator))
```

The next network event concerns the arrival of GOTO messages, which are the only ones that the server deals with:

```
(define (goto p iw msg)
  (define c (make-rectangular (second msg) (third msg)))
  (set-play-players! p (add-waypoint (play-players p) c iw))
  (broadcast-universe p))
```

First, goto creates a complex number representing the new waypoint. Second, it modifies the current list of players with that waypoint added to the client who sent the message. Finally, it broadcasts the new state of the universe. This broadcast allows the client to see that its waypoint message was accepted and to draw an appropriate path. Indeed, all clients get to see the new waypoint, and that may concern you.

The only undefined auxiliary function in goto is add-waypoint:

```
(define (add-waypoint ps c iw)
  (for/list ([p ps])
    (cond [(iworld=? (ip-iw p) iw)
           (ip (ip-iw p)
               (ip-id p)
               (ip-body p)
               (append (ip-waypoints p) (list c)))]
          [else p])))
```

This function traverses the given list of players, and when it finds the player with an iworld matching the one that sent the new waypoint, it reconstructs the given player, adding the provided complex number to the end of its list of waypoints.

The last kind of network event to worry about is a client disconnection:

```
(define (drop-player p iw)
  (broadcast-universe (play-remove p iw)))
```

Disconnecting from the `play` universe is like disconnecting from the `join` universe with the difference that we broadcast the new state to all players so that they know some client has dropped out. The `play-remove` function has a straightforward definition:

server.rkt

```
(define (play-remove p iw)
  (define players (play-players p))
  (define spectators (play-spectators p))
  (play (rip iw players) (play-food p) (rip iw spectators)))
```

The only difference between `join-remove` and `play-remove` is that the latter uses `rip` on both `players` and `spectators` because we don't know whether a player or a spectator has dropped out.

The Play State and Tick Events

We have one server handler left to deal with: the clock-tick handler. It is a large one because this function deals with all the game logic. We start with `move-and-eat`:

server.rkt

```
(define (move-and-eat pu)
  (define nplayer (move-player* (play-players pu)))
  (define nfood (feed-em-all nplayer (play-food pu)))
  (progress nplayer nfood (play-spectators pu)))
```

For doing so much, this three-line function definition looks almost trivial, but bear with us—it gets a little complicated. First, `move-and-eat` uses `move-player*` to move the players in the appropriate direction at an appropriate speed. Second, a new list of food is generated that doesn't contain any cupcakes that a player has eaten. The function `feed-em-all` also mutates the bodies of players who are eating; remember that they grow in size. Finally, these two lists, along with the list of spectators, are sent to the `progress` function. It will either progress the game by sending the new `play` state to all clients or transition to a `join` state by sending out the final score message.

Here is how we move all the players:

server.rkt

```
(define (move-player* players)
  (for/list ([p players])
    (define waypoints (ip-waypoints p))
    (cond [(empty? waypoints) p]
          [else (define body (ip-body p))
                (define nwpts
                  (move-toward-waypoint body waypoints))
                (ip (ip-iw p) (ip-id p) body nwpts)])))
```

For every player with waypoints, we mutate the player's body with `move-toward-way-point`. If the player reaches her first point, `move-toward-waypoint` chops off the first waypoint and returns the new list. If the next waypoint has not been reached, the list remains the same. A player without waypoints is left unchanged.

Moving individual players takes a bit of tricky math, but using complex numbers makes our lives pretty easy:

server.rkt

```
(define (move-toward-waypoint body waypoints)
  (define goal (first waypoints))
  (define bloc (body-loc body))
  (define line (- goal bloc))
  (define dist (magnitude line)) ;;in pixels per clock tick
  (define speed (/ BASE-SPEED (body-size body)))
  (cond [(<= dist speed)
         (set-body-loc! body goal)
         (rest waypoints)]
        [else ; (> dist speed 0)
         (define velocity (/ (* speed line) dist))
         (set-body-loc! body (+ bloc velocity))
         waypoints]))
```

The main part of the function is the conditional block. It checks the distance the player moves in this tick. If this condition is satisfied, the function sets the location to the goal to avoid overshooting it. Then, the function returns the rest of the waypoints. Otherwise, we add `velocity` to the current location, where `velocity` is the fraction of the complex number by which the body should move toward the next waypoint. Also notice that `speed` depends on the size of the body, meaning that a player's body slows down as it gets bigger.

If this looks to you like a bunch of complicated vector math, hidden behind complex arithmetic, then you're right. We recommend that you browse the Web for more information on vector-based movement. You should admire, however, how this avoids all uses of `sin`, `cos`, and other trigonometry.

Now think about the `ip` structure for a moment. Don't we have an internal `player` that needs updating? No, we don't. We got away with this because `body` in the `ip` and `player` structure is the *same* body, so mutating one mutates the other. Because they are really `eq?`, no extra modifications are needed.

It is time to feed the players. We start with `feed-em-all`:

server.rkt

```
(define (feed-em-all players foods)
  (for/fold ([foods foods]) ([p players])
    (eat-all-the-things p foods)))
```

This function folds across the players, accumulating a new list of food by removing any food that a player collides with. The function `eat-all-the-things` is the workhorse here, filtering out the eaten cupcakes and face-stuffing players:

server.rkt

```
(define (eat-all-the-things player foods)
  (define b (ip-body player))
  (for/fold ([foods '()]) ([f foods])
    (cond
      [(body-collide? f b)
       (set-body-size! b (+ PLAYER-FATTEN-DELTA (body-size b)))
       foods]
      [else (cons f foods)])))
```

This function also uses `for/fold`, but this time, it folds across the list of cupcakes. If the current food collides with the given player, it is not accumulated; instead, the player is fattened. Otherwise, the food is put back in the list.

The collisions themselves are straightforward:

server.rkt

```
(define (body-collide? s1 s2)
  (<= (magnitude (- (body-loc s1) (body-loc s2)))
      (+ (body-size s1) (body-size s2))))
```

This function compares the distance between the centers of the two bodies with the sum of their sizes. If the distance is less than the combined radius, then it must be a collision. And that's it.

Finally, we must discuss the `progress` function:

server.rkt

```
(define (progress pls foods spectators)
  (define p (play pls foods spectators))
  (cond [(empty? foods) (end-game-broadcast p)]
        [else (broadcast-universe p)]))
```

If all cupcakes have been eaten, `progress` ends the game by transitioning to a `join` state and sending the score list to all clients. If not, it just uses `broadcast-universe` to send out the current state.

Ending the game is simple:

server.rkt

```
(define (end-game-broadcast p)
  (define iws (get-iws p))
  (define msg (list SCORE (score (play-players p))))
  (define mls (broadcast iws msg))
  (make-bundle (remake-join p) mls empty))
```

All that happens here is that we build a score message, broadcast it to all players, and create a new `join` state from the current players and spectators. To accomplish this, we need the `score` function, which builds an association list linking each player's `id` to her score:

server.rkt

```
(define (score ps)
  (for/list ([p ps])
    (list (ip-id p) (get-score (body-size (ip-body p))))))
```

In truth, this function builds the second half of the score message. In order for the client to recognize this message, it needs to be placed in a list with SCORE as the first element. But the only part of this function that might be a little tricky is getting a player's score from its weight. Recall that a player's weight is increased by some amount whenever it eats. Hence, its weight is directly proportional to the number of cupcakes eaten:

shared.rkt

```
(define (get-score f)
  (/ (- f PLAYER-SIZE) PLAYER-FATTEN-DELTA))
```

We leave the explanation of this math up to your grade school math teacher.

Last, but not least, we turn our eyes to the `remake-join` function. Given a `play` state, this function constructs a new `join` state:

---

server.rkt

```
(define (remake-join p)
  (define players (refresh (play-players p)))
  (define spectators (play-spectators p))
  (join (append players spectators) START-TIME))
```

To do this, we refresh the current list of players. This moves them to a new location with an unfattened body. This list is joined with the spectators list to make the list of clients for the new state. Add `START-TIME` to the new `join` state to get the countdown going, and you have a complete new `join` state.

14.8 See Henry Run

The game is complete, but we need to see it run so that we can correct problems that unit tests don't uncover. While it is possible to run the game with the existing code, doing so is cumbersome—politely put. If we write a bit of extra code, life becomes easy.

As in the preceding chapter, let's create a new file to run the game and require all necessary pieces into this fourth file:

---

run.rkt

```
#lang racket
(require (only-in "server.rkt" bon-appetit)
         (only-in "client.rkt" lets-eat)
         2htdp/universe)
```

The `require` specification tells Racket to include one function from **server.rkt** and another one from **client.rkt**, plus everything that **2htdp/universe** provides.

With these functions, we define `serve-dinner`, launching a server and two clients:

---

run.rkt

```
(define (serve-dinner)
  (launch-many-worlds (bon-appetit)
                      (lets-eat "Matthias" LOCALHOST)
                      (lets-eat "David"    LOCALHOST)))
```

And bam! We can play the game just by running one simple function. It doesn't even take any arguments. With this last file, the game is complete. Go play.

`On-disconnect`—**Chapter Checkpoint**

In this chapter, we created an interesting distributed multiplayer game:

- Distributed programming requires a planned-out communication protocol. Ours fits into a one-page diagram.
- Designing a good protocol can save you a lot of work. Spend time on it.

Chapter Challenges

- **Easy**   Modify the game so that new cupcakes appear on the screen every other time one is eaten.

- **Medium**   Right now, a clever player could write a client that takes advantage of the other player's waypoints. Modify the data protocol so that this security breach cannot happen.

- **Difficult**   Write an AI that follows the modified protocol.

;; Good–Bye
(Close Paren)

```
#|
This book only scratches the surface of Racket. In this chap-
ter, we will give you a glimpse of what else you can find in
the depths of Racket: realms of unique and powerful programming
ideas. We hope you find the ideas intriguing and will continue to
explore Racket. If you need help, Help Desk and the Racket users
mailing list are there for you.
|#
```

).1 Run Racket Run

Due to some old, silly tradition, most books on programming languages start with a program that prints "Hello, world." You may think we missed our chance, but here we go:

```
"Hello, world."
```

This is the entire program. No command for printing is needed. Racket knows what to do. Yes, you need to tell the Racket implementation that you've written the program in one of its many dialects:

```
#lang racket/base
"Hello, world."
```

Click "Run," and you will see that it really prints `"Hello, world."` in the interactions panel. Did you notice that the `#lang` line looks different? Don't worry about this for now, but rest assured that you will see many different `#lang` lines before this chapter is over.

"Wait!" you might object, "In real programming languages, you write programs that run from the command line. People shouldn't have to open a development environment to run their programs." Don't worry; be happy. In Racket you can do this, too. Save the file as **hello-world.rkt**, open a command shell, go to the folder where you saved the program, and enter this:

```
$ racket hello-world.rkt
```

Ta-da! The string `"Hello, world."` appears. Your first program is complete.

But maybe you're starting to worry that your grandmother wouldn't know she has to type `racket` to run the program, right? You are too easily worried. Here's what you do.

Go back to your command shell and run these commands:

```
$ raco exe -l hello-world.rkt
$ ./hello-world
```

And eureka, once again you see the magical words. No one will know from the name of the file or the command line that you are using Racket. From now on, it's your secret weapon.

In case you're wondering, `raco exe -l` creates an executable script from a Racket program on all platforms: Windows, Mac OS X, and all *nixes. For the name of the script, it removes the `.rkt` suffix so that no one knows it was created from a Racket program.

There is much more to learn about running Racket programs, but we need to move on. Read the documentation if you need more information. Also, check DrRacket's "Racket" menu for the "Create Executable" item.

).2 Racket Is a Programming Language

If you have learned programming in the past 20 years or so, chances are that you grew up with classes, fields, and methods. And if so, you may be wondering whether Racket is the only language that comes without classes. We admit that many of our game programs would benefit from classes, but we wanted to show you a programming style so light and so simple that your little brother in high school could see how to do it. It is the style that makes mathematics come alive.

Racket is a regular programming language, and as such, it does come with classes and objects. For example, the snakes from chapter 6 could be presented as a short class in a rather compact way:

```
(define snake%
  (class object%
    (super-new)
    (init-field dir head tail)

    (define/public (slither)
      (set! tail (cons head (all-but-last tail)))
      (set! head (next-head)))

    (define/public (grow)
      (set! tail (cons head tail))
      (set! head (next-head)))

    (define/public (can-eat goos)
      (findf (lambda (goo) (close? goo head)) goos))

    (define/private (next-head)
      (cond
        [(string=? dir "up")    (posn-move head  0 -1)]
        [(string=? dir "down")  (posn-move head  0 +1)]
        [(string=? dir "left")  (posn-move head -1  0)]
        [(string=? dir "right") (posn-move head +1  0)]))))
```

Like the original game, this class supports the most basic snake actions: slithering, growing by one segment, and checking whether some food is in close proximity. Technically, the class says that it is a subclass of object%; that it has three fields, which are also initial parameters; and that it comes with three public methods and one private one.

Here is the conventional way to create an instance of this class:

```
(define snake1
  (make-object snake% "left" (posn 1 2) '()))
```

As in Java, this expression creates an instance by passing in the three required initialization arguments. When a class has three initialization arguments, you might remember the order in which you need to pass the arguments to the constructor. But even then, it is better to say which argument populates which field, and in Racket, you can do so easily:

```
(define snake2
  (new snake% [head (posn 3 9)] [tail '()] [dir "up"]))
```

With this second method of object instantiation, you can clearly see which fields you are initializing in what way.

It shouldn't come as a surprise that you can extend Racket classes and that doing so looks like it does in any pedestrian programming language:

```
(define snake-render%
  (class snake%
    (super-new)
    (inherit-field dir head tail)

    (init-field [bgrd THE-EMPTY-SCENE] [img-db "image-file"])

    (define/public (render)
      (define head-img (select-head dir img-db))
      (define tail-img (img-list+scene tail SEG-IMG bgrd))
      (img+scene head head-img tail-img))))
```

Note how this class definition explicitly specifies which fields it inherits; we will explain why in a moment. More importantly, the class has two optional initialization arguments, which you may or may not supply when you create instances:

```
(define snake3
  (new snake-render% [dir "down"] [head (posn 4 3)] [tail '()]))

(define snake4
  (new snake-render% [dir "down"] [head (posn 4 3)] [tail '()]
       [img-db "new-image-file"]))
```

If you now think Racket classes are as boring as the ones you got to know in your favorite object-oriented language, you are gravely mistaken. In most languages, objects are values, and this is true in Racket as well. But in Racket, classes are values, too, just like numbers, Booleans, or functions. You already know that having functions as values is a powerful concept. You should have no doubts that having classes as values is an equally powerful idea.

Let's start with a couple of silly examples:

```
(define snake5
  (new (if (today-is-tuesday?) snake% snake-render%)
       [dir "down"] [head (posn 4 3)] [tail '()]))
```

The first one demonstrates that wherever an expression needs a class, it is acceptable to write an expression that evaluates to a class. In this case, the result is a snake with the render method on all days except for Tuesdays. You'll have a hard time doing this in Java, no matter what day of the week it is.

This second example shows the same idea in a different context:

```
(define some-snake%
  (class (if (today-is-sunday?) snake% snake-render%)
    (super-new)))
```

Yes, even the superclass of a class can be determined at runtime, as long as the expression in this position returns a class.

A somewhat more serious example is a function that consumes and produces a class:

```
(define (add-render %)
  (class %
    (super-new)
    (inherit-field dir head tail)
    (init-field [bgrd THE-EMPTY-SCENE])

    (define/public (render)
      (define head-img
        (cond
          [(string=? "up" dir)    HEAD-UP-IMG]
          [(string=? "down" dir)  HEAD-DOWN-IMG]
          [(string=? "left" dir)  HEAD-LEFT-IMG]
          [(string=? "right" dir) HEAD-RIGHT-IMG]))
      (define tail-img (img-list+scene tail SEG-IMG bgrd))
      (img+scene head head-img tail-img))))
```

Take a look at the function parameter. It is %, which is the Racketeering convention for saying that this function expects a class as an argument. Once the function is applied to some class, say, snake%, it constructs a class extension from it:

```
(define snake-render-again%
  (add-render snake%))
```

It does so by first checking that the given class has three fields: `dir`, `head`, and `tail`. The superclass is forced to have these fields because we require them with `inherit-field`. Next, it creates an extended class with a render method, more or less the way `snake-render%` does.

The best aspect is that if you wish to introduce renderable crocodiles into the Snake game, you can easily do so:

```
(define crocodile%
  (class object%
    (init-field dir head tail)
    ...))
```

Adding the render method would be a two-line definition:

```
(define crocodile-render
  (add-render crocodile%))
```

In other words, functions such as `add-render` allow a programmer to dynamically splice entire classes into the class hierarchy.

Cool, right? What is even better is that the class system isn't a part of the Racket core. It is really shorthand for structures and functions, though you'd never know. The trick is called a macro, and we will explain macros next.

).3 Racket Is a Metaprogramming Language

All members of the Lisp family come with incredibly powerful ways to add new syntax to the language. For better or worse, pedestrian programmers call this idea metaprogramming, and Lispers say **macro programming**. Regardless of what you call them, macros allow you to expand the vocabulary of your language.

Racket comes with the most expressive and powerful macro system of them all. No other Lisp even comes close. Here, we provide you a glimpse of these magical macros.

We start with a definition for adding and-like expressions:

```
(define-syntax-rule
  (my-and a b)
  (if a b #f))
```

The advantage of re-implementing existing expressions is that we can compare our work with Racket's version to see whether we're on the right track. The definition of my-and tells Racket that whenever it encounters an expression of the form (my-and a b), it rewrites the expression to `(if a b #f)`. This `if` expression truly computes the and-like composition of a and b. Let's try it out in the interactions panel:

```
> (my-and (< 10 11) (< 11 12))
#t
> (my-and (< 10 11) 'ready!)
'ready!
> (my-and (> 10 11) (+ (/ 1 0) 10))
#f
```

The last two interactions show how closely `my-and` mimics and. First, it evaluates to more than plain Boolean values. Second, it shortcuts the evaluation of its subexpressions so that the division by 0 never gets to signal an error.

This last point also explains why it is impossible to define `my-and` as a plain function. If you were to try, you would quickly realize that an application of a `my-and` function forces all arguments to be evaluated *before* the function has a chance to break out of the sequence when an `#f` shows up. Put differently, if `my-and` had been defined as a function, the last interaction would signal an error concerning the division by 0.

If we now asked you to re-create or with a macro, you would probably come up with something like this:

```
(define-syntax-rule
  (my-or a b)
  (if a a b))
```

It is close enough for government work, which the following interactions show:

```
> (my-or (> 10 11) (< 10 11))
#t
> (my-or (< 10 9) 'okay)
'okay
> (my-or (< 9 10) (+ (/ 1 0) 10))
#t
```

We will let you figure out why the results are as expected. It should worry you, however, that Racket is told to duplicate a when it encounters `(my-or a b)` in your program. The result, `(if a a b)`, seems to compute whether a or b evaluates to true, but it does so by reevaluating a when a produces true. This reevaluation is acceptable for a simple a, but it isn't innocent:

```
> (my-or (begin (displayln "hello world") 'okay) #f)
hello world
hello world
'okay
```

If a prints a string, then that printing is performed twice. But with or, we don't get this kind of double execution:

```
> (or (begin (displayln "hello world") 'okay) #f)
hello world
'okay
```

Amazingly, or just knows that a produced a true value, and it returns that value.

Now it is time to remind you of let expressions. Even though they have played only a minor role so far, many macros use them extensively. So take a look at this:

```
>   (let ((temp (* 2 2))) (+ temp temp temp))
12
```

A let expression evaluates expressions such as (* 2 2) and names the resulting value, temp. The body of our let expression is (+ temp temp temp), meaning it adds temp three times, and that is how we get 12.

Here is another variant of this let expression:

```
> (let ([temp (begin (displayln "H")
                      (+ 2 2))])
    (+ temp temp temp))
H
12
```

As you can see, temp really stands for 4 and displayln is run only once. And now we will take a second look at an or-style macro definition:

```
(define-syntax-rule
  (your-or a b)
  (let ((temp a)) (if temp temp b)))
```

This macro says evaluate a, name the value temp, and then test whether temp stands for true. If so, return temp, meaning the value that this name represents. And voilà, you get what you expect:

```
> (your-or (begin (displayln "hello world") (> 10 9)) temp)
hello world
#t
```

The printing is no longer duplicated in this version of or.

At this point, you may wonder whether the `temp` inside `let` could interfere with variables that show up in a or b. Suppose we define another `temp` with a `define` in the interactions panel:

```
> (define temp 'okay)
```

When Racket now encounters `(your-or (> 10 19) temp)`, it is supposed to replace it with `(let ((temp (> 10 19))) (if temp temp temp))`. But if it did so, `(your-or (> 10 19) temp)` would evaluate to `#f`, and that contradicts what we expect from an or-style macro. With `or`, you should expect to get `'okay` back because `(> 10 19)` evaluates to false, but `temp` just stands for `'okay`, and that is true.

Fortunately, Racket knows how to separate the variables that show up in macro definitions from those that show up in macro uses, so everything works out fine:

```
> (your-or (> 10 19) temp)
'okay
```

We don't have the space here to explain how Racket accomplishes this feat. You just need to know that it uses the `gensym` function mentioned in chapter 14. And therefore, you can write macros that work.

Before we move on, let's show you one more macro definition for a regular Racket form. Since we have just reminded you of `let`, we thought we'd show you its essence:

```
(define-syntax-rule
  (my-let.v1 name initial-value-exp body)
  ((lambda (name) body) initial-value-exp))
```

This first version of the macro can introduce one variable, initialize it to a value, and evaluate a `body` expression in which the variable may occur as many times as needed. Here is a simple use of the macro:

```
> (my-let.v1 x 10 (+ x 19))
29
```

The key is that Racket's functions are plain values, and you can make one up on the fly. In this case, the macro makes up a function whose sole parameter is the newly introduced variable x and whose body is a subexpression from the `my-let.v1` expression. By applying this function to the expression that is supposed to initialize the variable, the macro evaluates `body` in a world where `name` stands for the value of `initial-value-exp`, and that is exactly what `let` promises to do.

Racket's `let`, though, is far more flexible than `my-let.v1`. In particular, `let` empowers programmers to define several variables at once. With macros, it is possible to mimic this behavior, too:

```
(define-syntax-rule
  (my-let.v2 ((name initial-value-exp) ...) body)
  ((lambda (name ...) body) initial-value-exp ...))
```

This definition may not look real to you because of all the occurrences of ... in the input and output pattern. But Racketeers really describe many macros by example. This one translates as follows:

```
(my-let.v2 ((a b)) yyy) to ((lambda (a) yyy) b),
(my-let.v2 ((a b) (c d)) yyy) to ((lambda (a c) yyy) b d), and
(my-let.v2 ((a b) (c d) (e f)) yyy) to ((lambda (a c e) yyy) b d f).
```

In other words, in the first line of the macro definition, the dots stand for "zero or more occurrences of the preceding *S*-expression pattern," and in the second line, they mean "whatever you saw when you matched that pattern." And it really works:

```
> (my-let.v2 ((x 1) (y 2)) (+ x y))
3
> (my-let.v2 ((x 1) (y 2) (z 3) (w 4) (u 5)) (+ x y z w u))
15
```

Indeed, it even works when we do not define any temporary variables:

```
> (my-let.v2 () 55)
55
```

What you have seen so far is the most trivial form of defining macros. At this point, you can't fortify your macros against the most basic misuses. Even with these trivial macros, however, you could create a simplistic, albeit difficult to use, class system. Better still, these simple macros suffice to create programming languages from scratch, and doing so is as easy as writing a module.

).4 Racket Is a Programming-Language Programming Language

Many computational problems require substantial knowledge about the problem area, also known as the **domain**. For example, dealing with time series from medical trials calls for a statistician who is familiar with medical procedures and Bayesian mathematics. Similarly, the core of an engineering system may rely on a module that deals with system-specific partial differential equations. When programmers express solutions to these problems with classes, methods, and `for` loops, experts have a difficult time communicating with them. Experts would much prefer to articulate solutions in a language that they understand, even if the language is just a special-purpose programming language from our perspective.

Racket makes it particularly easy to create new programming languages, including special-purpose languages. The goal of this section is to provide you with a taste of language engineering. We want to show you how easy it is to engineer languages, and we hope you will find this idea intriguing and interesting enough to check out the documentation.

When a module defines a macro, other expressions and definitions in the module can use this syntactic abbreviation right away. If the module also provides the macro, other modules can require the module and use the macro, too. To create an entire language, a Racketeer has to change just one step of this procedure: the providing module must be used as the language name of the module. Here is how this is done:

```
#lang s-exp "silly-lang.rkt"
```

Stop! This module is the first one in this book that does not specify `racket` or `racket/base` as the name of the language. Instead, it uses `s-exp`, which then expects a path to a file that implements the actual language.

```
#|
NOTE: It is also possible to get rid of s-exp and to use the name
of a folder as the name of a programming language, which is what
Racket does. We do not have room in this book to explain the second
variant of making languages. If you are interested, see the Racket
documentation.
|#
```

Like a compiler, the macros translate programs from the new language to plain Racket. If these generated Racket programs need functions or other values when they are run, the module supports these, too. Following traditional terminology, we call these the **runtime** system.

Now consider the following definitions:

```
#lang racket

(define-syntax-rule
  (count-and-print f)
  (begin (count++ 'f) f))

(define count 0)
(define (count++ f)
  (set! count (+ count 1))
  (displayln `(evaluating form ,count : ,f)))
```

When Racket encounters (count-and-print (+ 1 1)), this macro definition tells it to use (begin (count++ '(+ 1 1)) (+ 1 1)) instead. Recall that a quote in front of an expression turns it into a list. Hence, count++ is not applied to 2 but to (list '+ 1 1). The call to count++ bumps the count variable and uses this number to remind the programmer how many expressions have been evaluated. It also displays the expression that is about to be evaluated.

```
#|
NOTE: See how ` and , work together to tell the quote expression to
use the actual values of count and f? For more information, look up
quasiquote, unquote, and unquote-splicing in the documentation.
|#
```

Here are some sample uses from the interactions panel:

```
> (count-and-print (+ 1 1))
(evaluating form 1 : (+ 1 1))
2
> (count-and-print (+ 1 2))
(evaluating form 2 : (+ 1 2))
3
```

Now you may be wondering why we bother with such a silly macro.

Imagine running a long definitions window and all the definitions and expressions it evaluates. Wouldn't it be nice if the interactions panel told you where the results came from? It is possible to implement this change easily by defining a language.

At a minimum, a language is a module that provides some key forms. The most important one is a form that tells Racket how to deal with the content of a module in the new language. Others are about dealing with function applications and data.

Languages provide three common forms:

- `#%module-begin`, which is a form like `begin` that is implicitly wrapped around the content of an entire module
- `#%app`, which is implicitly wrapped around each function application
- `#%datum`, which is implicitly wrapped around each occurrence of a literal piece of data

Otherwise, the module must provide everything else the language is supposed to have.

Given that much, we know how to turn our macro into a useful device. First, we define a macro that wraps `count-and-print` around every form in the new language:

silly-lang.rkt

```
(define-syntax-rule
  (module-count-and-print f ...)
  (#%module-begin (count-and-print f) ...))
```

Here, `#%module-begin` refers to the macro that `silly-lang.rkt` requires from the `racket` language. Second, we provide this macro with the name `#%module-begin`:

silly-lang.rkt

```
(provide (rename-out [module-count-and-print #%module-begin])
         #%app #%datum +)
```

Furthermore, we provide Racket's way of interpreting function application and literal data constants, plus the addition function.

And that is all there is to the creation of a new language. Save the file. Get ready. Here is the experiment you want to conduct now. Create the file **silly.rkt** like this:

silly.rkt

```
#lang s-exp "silly-lang.rkt"
(+ 2 3)
(+ 4 -1)
```

Save it in the same directory as the **silly-lang.rkt** file and click "Run." The output in the interactions panel looks like this:

```
(evaluating form 1 : (+ 2 3))
5
(evaluating form 2 : (+ 4 -1))
3
```

This is precisely what we wanted. But the interactions panel also says that it is no longer possible to interact with poor DrRacket.

Here is the reason for DrRacket's inability to interactively evaluate expressions in this language. If you want or need interactivity from a language, it must provide another form, one that deals with expressions at the interactions prompt: `#%top-interaction`. This form is implicitly wrapped around each and every form you enter at the prompt. If you wanted the interactions panel of the **silly-lang.rkt** language to evaluate forms like Racket, the file should provide `#%top-interaction` from Racket. If you wanted the interactions panel to continue counting your evaluations, you would have to define a macro that knows how to use `count++`:

silly-lang.rkt

```
(define-syntax-rule
  (interact-count-and-print . f)
  (count-and-print f))
```

Similarly, if your language needs to use `define`, just provide it; Racket makes it available. Indeed, you can easily provide everything from Racket with a simple `provide` clause:

silly-lang.rkt

```
(provide
  (rename-out [module-count-and-print #%module-begin])
  (rename-out [interact-count-and-print #%top-interaction])
  (except-out (all-from-out racket)
              #%module-begin #%top-interaction))
```

This last clause says make **silly-lang.rkt** like Racket except for two features, which are exported separately. Of course, as indicated with the first version of **silly-lang.rkt**, there doesn't need to be much or any overlap with Racket at all; + was all we needed to get going.

Let's look at another example of a Racket-made programming language:

delayed-lang.rkt

```
#lang racket
(provide
  (rename-out [delayed-args-app #%app])
  #%datum #%module-begin #%top-interaction
  define if force* (rename-out [+force +] [/force /]))

(define-syntax-rule
  (delayed-args-app f a ...)
  (#%app f (delay a) ...))
```

```
(define (+force a b)
  (+ (force* a) (force* b)))

(define (/force a b)
  (/ (force* a) (force* b)))

(define (force* x)
  (if (promise? x) (force* (force x)) x))
```

The first definition is the most interesting one. It tells Racket to rewrite all occurrences of this code:

```
(delayed-args-app a b c) to (#%app a (delay b) (delay c))
```

As we alluded to before, #%app is how Racket sees every function application, and this occurrence of #%app refers to the way the Racket language applies functions. The trick is that delayed-args-app is provided as the *new* #%app in the first line of the module, meaning every function application in a requiring module is rewritten in this manner.

The other definitions introduce functions: a +force function, which forces its arguments and adds the results; a /force function, which is like +force but for /; and force*, which calls force on its argument until it isn't a promise. The first two functions are provided as + and /, respectively, and the last one on an as-is basis. Other than that, the module provides the usual suspects, as well as define and if.

While **delay-lang.rkt** isn't quite enough to make the lazy flavor of Racket mentioned in chapter 12, it is a good start.

---

delayed.rkt

```
#lang s-exp "delayed-lang.rkt"

(define (f x)
  (+ 1 x))


(f (/ 4 2))
```
- -

As before, we use s-exp so that we can make **delayed-lang.rkt** the programming language of the module. The body of the module defines the function f and applies it like this: (f (+ 1 1)). Since **delayed-lang.rkt** employs #%module-begin from the Racket language, you will see a 3 printed in the interactions panel.

All in all, our experiment shows that **delayed-lang.rkt** acts like our familiar Racket language. To see the difference, we need to use bad expressions such as (/ 1 0). Consider the following extension of the module with a function g that throws away its argument and returns 2. Here it is applied to a bad expression:

delayed.rkt

```
(define (g y)
  2)

(g (/ 1 0))
```

Now if you run this module, you see 2 printed. Why? When Racket encounters this . . .

```
(g (/ 1 0))
```

. . . it uses #%app from the language module, which means (g (/ 1 0)) is rewritten as . . .

```
(#%app g (delay (/ 1 0)))
```

This second #%app is taken from the racket language. So (/ 1 0) isn't evaluated here but turned into a promise. Put differently, the argument to g is a promise, and this promise is discarded. Hence, (/ 1 0) never gets to signal its error.

You may be surprised to find out that in this **delayed-lang.rkt** language, if expressions are just functions, too:

delayed.rkt

```
(define (my-if tst thn els)
  (if (force* tst) thn els))

(+ (my-if #t 0 5) (my-if #f (/ 1 0) 1))
```

The function forces its first argument to find out whether it is true or false. Depending on the result, it picks one of the other two arguments and returns it. Run the extended module and watch how the test expression evaluates to 1, even though the then branch in the second my-if expression divides 1 by 0. Neat!

We could show you a whole lot more along these lines. Defining languages in Racket is so easy because Racketeers figured out how to reuse a lot of the underlying language. Better still, the reuse of underlying language constructs means that DrRacket also becomes reusable. The beneficiaries are the people who program in Racket, and you can be one of them now. Go forth and build your own language in Racket—you can do it.

So Long

This is it, the end. We have taught you everything we learned in our first semester, and this chapter is a bonus. Now don't stop here; there is a lot more to learn.

As this chapter explains, the Racket language is incredibly powerful, and language creation is a ubiquitous element in the world of Racket. Search for "web server" in the Racket documentation. It comes with its own special scripting language that allows for powerful ways of interacting with users. Take a look at Slideshow, a language for creating slides for lectures and presentations. And do play with Scribble, the language in which Racketeers write their documentation and research papers. You have not seen this incredible capability for language creation before. It makes Racket more interesting than any other language you may ever encounter.

Index

Numbers & Symbols

= function, 55
#:mutable keyword, 132
#:opaque keyword, 217
#:prefab keyword, 215
#:transparent keyword, 50
#:when keyword, 157
#%app top level form, 277, 279–280
#%datum top level form, 277
#%module-begin top level form, 277–280
#%top-interaction top level form, 278
#f value, 57
#lang lazy, 198
#lang racket, 21
#lang racket/base, 266
#lang s-exp, 275
#t value, 57
/force function, 279
+force function, 279
` (quasiquote), for lists, 276
' (quote), for data, 39, 44
, (unquote), for quasiquoted lists, 276
,@ (unquote-splicing), for quasiquoted lists, 276
2htdp/image library, 80

2htdp/universe library, 80. *See also* big-bang; universe

A

above function, 142
above/align function, 143
accessor, 48
add function, 186
add1 function, 33
add-3-to-state function, 81
add-board-to-scene function, 176
add-dice-to function, 184
add-path function, 243
add-player function, 247
add-player-info function, 176
add-players function, 243
add-progress-bar function, 240
add-spectator function, 252
add-territory function, 177
add-waypoint function, 252
add-waypoint* function, 243
age-goo function, 102
AI (artificial intelligence), 168, 203–208
ALGOL, 4
all-but-last function, 101

all-dead? function, 147
all-monsters-attack-player
        function, 150
and form, 61–64
andmap function, 118
app structure, 237
apply function, 122
argmax function, 208
arrange function, 146
artificial intelligence (AI), 168, 203–208
attackable? function, 187
attacking function, 181

B

bake-cupcakes function, 250
Barski, Conrad, i
Bayesian mathematics, 274
begin form, 271
beside function, 122, 142, 146
big-bang, 81–87, 98, 136, 174, 238
    clauses, 84
        name, 224, 238
        on-key, 84
        on-mouse, 238
        on-receive, 224, 238
        on-tick, 84
        register, 224, 238
        stop-when, 84
        to-draw, 84
    bigger function
        for Guess My Number, 33
            distributed, 223
    binary search, 29
    body structure, 234
    body-collide? function, 255
    bon-appetit function, 245
    boolean=? function, 55
    boolean? function, 53
    Booleans, 38, 63–65. See also false value;
            true value
    branch, 57
    brigand structure, 130. See also monster
        structure

broadcast function, 250
broadcast-universe function, 250
build-list function, 120
bundle type, 216

C

C, 4
C++, 4
can-eat function
    for Land of Lambda, 117
    for Snake, 99
case form, 150
check-= function, 70
check-equal? function, 68
check-false function, 70
check-not-equal? function, 70
check-not-false function, 70
check-pred function, 70
check-true function, 70
Church, Alonzo, 2
circle function, 243
class form, 267
clause. See big-bang; cond form
client, 214
client.rkt file, 220, 221, 224
close? function, 100
closure, 197
collects, 218
color-chooser function, 177
command line execution, 266
comments, 38
complex numbers, 39, 236. See also numbers
composite data, 55
compute-every-1000th function, 195
cond form, 58–59
conditionals
    and, 61–63, 66
    case, 140, 150
    cond, 58–59
    if, 56–58
    or, 61–63
    unless, 63, 72
    when, 63, 150

connect clause, 217

connect function

for Guess My Number, distributed, 222–223

for Hungry Henry, 245

cons cell, 42

cons function, 43–44

cons? function, 107

constant, 72

count++ function, 276

count-and-print macro, 276

create-player function, 247

create-world-of-dice-and-doom function, 174

current-target function, 149

D

damage-monster function, 149

data types. *See* Booleans; bundle type; iworld type; mail type; number type; package type; promise type; sequence type; string type; structures

d/dx function, 121

dead? function, 107

deal-with-guess function, 87

decrease-attack# function, 148

define form, 29–30, 71–75

define/private form, for classes, 267

define/public form, for classes, 267

define-syntax-rule form, 270

define-values form, 156

definitions. *See also* functions, defining

constants, 72–73, 86

local bindings, 73–75

structures, 47–48, 50, 132

definitions panel, 21

delay form, 198

delayed-args-app macro, 278

dice function, 182

Dice of Doom, 165–192. *See also* artificial intelligence (AI)

end of game, 189

game trees, 171–174, 181–188

handling input, 179–181

neighbors, how to find, 184–186

rendering, 176–178

rules, 166–167

dice-world struct, 171

dir? function, 103

direct-snake function, 103

disconnect function, 246

display function, 153

displayln function, 158

distribute function, 184

distributed programming, 2, 213–214, 218

domain, 274

domain-specific language

#%app, 277

#%module-begin, 277–280

creation, 274–281

domain, 203, 274

installation, 275

delayed-lang, 279

silly-lang, 275

draw-a-ufo-onto-an-empty-scene function, 81

draw-dice function, 178

draw-dice-world function, 175

draw-end-of-dice-world function, 175

draw-focus function, 177

draw-guess function, 224

drawing. *See* big-bang; images; to-draw clause

draw-square function, 73

draw-territory function, 177

drop function, 146

drop-client function, 248

drop-player function, 252

DrRacket IDE, 19–26

E

eat function, 100

eat-all-the-things function, 255

eighth function, 47

empty value, 43–44

empty? function, 54
empty-bundle function, 246
empty-scene function, 81
end-game-broadcast function, 256
end-of-orc-battle? function, 137
end-turn function, 147
ENIAC, 3
entree structure, 237
eq? function, 66
equal? function, 55, 65–66
equality, 55–56, 64–66, 133
equality predicate, 55–56, 64–66
error function, 72
even? function, 61
even-row function, 187
exact-integer? function, 54
except-out form, 278
execute function, 188
expt function, 39

F

false value, 57
fault tolerant, 223
feed-em-all function, 254
Felleisen, Matthias, 8
field, 48
field selector, 48
fifth function, 47
filter function, 118
findf function, 180
Findler, Robby, 8
find-move function, 180
first function, 45–47
flail function, 148
flame-thrower wielding squirrels, 199
Flatt, Matthew, 8
foldr function, 118
for form, 153
    for*/list, 159
    for/and, 160
    for/first, 160
    for/fold, 154, 156
    for/last, 160

for/list, 154
    for/or, 160
force function, 198
force* function, 279
for-each function, 150
form, 58
FORTRAN, 4
fourth function, 47
fresh-goo function, 102
Friedman, Dan, 8
functional programming, 131–135, 182
functions
    anonymous, 113–115
    calling, 21, 31–32
    defining, 30–33
    helper, 102, 143, 239
    higher-order, 112–113, 121
    recursive, 59–60, 99, 101

G

game structure
    for AI, 205
    for Dice of Doom, 171
game tree, 168–170. *See also* minimax
    branches, 169
    depth limit, 206
    pruning, 207
games
    Dice of Doom, 165–192
        AI, 206–212
    Guess My Number, 27–34
        distributed, 219–226
        GUI, 85–90
    Hungry Henry, 232–261
    Orc Battle, 128–152
    Snake, 95–110
game-tree function
    for AI, 204
    for Dice of Doom, 183
gensym function, 247
get-dice-img function, 178
get-iws function, 251

get-posns-from-goo function
   for Land of Lambda, 113
   for Snake, 106
get-random-numbers function, 190
get-row function, 182
get-score function, 256
get-x function, 182
get-y function, 182
give-monster-turn-if-attack#=0
     function, 150
goo structure, 97
goo-list+scene function
   for Land of Lambda, 113
   for Snake, 106
goto function, 252
graphical user interface (GUI), 79–89. *See*
     also big-bang
grow function, 100
guess function
   for Guess My Number, 31
     distributed, 223
     GUI, 88
Guess My Number, 27–34
   distributed, 219–226
   GUI, 85–90
GUI (graphical user interface), 79–89. *See*
     also big-bang

H

handle-appetizer-message
     function, 240
handle-entree-message function, 244
handle-goto-message function, 246
handle-keys function, 224
handle-msg function
   for client, 224
   for server, 223
handler function. *See* big-bang; universe
handle-server-messages function, 239
heal function, 147
hexagon function, 177
higher-order functions, 112

higher-order programming. *See* functions;
     higher-order functions; loops;
     memoization
Hudak, Paul, 8
Hungry Henry, 231–261
   appetizer, 237, 239–241
   entree, 237, 242–245
   join, 237, 247–252
   play, 237, 251–257
hydra structure, 130. *See also* monster
     structure

I

IDE (interactive development
     environment), 19. *See also*
     DrRacket IDE
if form, 56–57
image? function, 53
images. *See* above function; above/
     align function; beside function;
     circle function; empty-scene
     function
img+scene function, 106
img-list+scene function, 106, 118
Indiana University, 8
inherit-field form, for classes, 268
init-field form, for classes, 267
initialize-monsters function, 140
initialize-orc-world function, 137
initialize-player function, 140
in-list function, 160
in-naturals function, 195
in-range function, 159
inside-of-rectangle? function, 73
instance, 48
instructions function, 142
integer? function, 54
interactions panel, 21–26
interactive development environment
     (IDE), 19. *See also* DrRacket IDE
interact-count-and-print macro, 278
interact-with-board function, 175
interval structure, 86

ip structure, 238
iworld type, 216
iworld=? function, 217
iworld-name function, 233

J

join structure, 237
join-add-player function, 247
join-remove function, 248

K

keep-waiting function, 249
keep-waiting? function, 249
key=? function, 87
keyword, 29
Krishnamurthi, Shriram, 8

L

lambda, 111–123. *See also* closure
lambda form, 113–114, 121–122
Land of Lisp, i
launch-guess-client function, 224
launch-guess-server function, 222
lazy evaluation, 194. *See also* memoization
  delay, 198, 204–205
  force, 198, 204–206
left function, 179
length function, 148
let form, 135
lets-eat function, 238
Lisp language, i
list function, 41–47
list? function, 54
list-eater, 59
list-ref function, 144
lists. *See also* for form
  cons, 43–44
  cons cell, 42–43
  empty, 43–44
  first, 43, 45–47
  for/list, 154

list-eaters, 59
loop functions
  andmap, 116
  filter, 114–115
  foldl, 118
  foldr, 117
  map, 112–113
  ormap, 115
  rest, 43, 45–47
  traversals. *See* for form; list-eater; lists;
        loop functions; loops; recursion
local definitions
  of constants, 73–74
  of functions, 75
LOCALHOST constant, 217
loop functions
  andmap, 116
  filter, 114–115
  foldl, 118
  foldr, 117
  map, 112–113
  ormap, 115
loops, 153–160. *See also* for form
  in-naturals, 195
  in-range, 159
lose? function, 146

M

macro programming, 270–283
macros. *See also* domain-specific language
  gensym, 248, 273
  for languages, 275–281
mail type, 216
main functions, 33
make-bundle function, 216
make-connection function, 247
make-lazy+ function, 195
make-mail function, 216
make-object function, 267
make-package function, 216
make-rectangular function, 236
map function, 118
mark function, 180

max function, 33

member function, 64

memoization, 196

memoize function, 196

memoize.v2 function, 197

message function, 142

metaprogramming. *See* domain-specific language; macro programming

minimax, 206

MIT, 4

module, 71, 218–223

module-level definitions, 71–73

monster structure, 141

monster-alive? function, 147

move structure, 172

move-and-eat function, 253

move-player* function, 253

move-target function, 149

move-toward-waypoint function, 254

mutate, 131

mutator, 132

my-and function, 270

my-andmap function, 116

my-build-list function, 119

my-equal? function, 66

my-filter function, 114

my-first-program.rkt file, 23

my-foldl function, 117, 119

my-if function, 280

my-let.v1 macro, 273

my-map function, 112

my-or macro, 271

my-ormap function, 115

N

name clause, 224

named-player function, 247

neighbors function, 186

new form, 268

next-head function, 101

next-interval function, 223

next-pit function, 98

ninth function, 47

no-more-moves-in-world? function, 175

number type

  complex, 39, 236

  exact, 39

  floating-point, 39

  inexact, 40

  integer, 39

  natural, 74, 120, 195

  rational, 39

  real, 236

number? function, 53

number->string function, 88

O

object% value, 267

object-oriented language, 268

object-oriented programming

  classes, 267–269

  classes as values, 269

  methods, 266–268

  objects, 267

odd? function, 61

odd-row function, 187

on-key clause, 84

on-msg clause, 217

on-new clause, 217

on-receive clause, 217

on-tick clause, 84

only-in function, 257

opposite-dir? function, 104

or form, 61–64

Orc Battle, 128–152

  actions, 131–136, 147–150

  ending game, 146–147

  orc world

    initializing, 140–141

    rendering, 142–146

  setting up the world, 128–131

  starting game, 136–139

orc structure, 130. *See also* monster structure

orc-world structure, 136

ormap function, 118

overlay function, 88, 107
overlay/align function, 144
overlay/offset function, 178

P

package type, 216
Pascal, 4
pass function
   for AI, 208
   for Dice of Doom, 180
PDE (program development
      environment), 19
pit structure, 96
place-image function, 73
place-image/align function, 86
play structure, 237
play-add-spectator function, 252
player structure
   for Hungry Henry, 234
   for Orc Battle, 132
player-acts-on-monsters
      function, 138
player-dead? function, 146
player-health+ function, 134
player-remove function, 253
player-update! function, 134
posn structure, 96
posn=? function, 108
posn-move function, 101
predicate, 51–55
prefab (previously fabricated structure), 215
program development environment
      (PDE), 19
progress function, 256
promise type, 198
provide form, 219

Q

quasiquote (`` ` ``), for lists, 276
quote ('), for data, 39, 44

R

Racket, i
   conventions, 30, 37, 52, 59
   download, 20
   etiquette, 30
   history, 2–10
Racketeer, 20
racket-lang.org, 20
racket/promise library, 198
rackunit library, 68
raco, 266
random+ function, 140
random-number-of-attacks
      function, 140
random-quotient function, 140
random-stars function, 73
rate-moves function, 207
rate-position function, 207
rational? function, 54
reader, 37
read-eval-print loop, 21
real? function, 54
real-part function, 236
rectangle function, 143–144
recursion, 59–61
refocus-board function, 179
register clause, 217
remainder function, 195
remake-join function, 257
remove function, 100
rename-out form, 277
render function, 88
render-appetizer function, 239
render-avatar function, 243
render-end function, 107
render-entree function, 242
render-id+image function, 240
render-last-scene function, 88
render-monsters function, 144
render-orc-battle function, 137
render-orc-world function, 142
render-pit function, 105
render-player function, 143
render-scores function, 245

render-text function, 243

render-the-end function, 137

render-the-meal function, 239

renew function

for Land of Lambda, 115

for Snake, 102

require form, 68, 218–219

rest function, 45

restart function, 244

return-five function, 32

Rice University, 8

right function, 180

rip function, 248

roll-the-dice function, 174

rot function

for Land of Lambda, 113

for Snake, 102

rotate-until function, 179

rotten? function, 102

run function, 225

run.rkt file, 225

S

scope, 73

score function, 256

second function, 47

selector. *See* field selector

self-colliding? function, 107

semantics, 35, 38–50

sequence type, 160

serialize-universe function, 251

serve-dinner function, 257

server, 214

server.rkt file, 220, 222–223

set! form, 32

set-waypoint function, 239

seventh function, 47

S-expression type, 215

shared.rkt file, 220–221

single? function

for Guess My Number, distributed, 223

for Guess My Number, GUI, 88

sixth function, 47

slime structure, 130. *See also* monster
structure

slither function, 100

smaller function

for Guess My Number, 32

distributed, 223

GUI, 87

Snake, 95–110

ending game, 107–108

data representation, 96–97

functions in, 98–107, 108

snake structure, 96

snake-body function, 108

snake-change-dir function, 108

snake-head function, 108

snake-tail function, 108

snake%, 267

snake+scene function, 105

sort function, 245

squirrels, flame-thrower wielding, 199

sqrt function, 39

square function, 37

stab function, 147

start function

for Guess My Number, 33

GUI, 86

for Orc Battle, 136

start-game function, 250

start-snake function, 98

state machine, 232–233

state-is-300 function, 83

status-bar function, 144

Steele, Guy, 7

stop-when clause, 84

stop-with function, 87

stream type, 160

string type, 40

string=? function, 55

string-append function, 41

string? function, 53

struct form, 47

struct inheritance, 130

struct-out form, 219

structures. *See also* definitions, structures
  creating, 47–48
  field access, 48
  mutation, 131–135
  predicates, 52
sub1 function, 33
sum-territory function, 189
super-new form, for classes, 267
suspended computation, 194
Sussman, Gerry, 7
switch function, 183
switch-to-entree function, 241
symbol type, 39
symbol=? function, 52, 55
symbol? function, 53
syntax, 35–38. *See also* comments;
    conditionals; define form; form
  begin, 272, 276–277
  let, 135, 205, 238, 272
  set!, 32–34, 61, 196
syntax error, 36

T

take function, 146
teaching languages, 21
tenth function, 47
territory structure, 171
territory-build function, 181
test expression, in if expression, 57
testing, 68–70
text function, 86, 107, 142
the-ai-plays function, 208
then expression, in if expression, 57
third function, 47
thunk, 194
tick ('), for data, 39, 44
tick-tock function, 246
time-broadcast function, 249
time? function, 241
to-draw clause, 84
true value, 57
Turing, Alan, 36
type predicate, 53

U

universe, 214–223, 245
  clauses, 217
    on-disconnect, 245
    on-msg, 222, 245
    on-new, 222, 245
    on-tick, 245
universe form, 214
unless form, 63
unmark function, 181
unquote (,), for quasiquoted lists, 276
unquote-splicing (,@), for quasiquoted
    lists, 276

V

values form, 155
variable bindings, 154
view, 80
void function, 132

W

wait-or-play function, 249
wall-colliding? function, 108
Wand, Mitch, 8
when form, 63
win? function, 146
winners function
  for define define 'define, 74
  for Dice of Doom, 189
won function, 189
world-change-dir function, 103
worlds, 80

Y

your-or macro, 272

Z

zero? function, 52
Zuse's Z3, 3

The Electronic Frontier Foundation (EFF) is the leading organization defending civil liberties in the digital world. We defend free speech on the Internet, fight illegal surveillance, promote the rights of innovators to develop new digital technologies, and work to ensure that the rights and freedoms we enjoy are enhanced — rather than eroded — as our use of technology grows.

EFF.ORG

ELECTRONIC FRONTIER FOUNDATION

Protecting Rights and Promoting Freedom on the Electronic Frontier